The Management of Consumer Credit

Also by Steven Finlay

CONSUMER CREDIT FUNDAMENTALS SECOND EDITION

The Management of Consumer Credit

Theory and Practice

Second Edition

Steven Finlay

First published 2010 by
PALGRAVE MACMILLAN

Palgrave Macmillan in the UK is an imprint of Macmillan Publishers Limited, registered in England, company number 785998, of Houndmills, Basingstoke, Hampshire RG21 6XS.

Palgrave Macmillan in the US is a division of St Martin's Press LLC, 175 Fifth Avenue, New York, NY 10010.

Palgrave Macmillan is the global academic imprint of the above companies and has companies and representatives throughout the world.

Palgrave® and Macmillan® are registered trademarks in the United States, the United Kingdom, Europe and other countries

ISBN 978-0-230-23830-5   hardback

This book is printed on paper suitable for recycling and made from fully managed and sustained forest sources. Logging, pulping and manufacturing processes are expected to conform to the environmental regulations of the country of origin.

A catalogue record for this book is available from the British Library.

Library of Congress Cataloging-in-Publication Data
    Finlay, Steven, 1969–
    The management of consumer credit : theory and practice / Steven Finlay. – 2nd ed.
        p. cm.
    Summary: "This book explains how financial institutions, such as banks and finance houses, manage their portfolios of credit cards, loans, mortgages and other types of retail credit agreements. The second edition has been substantially updated, with new chapters on capital requirements and scorecard and portfolio monitoring"–Provided by publisher.
    Includes bibliographical references and index.
    ISBN 978-0-230-23830-5 (hardback)
    1. Consumer credit–Management. I. Title.

    HG3755.F54 2010
    658.8'83–dc22   2009048422

10   9   8   7   6   5   4   3   2   1
19 18 17 16 15 14 13 12 11 10

Printed and bound in Great Britain by
CPI Antony Rowe, Chippenham and Eastbourne

To Ruby & Sam

Contents

List of Tables and Figures

Tables

Figures

Preface

Consumer credit is an integral part of many societies and a key driver behind the culture of consumerism. Everywhere you look credit transactions are occurring; in banks, shops, over the internet and on the phone. Long gone are the days when it was common to save, maybe for years, for the things you wanted, and only those considered spendthrifts bought items on credit. Today, it is almost unheard of not to have the option to purchase any type of good or service using some form of credit, and many people wouldn't dream of waiting to buy something when a loan, credit card or some other form of borrowing was available to fund their purchase. Not surprisingly, the consumer credit industry has grown to become one of the largest and most profitable sectors of many economies around the world, each year generating many tens of billions of dollars/euros/pounds for the financial services industry.

Given the economic and social importance of consumer credit, the principles and practices that underpin the way credit agreements are created and managed are clearly important subjects that deserve extensive and detailed study. However, while there is a large body of published material about the theory of money, banking and credit, there is very little about how credit granting institutions actually operate in practice, and the subject has not received anything like the attention it deserves. Why should this be the case? From a historical perspective, credit management has not usually been seen as a subject in its own right. The different aspects of credit management have been treated as sub-specialisms of disciplines such as law, marketing, mathematics, IT, accounting and finance and operations management. Therefore, to gain a complete understanding of the activities that need to be undertaken to support commercial credit granting activities one needs to be something of a jack-of-all trades, drawing upon an array of skills and experience from across all of these disciplines. This is probably the main reason why credit management has been a somewhat neglected topic of study, with there being only a handful of professional and academic books about the subject.

Having worked in the consumer credit industry for a number of years before moving to a university research post, it appeared to me that there was a need for a book that combined an academic perspective with the practical aspects of the subject. There was also a need for a book that embraced the different disciplines which have traditionally come together to deliver consumer credit to the public, and which presented a coherent and integrated view of how a credit granting business should be managed. The result is this book.

I hope I have written something that is informative and provides in-depth coverage of the subject, but which is also accessible to the general reader, whatever their background may be. I very much look forward to readers' comments to let me know how successful I have been in achieving this goal.

Steven Finlay, January 2008.

Acknowledgements

I am deeply indebted to my wife Sam and my parents Ann and Paul for their help and support while writing this book; their input and ideas, and for their proof reading services. My thanks to Phil Level for lending me several books that took me a considerable period of time to return. My thanks also to Hywel Davies and Terry Hancock for their help with Basel II and provision calculation respectively, and to Ade Lingard, Andrew Jordan, Karen Snape, Katie Stones, Nick Sime, Pete Sewart, Sarah Dover and everyone else at Jaywing (too many of you to name you all) for their support over the last few years. I am also indebted to Professor Robert Fildes and Dr Didier Soopramien of Lancaster University, and Professor Lyn Thomas of Southampton University, whose comments on my PhD thesis led to a number of improvements and corrections to the text of the book.

1

Consumer Credit Management: An Introduction

This is a specialist book, but not an overly technical one. It is suitable for anyone interested in the granting and management of consumer credit and who wants to know more about the processes involved. It covers the theory underpinning credit management and the practices employed by real world organizations to deliver their products and services to the general public.

1.1   Structure and content

This preliminary chapter covers introductory material and lays the groundwork for the remainder of the book. The nature of consumer credit is discussed, the most common forms of consumer credit are described and the different types of organization that provide consumer credit are introduced. The 'five phase credit model' is also presented, which describes the way credit providers manage their relationships with individuals over time.

Chapter 2 discusses the environment in which consumer credit management takes place. It begins by introducing the business functions required to operate a successful consumer credit business. These functions are then discussed within the context of the different organizational frameworks that credit granting institutions can adopt in support of their strategic objectives. Legal and ethical aspects of credit and debt are also discussed in this chapter. Chapters 3 through 8 discuss the role of credit management within each phase of the five phase credit model. Chapter 3 begins with the marketing of credit, and describes how a product proposition is put together and delivered to market through the implementation of an appropriate marketing plan. Particular emphasis is placed on the use of direct marketing to target prospective customers on a one-to-one basis. Chapter 4 describes how consumer behaviours are predicted, and how these predictions are used to make decisions about how relationships are managed. In particular, scoring and segmentation are introduced. These are two of the most widely used methods for predicting behaviour in consumer credit markets and are used in many different areas of credit management. In Chapter 5, the customer acquisition process is examined; covering issues such as application processing, credit scoring and the role of credit reference agencies. Chapter 6 is about customer management and the actions that can be taken to maximize the financial contribution from customers over the lifetime of the relationship with them. Chapter 7 discusses early stage delinquency. This is when a customer is in arrears with their repayments, but there is some hope of salvaging the relationship with them. Chapter 8 looks at the later stages of delinquency and debt recovery. This covers topics such as the use of third party debt collection agencies and legal action to recover unpaid debts. Chapter 9 examines the types of credit related fraud that can occur, in conjunction with the actions lenders can take to mitigate against fraud losses. Chapter 10 is in two parts. The first part describes the ways that lenders can obtain funds to support their lending activities. The second part of the chapter covers provision. This is money an organization 'puts aside' to cover bad debts that have not yet occurred, but can be expected to arise at some point in the future. The final chapter discusses capital requirements within the context of the BASEL II Capital Accord. A technical discussion about the processes involved in developing models of customer behaviour is contained in Appendix A. This is followed in Appendix B with an introduction to scorecard and portfolio monitoring.

The principles underpinning credit management and the practices employed by credit managers are largely universal. Therefore, the book has been written from an international perspective. For purposes of convenience, all financial values are quoted in US dollars.

1.2   The nature of consumer credit agreements

Ideas of credit and debt are ancient. We live in a society that is, and always has been, heavily reliant on formal and informal credit-debt relationships. We have all borrowed items from and lent things to friends, relatives, neighbours and colleagues. Everyone understands the idea of 'you scratch my back and I'll scratch yours' and the network of favours and goodwill that oils the relationships between us at home, work and in society at large. Even the giving of gifts can be viewed as a form of credit-debt relationship, placing an obligation on a person who receives a gift to give a gift in return. It has even been suggested that an understanding of such relationships and ideas of debt and obligation may have been one factor that enabled modern humans to supersede Neanderthals as the dominant primate species (Horan et al. 2005).[1] At some point in early human society individuals began helping one another to hunt, lending tools and food to each other, caring for each others' children, the sick and so on. These tasks were undertaken with the understanding that they created an obligation that would be reciprocated. This meant that people were better able to overcome short term hardships, leading to greater survival rates and an increased population. The Neanderthals may have been unable to grasp such concepts and were therefore, not able to benefit from the survival advantages that these credit-debt relationships provided.

A consumer credit agreement is just one form of credit-debt relationship that reflects a formal monetary commitment between two parties that is recognized as a legally binding contract. One party (the lender/creditor) provides funds in the form of cash, goods or services, to the other (the borrower/debtor), who undertakes a commitment to repay the debt at some point in the future. For the purposes of this book we restrict the definition of consumer credit to cover only credit agreements where the debtor is an individual. It doesn't matter what the purpose of the credit is, the amount of credit, the length of the agreement or anything else. The key thing is that the responsibly for the debt lies with an identifiable person, not a company or some other type of institutional entity. This is a broad definition of consumer credit. It is worth pointing out that many observers adopt a more restricted definition; in particular, lending secured against an individual's home (a mortgage) is traditionally classified as a different category of borrowing, and therefore, not consumer credit.[2] While there are some features of mortgages that differentiate them from other types of individual borrowing there are also many similarities. From a management perspective, many of the principles of consumer credit management can be applied across all forms of individual borrowing. That is not to say there aren't important factors that differentiate one type of credit from another, or that there are not certain practices and legal requirements that apply to specific types of credit. However, many of the general principles by which credit is granted and the practices used to manage it are universal, and can be applied regardless of the type of credit in question.

Consumer credit comes in a variety of different forms, all of which can be described in terms of the following features:

- **Secured or unsecured**. Credit is secured if the credit agreement details specific assets the lender can take in lieu of the debt should the borrower default; for example, their home or car. Otherwise, the credit is unsecured.[3]
- **Amortized or balloon**. Credit is amortized if debt is repaid in instalments covering both interest and capital, so that by the end of the agreement the debt has been fully repaid. With balloon credit the debt is repaid in full at the end of the agreement. Interest may be paid at regular intervals throughout the agreement or as a single payment at the end. Credit agreements where irregular repayments are made are also defined as balloon (Smullen and Hand 2005 p. 30) as are credit agreements where the final payment is greater than all previous payments (Collin 2003 p. 28).[4]
- **Fixed sum or running account**. A fixed sum credit agreement is where a known amount of credit is advanced (usually at the start of the agreement). When the debt has been repaid the agreement is terminated. With a running account agreement the amount of credit is not set when the agreement is made, but a credit facility is made available. The outstanding debt fluctuates as new credit is extended and repayments are made. Running account agreements are also known as open-ended credit agreements or revolving credit agreements.
- **Unrestricted or restricted**. If credit is obtained in the form of money, that can be spent however the borrower wishes, then the credit is unrestricted. If credit is restricted it can only be used to obtain a limited range of goods or services; that is, credit is provided to buy specific items which are then paid for on credit terms.
- **Credit sale, conditional sale or hire-purchase**. These features apply only to restricted credit agreements. If goods are sold on a credit sale basis they become the immediate property of the customer. The merchant can not reclaim/seize the goods if the customer subsequently fails to repay their debt. With a conditional sale, ownership of goods transfers to the borrower only when the terms of the agreement have been complied with.[5] Therefore, the lender can repossesses the goods should the terms of the agreement be broken. Hire-purchase is similar to conditional sale, but the important difference is that the customer is only hiring the goods with an option to buy at the end of the agreement.[6] Therefore, the hirer can choose not to exercise their option to

buy and return the goods. With a conditional sale the borrower is committed to the purchase; the goods can not be returned once the agreement has been signed.

- **Debtor-creditor** or **debtor-creditor-supplier** agreement. A debtor-creditor agreement exists where the transaction that led to the creation of the credit agreement involves only the debtor and the creditor. A debtor-creditor-supplier agreement exists when goods or services are purchased from a merchant, with credit provided by a third party. The purchaser is then indebted to the third party not the merchant. In many countries the distinction between a debtor-creditor and debtor-creditor-supplier agreement becomes important when there is a dispute over the goods purchased. With a debtor-creditor-supplier agreement the credit provider has joint liability for the goods. For example, if you purchase a television using a credit card, a debtor-creditor-supplier agreement will exist because the card issuer is providing the credit – not the retailer.[7] If the retailer subsequently goes bust the card company will be liable should the television prove faulty within the warranty period.

Table 1.1 shows the types of consumer credit offered by most large credit granting institutions.[8] However, it is important to note that the features in the 'Typical features' column in Table 1.1 are just that – typical. It is always possible to find a lender offering something atypical. Nearly all personal loans are amortizing, but a few are not. Most credit cards provide an unsecured form of borrowing, but there are some where the card issuer will demand that customers who have a poor credit history provide a cash deposit as security.

It can also be argued that Table 1.1 presents a somewhat traditionalist view. As the technology employed by lenders has become more sophisticated many credit providers have begun to move away from the idea of a set of individual credit products provided to customers on a piecemeal basis, towards a holistic view that considers all of the financial products and services that an individual requires. Today there are offset loans that take into account money the borrower has in their savings accounts to calculate a reduced amount upon which interest is charged. There are credit cards that give the user the ability to pay for high value purchases over a fixed period of time in the same way as an instalment loan, as well as providing revolving credit facilities for low value purchases. There are also home equity lines of credit (commonly abbreviated to HELOC) that combine credit secured against one's home with current account, overdraft and short term loan facilities. This trend is

Table 1.1 Types of consumer credit

Credit product	Also known as[1]	Typical features	
• Repayment mortgage	• Amortizing mortgage	• Secured on home • Amortizing • Fixed sum	• Restricted • Credit sale • Debtor-creditor
• Interest only mortgage	• Balloon mortgage	• Secured on home • Balloon • Fixed sum	• Restricted • Credit sale • Debtor-creditor
• Unsecured personal loan	• Instalment loan • Instalment plan • Signature loan	• Unsecured • Amortizing • Fixed sum	• Unrestricted • Debtor-creditor
• Secured personal loan	• Instalment loan • Instalment plan • Title loan	• Secured on home, car or other asset • Amortizing	• Fixed sum • Unrestricted • Debtor-creditor
• Retail credit (including motor finance)	• Retail instalment plan • Retail instalment credit	• Unsecured • Amortizing • Fixed sum • Restricted	• Credit sale, conditional sale[2] or hire-purchase • Debtor-credit-supplier[3]
• Credit card[4]	• Bank card • Universal credit card	• Unsecured • Amortizing or balloon[5] • Running account • Restricted (purchases) and unrestricted (cash withdrawal)[6]	• Credit sale (purchases) • Debtor-creditor-supplier (purchases)[6] • Debtor-creditor (cash withdrawal)[6]
• Store card[4]	• Retailer card • Credit card	• Unsecured • Amortizing or balloon[5] • Running account	• Restricted • Credit sale • Debtor-creditor-supplier[3]

Table 1.1 Types of consumer credit – *continued*

Credit product	Also known as[1]	Typical features
• Charge card[4]	• Credit card	• Unsecured • Balloon • Running account	• Restricted & unrestricted[6] • Credit sale • Debtor-creditor-supplier
• Overdraft		• Unsecured • Balloon • Running account	• Unrestricted • Debtor-creditor

Notes:

1. Some types of consumer credit are known by different names in different regions. Standard UK terminology is used in the credit product column.
2. In the UK most (non-motor) retail credit is granted on a credit sale basis. In the US conditional sale agreements are more common. Motor finance is usually provided as a hire purchase agreement.
3. Retail credit is often provided by a third party such as a bank or finance house, but there are no reasons why retailers can't provide credit if they wish.
4. In some regions 'credit card' means any type of card account. In others 'credit card' refers to a revolving account that can be used to purchase goods in a wide range of stores (such as VISA and MasterCard cards). The term 'store card' is used to refer to cards that can only be used in a single store.
5. These products are both amortizing and balloon. This is because the customer has the choice to repay all the credit at once, or to make regular payments of varying amounts.
6. Goods purchased using a credit card represent a form of restricted credit. This is because although the range of goods and services is very extensive, there are some things that can't be bought with a credit card. However, most credit cards can also be used to make cash withdrawals which is an unrestricted form of credit (Dobson 1996 p. 285). Credit card purchases create a debtor-creditor-supplier relationship while cash withdrawals create a creditor-debtor relationship.

likely to continue, and it is probable that in future consumers will simply be offered a 'credit account' that provides for all types of personal borrowing, be it a mortgage to buy their homes or retail credit to purchase a new kitchen appliance. The customer will simply choose the credit option and associated repayment terms that best suit their current circumstances at the point of purchase. However, this is not yet reality, and nearly all consumer credit can be classified as falling into one of the product categories within Table 1.1.

All credit agreements possess three additional features which can be used to differentiate between different products of the same type:

- **The amount of credit.** For fixed sum agreements this is the sum lent at the outset of the agreement. For running account agreements the amount will vary up to a maximum amount determined by the customer's credit limit.
- **The term (length) of the agreement.** For fixed sum agreements this is the time between a credit agreement being entered into and the date when the final repayment is made. For running account credit this is the date when the facility is withdrawn or reviewed, with the parties having the option to terminate or renew the agreement.
- **The cost of credit.** All commercial lenders apply charges to cover their costs and to allow them to make a return on their investment. This includes interest (the finance charge) that accrues over time, but also arrangement fees, transaction fees, annual fees, option to buy fees and so on. Sometimes credit may appear to be provided free of charge – something often seen in the retail sector where goods are routinely offered on 'interest free' terms. In reality there is no such thing as interest free – the credit provider's costs are factored into the price. If interest free credit wasn't available, then the merchant could sell the goods at a lower price and still maintain the same level of profitability. The APR (Annual Percentage Rate) is a legally defined way of representing the cost of credit in a standardized form.

1.3   Credit granting institutions

The vast majority of consumer credit is provided by the following four types of institution:

- **Banks.** Historically banks have been categorized by the type of customers they deal with and the services they offer. Merchant banks dealt mainly with international and corporate finance, while retail banks[9] provided current account and loan facilities to individuals and small to medium-sized businesses. Today, most large banks are described as 'universal banks', with a mixture of merchant and retail interests. The main providers of retail banking services have also diversified into other areas of financial services, and now offer a wide range of products including mortgages and credit cards, as well as insurance, savings accounts, pensions and other types of investments.

- **Saving and loan associations** (building societies in the UK, Ireland and Australia). These are mutually owned profit making organizations that traditionally provided mortgages, funded by the savings accounts of their members. Modern saving and loan companies now offer broadly the same range of financial services as retail banks.
- **Credit unions.** Credit unions are mutually owned financial cooperatives that have traditionally shared many features with saving and loan associations. Credit unions are owned by their members, with the funds contributed by members used to supply credit to other members.[10] Credit unions are usually created around specific interest groups sharing some 'common bond', such as members of a trade union or residents of a town or city. Consequently, many credit unions operate on a relatively small scale compared to the major banks and saving and loan companies. However, some of the largest US credit unions have hundreds of thousands of members and billions of dollars worth of assets. US credit unions offer a wide range of credit products including mortgages, personal loans and credit cards and are known for offering competitive credit terms because they are run on a not-for-profit basis and enjoy a tax exempt status. In other countries the popularity of credit unions varies enormously in terms of the number of members, the size of unions, and the range of products they offer. In Ireland for example, about 45 percent of adults are members of credit unions. In the UK the figure is only about 1 percent (Goth et al. 2006 p. 1).
- **Finance houses (finance companies).** These organizations provide consumer (and sometimes institutional) credit, but not savings or deposit accounts. Their lending activities are mainly funded by commercial loans obtained from merchant banks or other large financial institutions. Finance houses mainly provide credit in the form of secured and unsecured personal loans, hire-purchase agreements and card accounts. Some large finance houses also act as third party-credit providers, acting on behalf of retailers and other service providers

for the provision of store cards, retail credit and hire-purchase agreements.

From a consumer perspective there is very little difference between the financial products offered by these four institutions. What differentiates them is ownership, the objectives that drive their activities and the legislation under which they operate. Banks and finance houses are almost always driven by the profit motive, aiming to maximize shareholder return. Saving and loan associations are profit making organizations, but look to maximize the benefits to their members. Credit unions are also member owned but non-profit making. Banks, saving and loan associations and credit unions are all categorized as deposit taking institutions. This means that as well as providing credit, they also provide current accounts and/or savings accounts. This puts a number of legal obligations on them to ensure that they can maintain their liquidity so that depositors' funds are protected. Finance houses do not offer such services, and therefore tend to be subject to less stringent regulatory requirements than deposit taking institutions.

Between them banks, saving and loan companies, credit unions and finance houses account for the vast majority of consumer credit throughout the world. Other types of credit granting institutions do exist, such as mail order catalogue retailers, pawnbrokers, door-to-door lenders, cheque cashing services and payday lenders. However, most of these operate on a small scale, specialize in providing credit to those on low incomes and/or who have a poor credit history, and account for only a very small proportion of the total consumer credit industry.[11]

1.4   The five phase credit model

All credit agreements represent a relationship that displays different characteristics and behaviours as the relationship develops over the term of the agreement. Consequently, different actions are required to maximize the value of the relationship at different times. Many observers discuss the management of credit agreements within the context of the credit cycle (or lifecycle),[12] with a credit agreement existing in one of a number of phases during its lifetime (McNab and Taylor 2008 pp. 9–11; Bailey 2004 p. 5; Finlay 2009 pp. 191–2). For the purposes of this text a five phase model of the credit cycle is adopted, as shown in Figure 1.1.

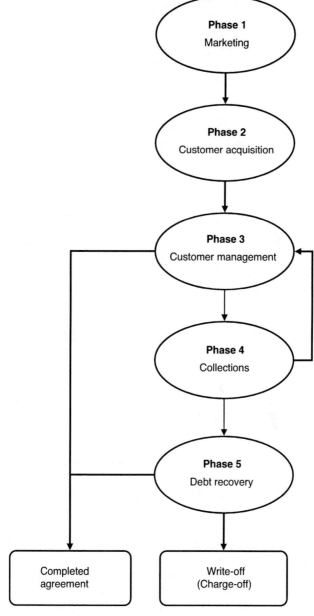

Figure 1.1 The five phase model of credit management

Each phase is characterized by a number of activities that the borrower or lender undertakes, and in each phase the lender looks to facilitate different types of customer behaviour. The goal during phase one is to encourage creditworthy people to apply for credit. Creditworthiness is primarily based on the likelihood that someone will repay the credit they are provided with, but it also captures other aspects of customer behaviour such as the potential revenue they are likely to generate and the opportunity to cross sell additional products and services. To put it another way, a creditworthy customer is someone who is likely to generate a positive contribution to profit and an uncreditworthy customer is someone who is likely to generate a loss. The measure of someone's creditworthiness is not an absolute measure. Every lender has different operational overheads, prices their products differently and calculates profitability in different ways. Therefore, each lender has their own perspective on how creditworthy someone is, and it is quite possible that someone deemed uncreditworthy by one lender will be considered creditworthy by another.

If someone responds to promotional activity by applying for the product the relationship moves to phase two. At this stage more information about the applicant becomes available, allowing a more accurate and up-to-date assessment of creditworthiness to be made. A decision will then be made whether to accept or decline the credit application. Decisions will also be taken about the terms of business (the terms and conditions) to offer successful applicants; that is, the credit limit, APR, term of the agreement and so on. If the applicant agrees to the terms, any paperwork that is needed for a legally binding credit agreement will be produced and passed to them to sign. Once the agreement has been signed some form of account record will be created (usually within a computerized account management system) to maintain details of the current and historical status of the agreement. The account record will then be used as the basis of phase three – the customer management phase of the credit cycle – as repayments are made, further credit advanced and other products and services are marketed to the customer.

Phases four and five are only required if the customer breaches the terms of the agreement, causing their account to become delinquent. At this point the relationship enters phase four where collections action is taken in an attempt to nurse the account back to an up-to-date status – returning it to phase three. At this stage the relationship is still viewed as a positive one, and much effort may be expended to try and persuade the customer to pay the arrears on their account. However, if the customer consistently fails to comply with the terms of the credit agreement, falling further behind with their repayments, the relationship moves to phase five – debt recovery. In phase five the objective is no longer to maintain a good customer relationship, but to recover as much of the outstanding debt as possible before terminating the agreement.

A credit agreement ends in one of two ways. It may end naturally when the debt has been repaid according to the terms of the agreement and the account closed, or if debt recovery action fails to recover the debt it is written-off (charged-off).[13]

Figure 1.1 shows the five main areas of credit management; the initial marketing of products and services, the acquisition of new customers, customer management, collections and debt recovery. In order to maximize their return a lender must manage all of these areas effectively. In addition, there is a need for an integrated strategy across each of the five phases to ensure consistency and that contradictory action is not taken within different phases. For example, it is generally not a sensible idea to try and promote further credit to customers whose accounts are in debt recovery because they have failed to honour the terms of their existing agreement. Therefore, marketing departments need to have knowledge of customers' accounts, not just to determine if someone already has the product, but also to see how their accounts are performing.

1.5   The role of credit management

A key point to note from Figure 1.1 is that movement between all five phases is driven by consumer behaviours. The customer chooses whether or not to apply for the product. If offered credit they then choose whether or not to accept the terms under which it is offered. If collections action is required, this is because the customer has, for whatever reason, chosen not to pay and so on. In order to move customers into or out of various phases, the activities of the lender are geared towards trying to persuade (or in some cases force) the customer to behave in a certain way. Therefore, it is possible to sum up the framework within which credit management operates, with all of the key activities, processes and systems employed by lenders, focused on the following.

1. Predicting how individuals will behave in future.
2. Undertaking actions in response to these predictions that maximize the organization's objectives, by attempting to influence (manage) the behaviour of the customer.

So, for example, when someone applies for a loan, the lender is interested in identifying whether the person will:

A. Repay the credit advanced to them according to the terms of the credit agreement, generating a positive contribution to profits.

or:

B. Default on the agreement, leading to a negative contribution to profits.

The lender will acquire information about the applicant from a variety of sources, such as the application form completed by the applicant and a credit report supplied by a credit reference agency. This information will then be used to predict the likelihood of behaviour A or behaviour B occurring. If the chance of the debt being repaid is high enough, then the customer will be offered the opportunity of signing a credit agreement and receiving the funds they applied for. However, if it is likely that the individual will default on the agreement, then their request for credit will be declined – thus removing the individual's option to default in the future.

Of course there are a host of other activities undertaken in the management of credit agreements. Large numbers of people are involved in maintaining the physical infrastructure required to deal with customers and to enable suitable actions to be taken in response to specific customer behaviours. IT systems are required to monitor the status of the business to see how well it is performing and to understand the consequences of past decisions in order to facilitate better decision making in future. Legal expertise is required to ensure compliance with relevant legislation, and accounting and finance functions manage the cash flows within the business and produce company accounts. However, these are all secondary to the two main activities of predicting how people will behave, and then taking appropriate action in order to manage relationships with individuals effectively.

1.6 Chapter summary

Consumer credit management is about predicting and controlling the behaviour of customers in order to meet the objectives of the credit provider. The relationships between individuals and credit providers can be represented by the five phase model of credit management, where each phase is concerned with different types of individual behaviour. In phase one the goal is to identify suitable individuals and to encourage them to apply for the product. Phase two deals with processing applications for credit, and the corresponding decisions and processes that need to be undertaken to facilitate the creation of a credit agreement. In phase three the relationship with the customer is managed in order to maximize the contribution from the customer; for example, reviewing the credit limit granted to a credit card customer and looking for opportunities to cross sell additional products and services.

When a customer does not comply with the terms of a credit agreement they move to phase four, collections, where action is taken to try and recover the account to an up-to-date status. If this fails then the relationship enters the final fifth phase, where action is taken to recover as much of the outstanding debt as possible before terminating the agreement. In order to run a successful consumer credit business, all of these five areas must be managed in an efficient, integrated and coherent way.

2
Organizational Matters

Before entering into the detail of the five phase credit model introduced in Chapter 1, it's worth taking a step back to consider the organizational structures and environmental conditions that influence and constrain the operation of consumer credit businesses. In the first part of this chapter the business functions needed to deliver consumer credit services to the public are discussed within the context of the different organizational structures that can be employed to manage them. The second part of the chapter discusses legal and ethical issues that need to be considered within the credit management process.

2.1 The business functions required for credit management

All large organizations are comprised of a number of discrete business functions. Each function has its own responsibilities and undertakes relevant tasks in order to facilitate the delivery of the organization's products and services. Each function can be classified into one of three types:

1. Strategy. These functions are directly concerned with the analysis of consumer behaviour, and the derivation of appropriate strategies to manage the relationships between the organization and individual consumers.
2. Operational. These deal with the logistical aspects of credit management; that is, they provide the infrastructure to run the business on a day-to-day basis and the interface between the business and its customers.

3. Corporate. Corporate functions are not involved in the day-to-day management of individual credit agreements. Rather, they are responsible for the administrative functions needed to ensure that the business runs smoothly and complies with relevant legislation.

The business functions within each of these areas are discussed in more detail in the following sections.

2.1.1 Strategy functions

There are two strategy functions within a typical consumer credit business. These are:

* Marketing.
* Credit risk (sometimes called credit strategy or risk management).

The marketing function is responsible for product design, customer acquisition and maximizing the contribution from existing customers. This includes the following tasks:

* Identifying each product's target audience.
* Branding; that is, creating a unique image of the organization and its products that meets, or ideally exceeds, the expectations of the target audience.
* Determining product features. This covers things such as the typical APR to charge, the amount of credit to offer, the nature of any loyalty schemes, the operation of payment holidays and so on.
* Formulating promotional campaigns to raise the profile of the brand and to encourage members of the target audience to apply for the product.
* Customer interface design. This covers all points at which there is contact between the organization and customers. As well as the look/feel of promotional material, this also involves working with operational functions to design application forms, websites, telephone scripts and any other material individuals are likely to come into contact with.
* Formulating customer relationship management (CRM) strategies to target existing customers with the most appropriate cross sell and up sell opportunities in order to maximize the revenue generated from each customer.

- Delivering, tracking and monitoring promotional campaigns and CRM strategies in terms of response rates, volume of new customers, customer contribution to profits and so on.

The credit risk function is responsible for making decisions about individual customer relationships on the basis of the risk profile of customers and their expected contribution to profit. The responsibilities of the credit risk function include:

- Working in conjunction with marketing during the marketing phase of the credit cycle to identify individuals who are uncreditworthy. These individuals can then be excluded from direct marketing activity.
- During the customer acquisition phase of the credit cycle, deciding who is creditworthy and who is not. This is usually on the basis of credit scoring and/or judgemental decision rules.
- For those deemed creditworthy, setting the terms of the credit offer. The marketing function will dictate the general terms of the product, such as the typical APR quoted within promotional literature. However, the credit risk function will decide the specific terms for each individual. Most people may be offered the typical 9.9 APR for a loan, but less creditworthy people may only be offered the loan at a higher rate, say 12.9 APR.
- During the account management phase of the credit cycle, regularly reviewing the terms of business under which agreements operate. For example, undertaking monthly reviews of customers' credit limits on their credit cards.
- Implementing, tracking and monitoring accounts in terms of revenues, write-off, provision estimates, overall contribution to profits and so on. This will then act as an input to financial analysis undertaken at a portfolio level by the corporate functions.
- Designing collections and debt recovery action plans, to apply to accounts when they become delinquent. This will be undertaken in conjunction with the operational team(s) responsible for collections and debt recovery processing.
- Devising strategies for identifying fraudulent applications for new credit, and fraudulent transactions for existing credit (this is mainly in relation to revolving credit facilities).

There is considerable overlap between the objectives of the marketing and credit risk functions. Therefore, it makes sense for these functions to be structured in an integrated manner with common business objectives set by senior management. However, in many organizations they remain separate entities with their own goals and objectives. This can lead to inter-departmental conflict if inter-functional relationships are not well managed or each function does not have a good understanding of the other's objectives. For example, it is common for marketing functions to be set volume based objectives to recruit a certain number of new customers each year. At the same time, the credit risk function may be tasked with keeping the total volume of bad debt below a specified amount. The credit function does this by ensuring that only the most creditworthy individuals are granted credit, and that applications from less creditworthy people are rejected – even if some of these customers might generate a positive contribution to profit. The problem that exists is what is termed the risk/response paradox (Finlay 2009 p. 216). The people who are most likely to respond to promotional activity by applying for credit are those who are least creditworthy and have the greatest risk of defaulting on any credit they are subsequently granted. Conversely, the most creditworthy people tend not to need or want credit. Therefore, they tend not to respond to promotional activity and are deemed poor prospects from a marketing perspective because they are very expensive to acquire. In order to deliver an optimal marketing/credit strategy there needs to be agreement to target those individuals somewhere in the middle; those who respond reasonably well to promotional activity and are acceptably creditworthy. The risk/response paradox is discussed in more detail in Chapter 4.

2.1.2 Operational functions

There are three main operational functions:

- Customer services.
- IT.
- Print production.

In most large organizations customer services are centered around branch networks and/or customer contact centres (call centres), and generally deal with the following activities:

- Satisfying requests for information from potential customers.
- Processing enquires and new credit applications during the customer acquisition phase of the credit cycle.
- Dealing with customers' enquiries and complaints about the running of their accounts.

- Maintaining customers' account records. This will include a filing system for paper based documentation such as signed credit agreements and customers' written correspondence.
- Undertaking collections and debt recovery activity to recover funds from delinquent customers. This will often be managed in conjunction with the credit department who will have overall responsibility for managing the volume of bad debt and write-off within the organization. The credit department will therefore have an interest in ensuring that the most efficient collections and debt recovery practices are being applied.
- Dealing with known or suspected cases of fraud.

Customer services departments need to be flexible and be able to respond to unexpected changes in the volume of customer contact activity that may occur from time to time. If the company receives an endorsement for its products in the national press, then a surge in customer enquiries and new applications can be expected. Alternatively, if there is disruption to the postal system, there may be more telephone enquiries about the whereabouts of customers' statements.

   IT plays an essential role in providing appropriate systems to meet the information and decision making needs of all groups across the organization. This includes systems in support of other operational areas, as well as the reporting systems employed by the strategy and corporate functions. Typical IT services include:

- Maintaining the prospects database, used by the marketing department, to target prospective customers with promotional materials.
- Maintaining the application processing system used to process new credit applications.
- Maintaining the account management system used to process transactions and maintain customer account records.
- Delivery of work flow systems to match customer contacts with appropriate customer service staff, while at the same time supplying those members of staff with the information they require to deal with customers in an efficient and timely manner.
- Managing external data links with organizations such as credit reference agencies and the VISA/MasterCard card networks.
- Providing operational reporting systems for customer services. This includes things such as daily transaction volumes, average call waiting times, staff performance levels and so on.

- Providing decision support systems for the marketing, credit and corporate functions to enable them to undertake the analysis necessary for them to gain a full understanding of the status of the business and the impact of their previous decisions.
- Providing software tools to facilitate implementation of new product strategies created by the credit and marketing functions. So, if the marketing function decides to raise the credit limits on some accounts, it should be possible for this change to be effected within the marketing department without needing to obtain programming resources from IT to make the change.

Print production is vital for ensuring written communications are dispatched to customers. Key activities of the print production function are:

- Production and dispatch of promotional materials designed by the marketing department[1] via letter, e-mail, phone and so on.
- Production and dispatch of credit agreements for new customers. This will also include dispatch of credit/debit/charge cards as required.
- Production and dispatch of statements and statement inserts.
- Production of standard letters. For example, notice of late/incorrect payments, or notification of changes to the terms of an agreement, such as an increase in a product's APR.

Print production can be a large and complex part of an organization's operational activities, with large organizations needing to produce and dispatch many millions of items each month.

The operational functions are the most resource intensive in the organization, requiring a large investment in buildings, people, IT and other equipment. This means there are significant time and cost implications whenever the demand for operational services changes. Consequently, there needs to be close cooperation with the strategy functions to ensure that the right resources are in place to meet the fluctuations in demand generated by the implementation of new business strategies. For example, if the marketing department goes ahead with a big recruitment campaign for new customers without giving customer services sufficient notice, then there will be insufficient resources to deal with the demand generated from the campaign. Service levels will suffer, resulting in frustrated and dissatisfied customers who may take their business elsewhere. What should happen is that the requirements of customer services (and other operational functions) are included as part of the overall campaign management, to ensure that suitable resources are in place – a process that could take weeks or months if new staff, IT systems or other resources need to be acquired. Conversely, if the credit risk function decides that write-off levels are to high and reduces the number of accepted applications, then the demand for customer services will decline and decisions will need to be taken as to what to do with staff that may be surplus to requirements.[2]

2.1.3   Corporate functions

All large credit granting institutions will also have a number of functions working in support of their general business activities. These include:

- Accounting and finance.
- Legal.
- Payroll.
- Human resources (Personnel).
- Estates and services.

The main responsibilities of the accounting and finance function are:

- Managing the flow of funds within the business to ensure there is sufficient capital available to fund the organization's lending activities and to repay creditors.
- Creating portfolio level forecasts of bad debt and provision.
- For deposit taking institutions, ascertaining capital requirements based on forecasts of future default rates and write-off amounts.
- Production of the organization's accounts.

Accounting and finance functions are concerned with the cash flow within the business and the income and expenditure figures required to produce company accounts. They will also provide senior management with a coherent view of the financial status of the business. Therefore, they need to liaise with other business areas to obtain the information they require. For example, in managing the supply of funds in support of consumer lending they will look to the marketing and credit functions to supply forecasts of expected demand for new credit and the expected income that will be generated from customer repayments. These funds then need to be acquired from the money markets that provide institutional credit. In deposit taking institutions there may also be some areas of joint responsibility with the credit risk function. For example, to translate individual estimates of the risk of customer default into portfolio level measures of risk for the calculation of capital requirements. Capital requirements are discussed in more detail in Chapter 11.

The legal function will mainly be concerned with contractual issues with suppliers and providing general advice to other areas of the business about relevant legislation. From an operational perspective there may be times when legal advice is sought about an individual customer's account, but this will be relatively rare because there should be a good working knowledge of standard legal practices within the operational areas. Therefore, only particularly unusual or sensitive cases will require the attention of specialist legal resources.

The responsibilities of the other three functions are common to almost all organizations. Payroll manages salary payments, pension contributions, tax deductions and so on. Human resources deals with personnel issues, draws up contracts of employment, defines disciplinary procedures, ensures compliance with employment legislation, organizes recruitment and arranges staff training. Estates and Services deals with procurement, general maintenance and cleaning services.

2.2 Structural orientation

The business functions responsible for credit management are usually structured in one of three ways. A divisional (product) orientated way, a functional (customer) orientated way or a mixture of the two.[3] If an organization is divisionally orientated, as shown in Figure 2.1, each credit portfolio (cards, loans, mortgages and so on) is managed as a separate business, with each making its own contribution to the overall profitability of the organization.

The main advantages of adopting a divisional orientation are:

- Each business function within the division is expert in dealing with the products that the division is responsible for. Therefore, it can be very efficient at designing and delivering those products.
- Within each division the business functions are usually well coordinated and work cooperatively to manage the customer relationship.

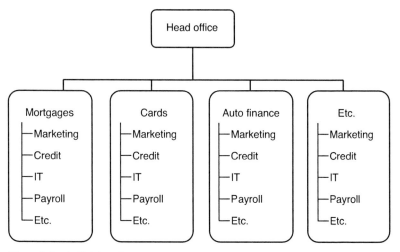

Figure 2.1　A divisional structure

- As each division is self contained, it is relatively easy to calculate the profitability of each division and the products that the division provides.

The main disadvantages are:

- Some activities will be replicated within each division, resulting in additional costs.
- There is little opportunity for staff to learn about the management of products and services within other divisions. Their expertise will therefore be narrow, unless effort is made by head office to move personnel between divisions.
- Contradictory actions may be taken within different divisions. This can result in poor customer service, increased rates of attrition and/or lost opportunities to cross sell additional products and services. For example, the mortgage division may be willing to grant someone a $200,000 mortgage, but the customer only requires $75,000, meaning that the customer has a potential unused credit line of $125,000. A short time later the card division declines the individual's application for credit card with a $5,000 limit, because they believe the customer won't use the card much and so won't generate much profit. Being rejected for the credit card is likely to upset the mortgage customer and increase the chance of them moving their mortgage to another provider.

- Opportunities for savings via economies of scale will be lost. For example, by operating separate call centres for each division instead of a single large call centre.

A functional orientation on the other hand, as illustrated in Figure 2.2, tends to focus on bringing together similar types of resources from across the business.

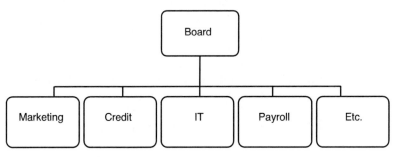

Figure 2.2   A functional structure

So, for example, there will be a single marketing function responsible for all of the products provided by the institution. The pros and cons of adopting a functional orientation tend to be a mirror image of those of the divisional approach. The main advantages are:

- Costs are reduced for two reasons. First, the duplication of business functions found within a divisional structure is reduced. Second, advantage can be taken of economies of scale.
- It is much easier for staff to gain a broader understanding of the business, outside of their own area of expertise. This facilitates staff development and retention, and better customer service.
- Customer relationships can be managed much more cohesively across all of the products and services that someone may possess. So if someone applies for say, a mortgage, a lending strategy for instalment loans, credit cards and overdraft facilities can be formulated in conjunction with the mortgage offer.

The main disadvantages are:

- There is less coordination and communication between different business functions. This can result in a more tactical view of the business being adopted, with each function focusing only on its own immediate problems and objectives. Insufficient consideration may be given to wider strategic objectives and organizational level issues. This is particularly true for organizations which provide a diverse range of products and services (Johnson and Scholes 2002 p. 423).

- Determining the profitability of individual products becomes difficult. This is because there is often dispute over how costs and revenues should be allocated within and between different business functions. It is not unheard of for each business function to have an independent methodology for calculating product profitability.
- There is increased competition for shared resources. For example, if the business wants to update the IT systems for both its card and loan portfolios, but has limited resources, a decision will have to be made as to which takes priority.

Few organizations adopt structures that are purely functional or divisional and there are many shades of grey. For example, organizations that operate in a primarily divisional way may set-up interdivisional functions to coordinate entry into new markets or to share information about customers. On the other hand, a functionally orientated organization may find it beneficial to impose a level of divisionalization when developing new products to ensure an integrated approach is taken across the organization (Johnson and Scholes 2002 p. 431). It is also common to find organizations where the corporate and operational functions are functionally orientated, while the strategy functions are divisionally orientated.

2.3   Legislative principles

Throughout the world consumer credit is subject to legislation that dictates how credit agreements are promoted, created and managed. Every country has its own legislation and within some countries the law can even differ between states and regions. Given the international nature of this book and the lengthy prose required to explore even a single piece of legislation in detail, an in-depth discussion of credit legislation is not attempted. Rather, certain principles can be found within many of the different legislative frameworks adopted by governments worldwide[4] and therefore, the goal in this section is to describe these general principles. It is then up to the reader to carryout the necessary investigative work to familiarize themselves with the specific legislation that applies to them. A short summary of the most important legalisation relevant to US and UK consumer credit markets is contained in Appendix C.

2.3.1 Transparency and disclosure

Organizations are required to provide clear information about the terms and conditions of credit agreements within promotional literature and the text of credit agreements. In particular, the typical APR[5] and the total cost of credit over the term of the agreement must be provided. Additional charges and fees must also be made clear. For example, penalty charges for missed payments or exceeding the credit limit on a credit card.

2.3.2 Use of personal data

Many countries impose restrictions on the way in which organizations gather, hold and use personal data about individuals. In EU countries controls over the use of personal data are enshrined within EU directives implemented within each member state's national legislative framework. The key principle underpinning EU data protection law is that it is the individual who controls information about themselves and how their personal information may be used. This means that an organization can only obtain and use data about someone if the individual has first given permission for them to do so. Permission is usually obtained by having a suitable clause within the application form that the individual signs, to confirm that they agree with the terms and conditions of the agreement. In many non-EU countries, including the US, a somewhat different perspective is taken. Personal data is a commodity that any organization can obtain and use. Legislation exists to prevent specific misuse of data. For example, the US Fair Credit Reporting Act 1970 gives every citizen a legal right to receive copies of the information that credit reference agencies hold about them. The Act also requires credit reference agencies to correct any errors in the data that may subsequently be found to exist.

2.3.3 Discrimination

Laws against discrimination on the grounds of sex, race, religion, sexual orientation and so on are common. This means it is illegal to use certain types of information when making lending decisions.

2.3.4 Collections and debt recovery action

When someone falls behind with their credit repayments action will be taken to encourage payment of the arrears, such as sending a reminder letter or calling the customer on the phone. In many countries legislation exists to limit the activities that can be taken to recover unpaid debts and/or the costs that can be charged for such activities. For example, the use of abusive or threatening behaviour, contacting customers at unsociable hours and forcing entry to a property to seize assets in lieu of unpaid debts are often prohibited.

2.3.5   Asset seizure and bankruptcy (Personal insolvency)

If a debt is unsecured, a lender can not force repayment or seize assets in lieu of the debt unless action is taken through the courts. You can not, for example, decide to take someone's car and sell it in order to cover a credit card debt even if the credit card was used to buy the car. The lender must obtain a court ruling permitting the car (or other assets) to be seized in lieu of the debt.[6] If an individual has debts but no means by which to pay them, a court may declare the individual bankrupt (personally insolvent). Various forms of bankruptcy are defined within different jurisdictions, but in general, once declared bankrupt an individual loses control of their assets, including their home[7] and these may be sold by representatives of the court/creditors in order to repay the individual's debts. After a period of time the bankrupt will be discharged. This means that the slate is wiped clean, with most[8] outstanding debts written-off.

2.3.6   Cancellation rights (Right of rescission)

In order to reduce the incidence of people being persuaded to take out loans that they don't really want by overbearing salespeople, many forms of credit come with cancellation rights (termed the right of rescission in the US).[9] This gives consumers a short period of time after signing a credit agreement (usually a few days) to notify the lender in writing that they wish to cancel the agreement. The lender must then cancel the agreement and refund any deposit or other up front payments made by the customer.

2.3.7   Linked transactions

In many regions the decision to grant credit and the terms under which credit is offered, can not be made on the condition that the individual purchases other financial products from the credit provider. In particular, a customer can not be forced to take out credit insurance as a condition of being granted credit.

2.3.8 Maximum interest rate

Interest rate ceilings exist in many US states, Canada, Germany, France, Australia and a number of other countries. These restrict the maximum interest rate (or the APR) that a lender can charge. The principal goal of such restrictions is to prevent extortionate lending, particularly to those who are already in financial difficulty or who do not have a sufficient level of financial literacy to fully understand the terms of the credit being offered. In some regions the maximum interest rate is a fixed amount, say 15 percent per annum. In others, the maximum rate is a function of the average market rate of the major lending institutions, perhaps double the average. The legal maximum is recalculated on a regular basis to reflect changes in market conditions. In the UK interest rate ceilings were abolished in 1974, but legislation does allow the courts to alter the terms of a credit agreement if they are deemed to be unfair or otherwise grossly contravenes the principles of fair dealing (Skipworth and Dyson 1997 p. 150).

In the US the laws regarding interest rate restrictions are complex due to the mixture of state and federal regulations that apply. In practice however, most credit granting institutions are relatively unrestricted in the interest rates they can charge their customers. This is for two reasons. First, retail credit; that is, credit cards, personal loans, hire-purchase and so on have been granted special exemptions from federal legislation. Second, if an organization operates in a number of states, the state law where the organization's head office is based applies to all of the organizations lending activities, wherever they may be. Therefore, most large credit granting institutions have head offices located in states that have lax laws about the rates that may be charged.

2.4 Ethical aspects of credit management

Why are ethical issues important in running a commercial credit granting operation? As long as the relevant legislation is complied with, then isn't that all that needs to be considered? Well yes, that is one point of view, but there is evidence to suggest that organizations that make some efforts to incorporate an ethical perspective within the scope of their business operations outperform those that do not (Webley and More 2003). At first sight this may seem counterintuitive because taking an ethical stance obviously limits the range of activities that can be engaged in, making it more difficult for an organization to achieve its business objectives. However, in the longer term there is often a positive impact of ethical behaviour in terms of company image and better customer relationships, which leads to improved bottom line performance. One should also be aware, that while there is often a degree of overlap between legal and ethical activities, just because something is legal does not mean it is ethical and vice versa. At best, the law captures the essence of ethical behaviour, but there are always areas that the law does not cover or areas where people have found ways to work within the letter of the law while flaunting the spirit of the law.

The other reason why ethical issues are important in credit granting is that there is a relationship between debt, poverty, social exclusion and mental health. Research has shown that the burden of debt can cause physiological stress and lead to depression (Nettleton and Burrows 1998; Drentea and Lavrakas 2000; Reading and Reynolds 2001). There aren't many (if any) cases of people committing suicide because they bought a dishwasher that wasn't ideal for their needs, or were mis-sold their car, but there are many examples of people committing suicide because of their debts. There is also a proven link between physical illness and debt (Jacoby 2002; Balmer et al. 2005) although reasons why this should be the case are yet to be determined. This is not to say credit and debt are bad things – far from it – but that there are concerns around its use and misuse that the reader should be aware of.

What does this mean for the credit professional operating in the market today? Well a number of things. From a personal perspective, if one wishes to display a degree of social responsibility, then there is scope to consider how the implementation of the organization's lending practices impact upon the wellbeing of its customers. From an organizational perspective there is a need to consider how to identify customers who may be over-indebted, have responsible lending criteria, and be sympathetic when dealing with people who inform the company that they are finding it difficult to repay their debts. This is not purely for reasons of legal compliance, but one of market prudence that can generate an improvement to the overall performance of the business.

2.4.1   Lessons from history

Anyone working within the credit industry should be aware that credit, and the practices associated with credit granting, have historically been (and remain) enormously controversial. There have always been great social concerns over the use and misuse of credit, often resulting in legislation to control the terms under which credit can be granted and managed in an attempt to safeguard the general public. One of the earliest pieces of credit legislation forms part of the Babylonian 'Code of Hammurabi', dating from around 1750 B.C. Amongst other things, The Code specified the maximum interest rates that could be charged and protected borrowers from being physically abused by their creditors should they experience repayment difficulties (Gelpi and Julien-Labruyere 2000 p. 3). In the fifth century B.C. Aristotle argued that interest bearing credit was 'unnatural' (Everson 1988) and for more than 2,000 years after his death, Aristotle's arguments were widely used to condemn commercial lending activities based on the charging of interest. The Bible, Koran and Torah all contain passages condemning the charging of interest (or usury as it was traditionally known). In many European countries there have been periods of history when usury was declared illegal and banned outright.

In many societies today, consumer credit is now widely accepted and openly practiced – after all most of us have credit cards, loans of one sort of another, and maybe a mortgage. However, it should not be forgotten that suspicions about the motives of the credit industry remain, and there is a perceived view that lenders are out to fleece their customers for every penny they can get using whatever means available, regardless of the true situation. Consequently, many governments regularly investigate the actions of the credit industry resulting in limitations and controls being imposed on the activities of credit providers. The reader should also be aware that while interest bearing credit is widely accepted by many parts of society, for the estimated 1.5 billion members of the Islamic community the charging of interest is forbidden. This doesn't mean that credit is not permitted in Islamic society, but that the forms of credit that are compliant with Islamic (Shari'ah) law are somewhat different from that which the reader may be familiar.

2.4.2   Credit – not just another consumer product

So what is it that differentiates a credit agreement from other types of trading relationship, and what is it that leads to such controversy over its use and misuse? When someone purchases something on a cash basis, goods and funds are exchanged simultaneously by the two parties involved. Certainly there is a risk of the customer being mis-sold a product that is inappropriate or over-priced, but the loss faced by the customer is usually limited to the value of the goods.[10] This is not the case with credit and two things differentiate a credit agreement from other types of consumer retail transaction. The first is the time dimension of the relationship and the risks to both parties that such a relationship creates. The debtor may receive funds up front, but the creditor has to wait for the debt to be repaid. This introduces an element of risk to the transaction because there is always the chance the debtor won't repay what they owe, leaving the creditor out of pocket. Therefore, all aspects of credit management are involved in the management of this risk in one form or another. From a customer perspective, the risk comes from the actions lenders take when the customer experiences repayment difficulties, and this brings us to the second point. Interest bearing credit is not static. It grows exponentially over time. It is quite possible for small debts, initially perhaps no more than a few hundred dollars, to result in an individual losing their home, their job and being declared bankrupt. One example of this which received considerable media attention at the time, was the case of a $9775[11] loan granted in the UK in 1989 at an interest rate of 34.9 percent. By 2004 the debt had risen to $652,800[11] due to the borrower falling into arrears a few months into the agreement, with interest continuing to be charged,[12] the penalty charges that were levied and interest that had already accrued. This is despite the borrower resuming repayments a few months after the initial difficulties arose. The debt was eventually written-off by the courts, but only because the credit agreement did not fully conform to the consumer credit legislation at the time.[13]

2.4.3   Whose responsibility is debt?

Given the comments in the previous section, if one wants to act as a responsible lender yet continue to manage a competitive business, then how can responsible lending be defined in a practical context? A common argument that is often touted – with some justification – is that every individual has responsibility for the agreements they enter into, and if they subsequently can't pay then it's their own fault and they should suffer the consequences – whatever they may be. The emphasis is firmly on the borrower not the lender. However, the vast majority of debt problems come about not because of borrowers acting irresponsibly, but due to unforeseen events that occur after debts have been incurred. In the US for example, it is estimated that about 90 percent of bankruptcy is due to unemployment, medical bills or divorce (The American Bar Association 2006 p. 201). It is also important to note that there is plenty of evidence to suggest that a large proportion of the population of the UK and US do not understand the terms under which credit is provided to them. This is despite legislation in the form of the US Fair Credit Reporting Act 1970 and the UK Consumer Credit Act 1974, which provide detailed and specific instructions about the information that must be provided in credit advertisements and credit agreements about the APR and repayment terms. In a survey carried out in the US, it was found that at least 40 percent of individuals did not understand the relationship between the interest rate and the quoted APR (Lee and Hogarth 1999). A UK survey in 2002 reported that 75 percent of those with hire-purchase agreements and 63 percent with loans did not know the interest rate they were being charged on their debts (Kempson 2002 p. 50). Why should this be the case? One answer is that credit agreements are, despite efforts to make them more understandable, quite complex. If you are reading this book, then you are very likely to be highly literate and university educated. We must remember that, while very few people are completely illiterate, in the US 34 percent of adults are reported as having only a basic or below basic level of literacy (Kutner et al. 2005 p. 4)[14] and in England 16 percent of adults are reported as having a level of literacy at or below that expected for an 11 year old (Williams et al. 2003 p. 18). Similar figures exist for numeracy. It is difficult to see how people without such skills can fully understand the nature of compound interest, the multiple interest rates applied to different types of transaction for products such as credit cards, or the host of additional charges and fees imposed by lenders in response to various customer behaviours. Given this situation, it is perhaps not surprising that the UK industry taskforce on over-indebtedness came to the conclusion that there was a joint responsibility for debt. Therefore, while the borrower shouldered some responsibility for their debts, the lender also had a duty to lend responsibly (Consumer Affairs Directorate 2001). This means that for those working within the credit industry in the UK there is a requirement to consider issues such as the affordability of debt when promoting credit to potential customers, and to also take an understanding approach with customers who inform them of their debt problems. For many lenders this means far more than paying lip service to a commitment to lend responsibly. In the UK, which has the largest consumer credit market outside of the US, lenders have been known to have written-off substantial debts when they have been shown to have lent money to those who clearly can not afford it, even though they had no legal obligation to do so. The *Guardian* newspaper reported a case where an individual who earned only $213[11] a week had debts with five major banks totalling around $170,000[11]. Most of the banks wrote-off the debts after agreeing that they had lent irresponsibly. This is despite the fact that the individual openly acknowledged inflating his salary details when originally applying for credit (Jones 2006).

Some of the approaches that can be adopted to develop a responsible lending framework are discussed in later chapters.

2.5 Chapter summary

The management processes required to run a successful consumer credit business sit within an organizational structure interlaced with a number of different business functions. The two strategy functions, credit risk and marketing, are concerned with planning the customer relationship strategy; that is, the actions that the organization should take in order to maximize the return generated from the universe of potential and existing customers. The operational areas provide the support and infrastructure required to implement the actions that have been planned by the strategy functions. Customer services controls the interface with the customer and print production manages the production and dispatch of written communications such as monthly statements, reminder letters and promotional literature. IT provides the computer systems to allow each business function to process and record the information it needs to fulfil its role within the organization. The corporate functions are common to all large organizations and are responsible for the administrative tasks needed to ensure that the business runs smoothly and complies with relevant legislation. The main corporate functions are Accounting and Finance, Legal, Payroll, Human Resources and Estates and Services.

There exists a long history of debate around the use and misuse of credit and what constitutes ethical good practice within the credit industry. This has led to detailed legislative frameworks in many regions that control or limit the actions that lenders can take when promoting their products, recruiting new customers and managing credit agreements on an ongoing basis.

3
Marketing

In this chapter we consider the first phase of credit management; the marketing of credit to people who do not have any sort of existing relationship with the credit provider. Marketing strategies targeted at existing customers to encourage greater product usage, foster brand loyalty and the take-up of additional products and services are discussed in Chapter 6.

Marketing is about far more than coming up with the best advertising strategy in order to try and sell as much product as possible. Marketing encompasses every aspects of a product that involves potential customers. This includes function, branding, price, service levels, communication channels and methods of distribution, which in many texts are described within the context of the four Ps of marketing – Product, Price, Place (distribution) and Promotion (Perreault and McCarthy 2004). To put it another way, the marketer's goal is to maximize the returns from a product by considering the customer's requirements across the entire product proposition from conception to delivery.

This chapter is in three parts. The first part covers product design and the features that define a credit product; that is, the terms of a credit agreement and the ways in which it can be differentiated from competitors through the implementation of an appropriate brand strategy. The second part is about product strategy and understanding the market in terms of the different types of consumers that comprise the market and the different product features that appeal to each. The third part of the chapter discusses promotional strategies and the ways in which demand can be generated to meet organizational sales objectives.

35

3.1   Product design

A credit product is characterized by a number of features that define its type, functionality and usage. These features can be categorized into three different types:

1. Primary features. These define the type of credit being offered and determine the way in which credit is advanced and repaid.
2. Secondary features. These are additional features that are not central to the credit offer, but which provide some additional tangible benefits to the customer.
3. Brand features. These are the less tangible features that consumers associate with a product that help differentiate it from competing products with similar primary and/or secondary features.

3.1.1   Primary features

Primary features define the conditions under which credit is granted and the terms under which credit is repaid. These features were described in some detail in section 1.3, and in summary are as follows:

1. Whether credit is provided on a secured or unsecured basis.
2. Whether repayments are amortizing or balloon.
3. Whether the credit agreement is fixed sum or running account.
4. Whether credit is provided on a restricted or unrestricted basis.
5. Whether credit is provided on a credit sale, conditional sale or hire-purchase basis (for restricted credit only).
6. Whether the credit agreement is a debtor-creditor or a debtor-creditor-supplier agreement.
7. The amount of credit available.
8. The term (duration) of the agreement.
9. The cost of credit. If several different charges are applied, then each of these can be considered to be a separate sub-feature of the product.

The first six features define the product type. If an unsecured personal loan is being offered, the features that define it as an unsecured personal loan are that it is unsecured, amortizing, fixed sum, unrestricted and debtor-creditor (item five does not apply as a personal loan is unrestricted). The product types offered by an organization is normally a strategic decision taken at board level. The directors of a retail bank may decide that the bank will offer mortgages, unsecured personal loans and overdrafts, but not credit cards or motor finance. The mix of product types is not something that is usually considered by marketing departments as part of their normal day-to-day operations. Instead, the marketing department is responsible for determining the organization's product strategy for each product type. This covers items seven, eight and nine on the list – the amount of credit, the term of the agreement and the charging structure (the costs) that will be imposed on different types of customer. At this point it is worth noting that in this chapter we are talking about the general features of a product that are determined prior to someone applying for credit. The actual amount of credit, the term of the agreement and the cost of credit will vary from one individual to the next, and in most cases will only be determined after a full assessment of their credit application has been made. The role of the marketing department prior to application is to come up with the general features of the product and the parameters within which the product will operate. For a mortgage the typical APR may be chosen to be 6.75 percent, and this is the rate that features within promotional literature. However, while 6.75 percent is the typical APR, some people will be charged a higher APR if they have a poor credit rating, or a lower APR if they have a very good credit rating – a strategy referred to as pricing for risk. Likewise, a lender may advertise that it provides unsecured instalment loans up to a maximum of $100,000, but in reality only the very best customers with a good income and who are extremely creditworthy will be allowed this much credit. Individualized credit strategies are discussed in more detail in Chapter 5.

Following on from the discussion in the previous paragraph, the minimum and maximum amount of credit to offer is a relatively simple decision. The minimum will be set to ensure that interest and other charges, at the very least, cover the cost of setting up and running the customer's account. Most lenders will not provide credit cards with limits of less than $500, personal loans for less than $1,000 or mortgages for less than $20,000. The theoretical maximum amount of credit is usually uncapped or set to some very high value, or limited by legislation in some regions. Some lenders will also set somewhat arbitrary limits on the amount they are willing to lend to a single individual. This is to ensure their risk from bad debt is spread evenly across a large portfolio of individuals, rather than concentrated towards a few individuals with very large debts.

Decisions about the term are also relatively simple. For standard fixed term credit a minimum term (often 6 or 12 months) will be imposed because a shorter term will not result in enough revenues to provide a sufficient return on investment after administrative costs have been taken into account. Maximum lending terms are less problematic. The only major considerations are whether or not the borrower is likely to retire (and hence find the loan unaffordable on a reduced income) or die before the end of the agreement (leaving the lender to decide whether or not to peruse the deceased's estate for the outstanding debt). For revolving products such as credit cards and store cards the term relates to the time until a decision is made about card renewal. Common practice is to set a renewal date between one and five years. The advantage of a short renewal period is that it provides an easy way to manage unprofitable agreements. For example, in cases where an account is no longer used (has become dormant), but costs are incurred for maintaining the customer's account details within the organization's account management system. In some cases the best option may simply be to close the account. In other cases card renewal can be seen as an opportunity for customer communication to encourage reactivation of the account using various incentives such as a reduced interest rate or a discount on items purchased from certain stores. A downside of frequent card renewal is that it incurs cost and can cause the customer to stop using their account. This is because the renewal process may require the account holder to do something to validate their new card. This may simply be to sign the card or make a phone call to confirm receipt, but in some cases the account holder can't be bothered to do this, preferring to make use of alternative credit facilities they have available.

The most prominent primary feature of a credit agreement is the cost of credit, which can be made up of a number of separate fees and charges. The interest (finance) charge is the most obvious way in which charges are imposed, and for credit cards, for example, around 70 percent of revenues are generated from interest charges (Evans and Schmalensee 2005 p. 223). However, significant revenue streams can also be generated from a range of other sources. These include:

- Arrangement (documentation) fees. These are charged for setting up a credit agreement. They are commonly applied to mortgage agreements, hire-purchase agreements and conditional sale agreements.
- Annual fees. These are often applied to card products.
- Option to buy fees levied on hire-purchase agreements.
- Redemption fees. These are applied to mortgages and loans when a borrower repays the loan before the agreed end date.

- Penalty charges. These include:
  - o Fees for missed/late/reduced payments.
  - o Fees for exceeding the credit limit.
  - o Fees for returned cheques/bounced payments.
- Duplicate statement fees, charged for providing additional copies of customer statements.
- Interchange fees. The interchange fee is the proportion of a credit card transaction that a card issuer receives from a merchant each time someone pays for something using a card. Interchange fees are discussed in more detail in Chapter 6.
- Cash withdrawal fees. These apply when a credit/charge card is used to obtain cash from a bank or ATM.
- Balance transfer fees. These are charged for transferring balances from one form of credit facility to another, and are most commonly associated with credit cards.
- Call charges. A significant income stream can be generated by setting up a premium rate line for customer enquiries.

Other features which impact on the cost of credit include:

- The timing between repayments. For most credit products repayments are made on a monthly basis, but some agreements specify annual, four weekly or weekly repayments.
- The minimum repayment for revolving credit accounts.
- Repayment holidays – where repayments are suspended for a period of time, although interest may continue to accrue.
- Introductory/reduced interest charges. These are usually applied at the start of an agreement, to encourage product usage or the transfer of a credit balance from a rival product.
- The repayment hierarchy. For credit cards different interest rates may be charged for retail transactions, cash withdrawals, balance transfers and so on. Decisions need to be made about which part of the balance is repaid first when a customer makes a payment.
- The value of cross sold products – for example payment protection insurance, which is discussed in greater detail in Chapters 5 and 6.

The total cost of credit is the sum of all the charges imposed over the life of a product. From a legal perspective, the cost of credit is defined as the sum of mandatory fees that a customer must pay; for instance, the interest charge on a loan. Charges such as those for exceeding the credit limit on a credit card are not mandatory because a customer can choose to keep within their credit limit and not pay the charge. The APR is calculated using only the mandatory charges that must be paid.[1] Optional charges are not included in the APR calculation. Whether charges are mandatory or optional has important implications from a marketing perspective, because there is usually a requirement for the APR to be displayed prominently on any promotional literature and within credit agreements. Public perception is that a lower APR will result in a lower cost of borrowing for the consumer. Therefore, for many lenders a key goal is to keep the interest rate and other mandatory charges as low as possible, and to encourage the take-up of the optional components. For example, within the UK personal loan market the largest contribution to lenders' profits comes from payment protection insurance and penalty charges – not the interest charges that are applied.

Another important consideration is the difference between the affordability of credit and the cost of credit. The cost of credit is the total amount that an individual pays over the term of the agreement. Affordability relates to how payments are managed within the context of someone's income and cash flow. It does not necessarily follow that the cheapest credit option is the most affordable. If two competing credit cards have the same APR, but one allows a minimum repayment of 3 percent of the outstanding balance per month and the other 5 percent of the balance per month, then the first card provides greater affordability, although the second will be cheapest overall, if only minimum repayments are made each month. Affordability is also affected by the split between up front fees paid at the outset of a credit agreement and the charges that accrue over the lifetime of the agreement. In the mortgage market many lenders will charge a large arrangement fee, sometimes several thousand dollars, in return for a medium to long term guarantee of a low interest rate. This may be attractive to some borrowers, but if cash flow is tight, a borrower may accept a higher interest charge in return for a lower arrangement fee. Likewise, a loan product that allows someone to change the monthly repayment date so that repayments fit better with their personal cash flow situation (such as immediately after payday rather than immediately before) is more attractive from an affordability perspective than an otherwise identical loan product that does not provide such an option.

3.1.2   Secondary features

Primary features define a product's core utility and usage. The variation in primary features for credit products of the same type, such as two competing credit cards, is in reality not that great. Any credit offer based on primary features alone can be imitated by competitors with relative ease. If you can offer a fantastic credit card deal with a 5.9 percent APR, then any other card provider could replicate this offer almost immediately if they so wished (whether or not they could do so <u>and</u> make a profit is a different issue). The overall result is that many competing credit products tend to be very similar, providing an almost identical set of primary features for the consumer. Therefore, to try and make a product more appealing than competitor products, a common strategy is to provide some additional features or 'perks' that encourage take-up of the product, but which are not directly relevant to the terms and conditions of the underlying credit agreement. Popular secondary features include:

- **Loyalty schemes.** These provide some type of incentive to use the product on an ongoing basis. This may be in the form of air miles, free travel insurance, discounts with certain retailers or 'cash back' where a proportion of retail expenditure (usually somewhere between 0.5 and 1 percent) is paid back to the customer each month. Loyalty schemes are most commonly associated with card products, but can also be provided as an incentive for loan and mortgage customers by giving them something if they maintain the agreement for its full term and do not redeem the product early.
- **Cash back on agreement.** For fixed term credit products, particularly mortgages, a lender may offer a cash payment as an incentive for taking out their product. If someone takes out say, a $100,000 mortgage, a 2 percent cash back would result in the customer receiving a $2,000 payment.
- **Payment holidays.** A payment holiday provides an option to suspend repayments for several months during course of an agreement, giving a customer greater control over their cash flow. With many agreements a payment holiday will be provided at the start of an agreement, delaying the first repayment by anything up to 12 months. In other instances, a customer may be given an option to miss their next repayment. Although a customer will make no repayments during the period of the repayment holiday, interest will normally continue to accrue.
- **Purchase discounts and product tie-ins.** For revolving credit products a discount may be offered on goods bought from retailers with whom the card provider has an agreement. For store cards it is common policy to offer a 10–20 percent discount the first time the

card is used, or for the first week or month that an account is open. The offer of a purchase discount can also be used as a customer management tool to encourage the reactivation of dormant accounts.

• **Product customization.** People like to be seen to be different. If a product be tailored in some way so that it is unique to an individual, then this can be a desirable product feature. In the UK, the Royal Bank of Scotland allows customers to personalize their credit cards by uploading any picture they like to the bank's website, which is then used to emboss the customer's credit card.

3.1.3   Brand features

'Brand' imbues a product with certain characteristics, perceived or real, that provide some added value over and above those defined by the primary and secondary features. Brand features are often emotive in nature, reflecting an individual's feeling and perceptions about the worth of the brand (De Chernatony and McDonald 2003 pp. 14–16). Consumers look to brands as a means of expressing their identity. A brand says something about how someone perceives themselves and how they want to be seen by others. Morgan Stanley put this to good effect in their credit card marketing campaigns during the early 2000s with their ad-line 'Only 7 percent of communication is verbal.' The ads conveyed the message that when someone saw you using your Morgan Stanley card this said that you shared Morgan Stanley's belief in only accepting the very best terms of quality and service. This in turn implied that when people knew you were a Morgan Stanley customer, you were part of an elite that demanded better treatment than people who used competitor products. Whether or not Morgan Stanley's credit card customers actually received better service than other people is irrelevant. The perception of better service is what gave Morgan Stanley a brand advantage over its rivals in this instance. Similarly Capital One has made a big effort to foster its image as a provider of credit products that are secure and help to prevent fraud. MBNA uses affinity marketing to associate itself with hundreds of organizations such as sports clubs, charities and trade associations in order to share the brand qualities that people associate with these organizations, while in the UK the Cooperative Bank emphasizes its ethical credentials when promoting its products.

Creating a strong brand is usually the result of many years of nurturing and a carefully orchestrated and well integrated corporate strategy; that integrates product marketing with the organization's public relations and social responsibility policies. The result is a set of brand features that are very hard for competitors to replicate and allows consumers to easily differentiate a product from its competitors.

3.2   Product strategy

As long ago as the seventeenth century, Adam Smith stated his belief that in order to succeed, organizations needed to be better at understanding and satisfying their customer's needs than their competitors (Smith and Sutherland 1998). This means that organizations need to understand the market and incorporate this understanding within their product strategy. Yet, it is only relatively recently that these ideas have come to the forefront of mainstream marketing activity (Levitt 1960). It is still common to find organizations that come up with what they think is a good idea for a credit product (or any other type of product or service) and then expend considerable time and money developing the concept without carrying out market research to see if anyone actually wants the product, how it compares against competitors and how profitable (or unprofitable) such a product is likely to be.

The starting point for any product strategy, before any of the products features have been defined, is to gain an understanding of the market. The sort of things a product strategist would need to know are:

- The size of the market in terms of the number of potential customers, annual turnover, total profitability and so on.
- The different sub-groups (segments) that make up the market and the geo-demographic characteristics that define each segment such as gender, age, income, education and occupation.
- The differences between different customer segments in terms of which product features are the most important to customers in each segment.
- The way people within each customer segment behave when using a product. In particular, how much customers want to borrow, the term over which they want credit and the losses that will result should they default. For card products it is important to know the proportion of balances that result from balance transfers, cash withdrawals and retail purchases because the income streams from each type of balance can vary enormously. The proportion of customers who revolve their balances each month is also important because interest revenue will only be generated from those that revolve.

- The average worth of individuals within each customer segment in terms of the revenues that are likely to be generated and the costs that will be incurred. This will usually be inferred from information that has been gathered about the way in which people within each customer segment behave when using a credit product, together with information about the cost of providing different product features.
- The competitors in the market. This is in terms of product features, consumer perceptions of brand features, market penetration and product profitability.

Such information will be used to produce a marketing plan covering the product launch and development over a period of somewhere between one and five years. A comprehensive marketing plan should include all of the following:

- The set of primary, secondary and brand features that define the product to be launched.
- A description of the product's target market.
- The expected demand for the product by month/quarter/year.
- A project plan. This contains details of all activities that need to be undertaken to launch the product, the resources required and the cost of these resources. The plan should cover all areas of the business, including customer contact centre and IT resources required to support the product.
- The promotional strategy. This will describe the types of promotional activity that are envisaged, the number/timing of individual campaigns, the cost of each campaign and the expected demand that will be generated.
- Ongoing costs. In addition to promotional expenditure, this will include account management costs, provisions for bad debt from customers who default and any infrastructure costs.
- A resource plan for the operational areas to ensure that customer demand generated by each promotional campaign can be dealt with.
- Cash flow. In the early stages of a product's lifetime far more will be paid out in new lending then is received in repayments. Therefore, plans need to be in place for acquiring the funds required to support new lending.
- Capital requirements. If the lender is a deposit taking institution, then the impact on capital requirements (as discussed in Chapter 11) will need to be considered.

• Risk analysis. This covers the chance of different problems (risks) occurring, the impact of those problems should they occur, and the actions needed to mitigate against them. For example, if initial demand is much higher than expected, then call centre resources may be insufficient to deal with demand. The impact will be a cost in terms of customer dissatisfaction and lost business. The risk could be mitigated by entering into an agreement (well before product launch) to have call centre resources, supplied by another organization, on standby should it prove necessary.

A comprehensive marketing plan is important because it helps provide a complete picture of the time, cost and effort required to deliver a product over the long term. One problem that I have witnessed time and time again is over enthusiastic marketing professionals getting carried away with providing a fantastic product with lots of great features, but who give little or no consideration to the cost of providing those features outside of the marketing domain. There is also a tendency to be driven by short term goals focused on recruiting large numbers of new customers quickly, without sufficient thought being given to more strategic objectives based on long term profitability. Perhaps the most common failing is to underestimate the amount of bad debt that a product will generate. The bad debt generated by new customers in the first few months of a credit agreement tends to be much higher than that from more established customers who have been on the books for a number of years. Another area that is often neglected is the impact of marketing activity on the operational areas of the business. In particular, sufficient consideration needs to be given to the resources required within customer contact centres to train staff about new products, adjust staffing levels to meet the demand generated by the product and make any changes that may be required to the organization's IT systems.

3.2.1 Market intelligence

A number of data sources and investigative tools can be employed to gather information about the market:

• General consumer surveys. Individuals are randomly selected and asked a series of questions about themselves, their lifestyles and product preferences. Surveys may be conducted via one-to-one interviews in the street or in individuals' homes, via mail, telephone or the internet.

- Existing customer surveys. Similar to a general survey, but the target group is selected from existing customers. This allows a more targeted approach to be applied based on information that is already known about individuals from the organization's customer databases.
- Existing customer databases. If an organization has previously offered a similar product to the new one being formulated, then patterns of past customer behaviour may give useful insights into how the new product might be used.
- Third party data. Organizations such as Callcredit, Experian and Equifax hold large amounts of information about consumer preferences and behaviours that they package and sell to their clients.
- Product testing. A small number of people (usually no more than a few hundred) will be recruited to test a prototype product. Response rates, product usage and profitability will then be monitored for a period of at least 3–6 months, but maybe much longer. Many organizations will undertake dozens or even hundreds of such tests as part of their market research, with each test offering a different set of product features and targeted at a different segment of the market. Capital One, for example, are reported to undertake around 45,000 different product tests worldwide each year (Ehrlich and Fanelli 2004 p. 24).
- Focus groups. Several individuals, often of a similar age and from similar socio-economic groups, will meet to discuss some aspect(s) of the product in question. Some incentive to attend will usually be provided in the form of a financial payment or a gift. The group will be led by an experienced facilitator who introduces various discussion topics to the group and guides the discussion. Ideally each focus group will be recorded, allowing a more complete analysis of the proceedings to be made after the event.
- Expert opinions. The views of marketing professionals will be sought about the product features that appeal to different types of consumers.
- Public information. Freely available information from journals, newspapers, industry magazines, government websites etc. about the current size, nature and trends in the market.

Each data source has its own strengths and weaknesses. The trick to gaining comprehensive and reliable market information is to use several methods in combination. Consumer surveys are a very popular way to gather quantitative data about a large number of individuals. The results can then be subject to formal analytical methods, such as data mining (discussed below) in order to discover statistically significant relationships between individuals and their product preferences. However, surveys are prone to a number of problems; in particular, issues surrounding non-response. In a postal survey it is not unusual for less than 20 percent of recipients to make a return. For internet surveys a response rate of 2 percent would be considered good. Response rates often differ depending upon the demographics of the individuals in question. This means that certain groups will be under or over represented within the population who complete the survey. Imagine a survey that asks people about their income. If older people have a greater tendency to complete the survey than younger people, and older people earn more than younger people, then the results of the survey will lead to an overestimate of the true income figure. In many cases it is possible to correct for such bias. If the distribution of age within the entire population is known (from government census data for example) then it is possible to check the age distribution of the responders against the wider population. If bias is found then more weight can be given to the responses received from under represented groups.

A great deal of thought needs to go into survey design. Questions should be simple, clear and objective. If options are provided, then it is important that all possible outcomes are covered and there is no ambiguity between options. So if part of a customer survey asked people about their preferences when being contacted on the phone, a reasonable question might be 'Do you prefer receiving calls on your mobile phone or landline when at home?' The two obvious answers that could be given in response to this question are 'Prefer mobile phone' and 'Prefer landline.' However, what if someone has a landline or a mobile but not both? Then the question is redundant. What if they don't mind which phone is used? In this case an incorrect answer will be given unless a third option: 'No preference' is also available. What if someone doesn't have a phone at all? Then the question will be left unanswered (and you won't know why it's been left unanswered) or maybe a random answer will be provided. The question should either include an additional option 'Don't have a phone' or the original question should be preceded with a question asking if they have a landline, mobile, both or neither.

Existing customer databases can be useful, but only if they contain information about a product that is similar to the new one being considered. A database containing information about the repayment behaviour of store card customers, for example, is likely to be of limited worth when considering a credit offer for the residential mortgage market. This limitation also applies to third party data, which sometimes suffers from being provided in a summarized form (for example Experian's MOSAIC products). The raw data may not be provided, and this can severely restrict the amount of detailed analysis that can be carried out. However, the converse is also true. If analytical resources within an organization are limited, then being supplied with summary information that has already been analysed in detail by third party experts can be extremely useful, lead to more rapid results and be far cheaper than carrying out detailed analysis of the raw data in-house.

Product testing can be extremely useful as it provides information about actual product usage, and if many different tests are undertaken then many different dimensions of customer behaviour can be analysed across different segments of the market. One downside of product testing is that it requires several months to observe how customers use the product before definitive conclusions can be arrived at. Another disadvantage of product testing is that it gives advance warning to competitors about your product strategy (Harrison 1999 p. 109). It can also be expected that some of the tests will be unsuccessful – possibly resulting in a loss. Therefore, this cost needs to be accounted for within the marketing plan.

Focus groups and expert opinions suffer from the problem that they don't tend to provide hard evidence and are based on responses from relatively few individuals. This can lead to skewed results and the data may be interpreted by different people in very different ways. One of the strengths of focus groups is that they allow less quantifiable views and more personal feelings to be captured in a way that would be difficult or impossible with more detached approaches such as a postal survey. Another strength of focus groups and expert opinion is that they can incorporate feedback as part of the information gathering process. This allows the facilitator to change their line of questioning so that new avenues are explored beyond the original scope of the investigation. Focus groups and expert opinion are often used at a preliminary stage to generate ideas and undertake exploratory investigation to establish the scope of future market research.

Public information can be useful for gauging the size of the market and for predicting future trends, particularly in markets where central banks or industry bodies publish regular market updates. The US Federal Reserve publishes monthly data about trends in the consumer credit market gathered from the major US lending institutions and similar information is provided by the British Bankers Association, APACS and the Bank of England in the UK. The drawback is that information may be patchy and it can be difficult to verify figures published in some newspapers and magazines, and on the internet. As with focus groups and expert opinion, public information tends to be of greatest benefit when used as an exploratory resource, to provide an initial view of the market before more exacting and reliable methods are used.

3.2.2 Competitor intelligence

In most consumer credit markets there are several organizations offering competing products. It makes sense to gather information about competitors' offers to ensure that the package of features that define your product are not inferior. At one level, competitor information can easily be obtained from promotional literature and websites. Product comparison websites can also be useful, such as moneysupermarket.com and gocompare.com in the UK, which provide details about mortgages, loans and credit cards. However, it is surprising how many marketing departments don't maintain an up-to-date competitor database, and therefore can't say with certainty how their products are positioned within the market. Competitor brand features are less tangible and more difficult to ascertain, but questions about how competitor brands are perceived can often be incorporated into focus groups or customer surveys.

At another level, what you really want to know is not just what the competition is offering, but which products are successful (profitable) and which are not. It is important to realize that just because a competitor is advertising what seems to be a fantastic credit offer or has acquired a significant market share, it does not mean that the product is generating a positive or sustainable contribution to profits. Information about product profitability is sometimes publicly available via annual reports or company trading updates.

3.2.3 Data analysis

To be of use, the data that's been gathered needs to be interpreted and acted upon. A number of data analysis tools are available:

- Data mining. Data mining is the application of statistical methods, such as regression and clustering, to large and complex data sets.[2] The data is analysed to identify relationships between individuals' characteristics, product preferences and product usage. For example, it may be found that the 25–34 age group make the greatest use of cash withdrawal facilities when using their credit cards. So, if the credit card provider wants to target 25–34 year olds, then providing attractive terms for cash withdrawals would be a good idea. Data

used in the analysis may come from consumer surveys, the organization's existing databases or from third party suppliers such as
credit reference agencies.

- Forecasting/trend analysis. Historical trends within the market and
  the geo-demographics of customers are analysed over a number of
  months or years. These are then projected forward to give forecasts
  of the future size and composition of the market.
- Expert opinion. Individuals with considerable industry experience
  will provide their interpretation of what the data means.

Each type of data analysis has its merits and drawbacks. Data mining
is attractive in situations where large amounts of diverse data are available
about many thousands of individuals. Various statistical techniques can
be applied in order to construct models of the relationships between individuals' characteristics and product usage. The limitations of data mining
are that it is often difficult to draw inferences about situations beyond the
domain of the existing data. If a finance company has historically offered
secured personal loans and is wondering whether or not there is market
for unsecured loans, then its database of existing customers will only be
of limited use because it won't contain any information about customer
behaviour when repaying unsecured loans.[3]

Forecasting market trends can be useful, but most forecasting techniques make inferences about the future based on what has happened
in the past. So if the market has grown consistently in the last few
years, most forecasting technique will predict that the market will continue to grow in the future as well – regardless of whether or not this
represents the true direction of the market.

Expert opinion is somewhat subjective in nature, but has the advantage that experts tend to be able to draw upon their wider experiences
and market knowledge to provide a view of the market that may be
more extensive and reliable than that drawn from statistical analysis
alone.

3.2.4   Decision analysis

One very useful tool that can be employed to evaluate customer preferences for different product features is decision analysis, which is used
to measure the value[4] of different options so that the best option (the
one of greatest value) can be identified. As a market research tool
decision analysis can be used to evaluate the relative value of competing product features so that the most desirable set of features can
be identified. The basic idea is that an individual is allowed to choose

the product features that they want, subject to certain constraints based on the cost of providing those features and the profit margin the organization wishes to achieve. Therefore, the customer must make trade-off decisions about the worth of different features.

Consider a bank that is planning to launch a credit card with just three features – two primary and one secondary. The primary features are the APR charged for purchases and the annual fee. The secondary feature is a cash back loyalty scheme based on a percentage of purchases made using the card. The decision analysis exercise is conducted as an interactive computer based process. It begins with an individual providing the computer with geo-demographic information about themselves such as their age, income, occupation, marital status, number of children and residential status. The individual also provides information about how they use their existing credit card(s) such as their average monthly spend, whether or not they revolve their balances and how often they make cash withdrawals. Given this information it is possible to construct a mathematical model[5] to estimate the expected costs, revenues and contribution to profit that will be generated from that person for any set of product features. It then follows that if an organization can say what level of contribution towards profit they wish to achieve, the model can be used to determine all of the different combinations of product features that will yield that level of contribution.

One set of product features is then selected (at random) and these are presented to the individual. For example:

APR (purchases): 19.99 percent.
Annual fee: $0.00.
Loyalty scheme: 1.0 percent cash back on purchases.

The person can then choose to change one feature. The computer then calculates how the other product features must change in order to maintain the same level of contribution. So if the person decides they would like a lower APR of say, 12.99 percent, they will enter this into the computer and the credit offer recalculated:

APR: 12.99 percent.
Annual fee: $15.00.
Loyalty scheme: 0.75 percent cash back on purchases.

So in this case, because the individual has chosen a lower APR, the computer has calculated that a $15 annual fee must be charged and the loyalty scheme reduced from 1.0 percent to 0.75 percent. The person then has the opportunity of changing the offer again. They might, for example, decide that they don't like the idea of an annual fee and set the fee to zero. This action results in the offer being recalculated again:

APR (purchases):   13.99 percent.
Annual fee: $0.00.
Loyalty scheme: 0.00 percent cash back on purchases.

So in order to maintain the same level of contribution from this customer, the computer has calculated that to remove the annual fee, the APR would need to be raised from 12.99 to 13.99 percent and the loyalty scheme no longer provided.

The process continues until the customer feels that the offer can no longer be improved. Therefore, the final set of features represents the best credit offer for that person that generates the desired level of contribution. Finally, the individual will be asked further questions about how they feel about the final credit offer. Most importantly, whether they feel the offer represents a better or worse proposition than their current credit card(s) and whether or not they would consider applying for such a product.

Ideally, the process will be repeated for hundreds of individuals from across many different segments of the market, and a range of different profitability levels will be explored. The results can then be analysed to estimate the following:

- The best credit offer for the target market; that is, the offer that is likely to generate the greatest overall contribution to profits.
- The best credit offer for individual segments within the population. It may be that rather than offering a single product with one set of product features, a better proposition is to target different segments with different credit offers. Some credit card providers have dozens, or even hundreds, of different products, each tailored to a different part of the market.
- Which types of customer should be excluded from promotional activities because they will not make a sufficient contribution towards profits.

Although decision analysis works best with large numbers of cases, it can yield useful information from only a few dozen cases based on expert interpretation of results and some simple statistics. If sufficient information is available then more formal mathematical approaches can be applied using methods such as game theory (Keeney and Oliver 2005; Thomas 2009 pp. 196–203).

3.2.5 The cost of providing credit

Good market intelligence will provide information about what customers want in a credit product, the size of the market and the revenues that can be generated. The other side of the coin is the cost of credit provision. The main costs that a credit granting organization will incur are:

- Cost of funds. Funds must be obtained before they can be lent to customers. Several different sources of funding exist, each of which has various benefits and drawbacks associated with it. Funding is discussed in more detail in Chapter 10.
- Bad debt write-off. Some customers will default on their loans resulting in all or part of the debt being classified as bad debt and written-off (charged-off). In the credit card and unsecured instalment lending markets, a typical lender can expect to write-off between 2 and 6 percent of their outstanding debts each year. In secured lending markets write-off rates are typically well below 1 percent due to the assets that can be seized in the case of default.
- Fraud. Consumer credit represents one of the largest areas of consumer fraud. A lender operating in the unsecured lending market can expect to write-off between 0.1 and 0.2 percent their outstanding debts per annum due to fraud. This is despite having sophisticated fraud detection procedures in place. Fraud losses are usually reported as a subset of bad debt losses.
- Promotion and advertising. Promotion and advertising are usually associated with promoting products using different media such as TV ads and mail shots. However, the costs of incentives such as loyalty points, interest-free periods and discount offers also need to be considered, as do the costs associated with targeting existing customers to retain their business and prevent defection to a rival product.
- Infrastructure costs. These include capital expenditure on things such as call centres, computer systems, depreciation, employee salaries, maintenance and other day-to-day running costs.

Costs vary considerably between lending institutions, but for an organization providing unsecured credit in the form of instalment loans and credit/charge cards, the cost of funds, bad debt and fraud typically account for around 70 percent of all costs. Infrastructure costs account for

20–25 percent and promotional activity around 5–10 percent. For mortgages and other high value long term secured credit agreements, the cost of funds may account for more than 80 percent of total costs. This is because once a mortgage application process has been completed there is very little that needs to be done to manage an account. Losses from bad debt and fraud tend to be very low due to the secured nature of the agreement.

3.2.6   Determining the offer

Significant market data may have been obtained and extensive analysis carried out, but there will always be some gaps in the data and questions about the nature of the market which remain unanswered. Therefore, it becomes impossible to say with absolute certainty what the ideal product offering should be. Rather, one tends to find that a range of potential offers emerge and there can be much debate about which offer the organization should actually take forward. Consequently, the final decision about the features of the product will often be somewhat subjective in nature, based partly on analysis of market data and partly on the opinions of members of the marketing team.

3.3   Promotional strategy

Once the product strategy has been determined the next step is to take the product to market. Promotional strategy encompasses the activities undertaken to create demand for the product in line with the targets specified within the marketing plan. Usually, the promotional strategy will comprise a number of separate campaigns. Each campaign will aim to generate a certain level of sales within a given period of time. The long term promotional strategy may cover a period of several years, but within this period separate campaigns may be planned to run each month, quarter or year. Each campaign will be set targets that will collectively lead to the targets set out in the marketing plan being met. One of the benefits of this approach is that it facilitates learning from one campaign to the next, allowing successful activities to be repeated and improved upon while less successful ones are discarded.

3.3.1   Communication channels

Two main types of communication channel are used to recruit customers as part of a campaign.

- Mass media. This communicates with general populations. Common mass media include TV, newspapers, flyers, billboards, internet pop-ups and radio.

- Direct media. Direct media communicates with people at an individual or household level. Direct media includes mail shots, telephone calls, e-mails and text messages.

The advantage of mass media is that it facilitates contact with a large number of people very quickly, normally at a far lower cost than contacting the same number of people individually. The advantage of direct media is that it can be used to target individuals much more specifically than mass media, and if there are people within the population you don't want to communicate with, these can be excluded. Therefore, mass media promotions are primarily used to raise brand awareness (although some demand will be generated). Direct media are then employed to encourage product take-up, and in most credit granting organizations the majority of new business is generated in this way. For this reason we focus on the use of direct marketing techniques in the sections that follow.

3.3.2 Direct marketing

Direct marketing aims to communicate with customers at an individual level. An organization will acquire a list containing names and contact details of potential customers. Individuals from the list will then be contacted directly on a one-to-one basis.

Traditionally, the most widely used direct marketing tool has been the mail shot, but the use of telephone calls, e-mail and SMS messaging has become increasingly common. A good direct marketing campaign will look to contact people using the medium that is most appropriate for each person.

Lists may be sourced from an organization's internal database(s), a third party list supplier, affinity partners (see below) or any combination of these. If a list is purchased from a third party, then in its simplest form it may contain contact details and little else. No work will have been done to pre-process the list and as a consequence the response rates that result from using such lists tend to be low. Lists of this type are usually sourced from national registers or publicly available information sources, such as the electoral (voter) roll and telephone directories.

Most list providers offer market and client specific lists that have been 'cleaned' in order to make them more suitable for their clients and deliver better response rates. Basic list cleaning will remove details of people who have recently died, been declared bankrupt, who have expressed a preference not to receive promotional material or who are known to have moved recently and therefore are no longer resident at the address on the list. Existing customers should also be removed – there is after all, nothing more frustrating than receiving junk mail for a product you already possess!

More advanced list processing applies rules to remove people who are unlikely to be interested in the products and services being offered. So if a list is to be used to target high earning professionals with an offer for an exclusive credit card, it makes sense to exclude people such as the unemployed and students, who are known to have low incomes. It would also be prudent to exclude people who live in deprived areas (usually identified by postcode/zip code) because high earners are unlikely to live there. The most advanced forms of list processing make use of complex scoring and segmentation methods which are discussed in more detail in Chapter 4.

Affinity partners are organizations that provide a lender with details of their customers/members. The belief is that both organizations will benefit from the relationships and brand associations that already exist, resulting in higher than average take-up of the product. The affinity partner may sell the list and receive a one-off payment, or take a percentage of the revenues that result.

The communication with the customer will tell them about the product and provide a mechanism for them to apply for it. This could be a paper based application form together with a pre-paid envelope provided as part of a mail shot, a contact number for them to call or a web address to allow them to apply on-line. Some specialist lenders may also employ a sales force to make home visits to potential customers, particularly if the individual is an existing customer who may be looking to acquire another one of the organization's products or services.

3.3.3   Campaign costs, response cost and cost per conversion

Every campaign incurs costs. Some costs are overheads associated with the planning of the campaign which may involve resources from within the marketing department as well as fees paid to external advertising agencies. For a mass media campaign other costs include the production of the advert(s) and the purchase of advertising space/time. For direct marketing activity there are two other important costs to consider. The first is the cost of buying a contact list or producing it in-house from the organization's existing database(s). The other is the cost of contacting people on the list.

One of the key measures by which promotional campaigns are assessed is the cost per response; that is, the average cost incurred for each individual who responds by applying for the product. The cost per response is calculated as the overall cost of the campaign divided by the number of responses (credit applications) received. Very different response rates can be expected for different types of media. For mass media promotions, including TV and newspaper adverts, response rates are typically between 0.01 and 0.05 percent of those who are exposed to the advert. So a TV commercial seen by five million people could be expected to generate somewhere between 5,000 and 25,000 customer responses. For a mail shot undertaken as part of a direct marketing campaign, average response rates of between 1 and 2 percent can be expected (Tapp 2008 p. 362).

A second measure of a campaign's success, which in consumer credit markets is far more important than the cost per response, is the cost per conversion; that is, the promotional costs incurred for each new credit agreement that is signed. The cost per conversion is calculated as the overall cost of the campaign divided by the number of new customers (converts) who actually sign a credit agreement. The cost per conversion will always be higher than the cost per response because some of those who apply for credit will subsequently not take up the credit offer. There are a number of reasons why this occurs:

- Some who respond will have their application declined because they are not creditworthy; that is, they are likely to default on any credit they are granted or otherwise be unprofitable customers.
- Someone may be offered credit on different/worse terms than advertised in the promotional literature that they received. A TV advert may offer loans of up to $100,000. However, the lender may only be willing to grant $100,000 to people with very high incomes: lower borrowing limits will be set for people on more average incomes. Therefore, if someone on an average income applies for $100,000 loan they are likely to be disappointed.
- In many countries a credit agreement is legally binding only if it has been signed by both parties. So, if someone agrees to a loan over the phone and is sent a credit agreement, if they don't sign and return the agreement then a legally binding agreement won't exist.
- A small proportion of responses can expect to be received from suspected fraudsters, and these cases will be declined.

Of the responses received from mass media campaigns for loans and credit cards, only about 25–50 percent can be expected to convert (although this figure varies widely depending upon the lender and the type of customers they wish to acquire). For direct marketing activity between 40 and 80 percent of responders can be expected to convert. Direct marketing results in a greater conversion rate than mass media because most individuals that are uncreditworthy can be excluded from contact lists. For mass media no such screening can take place. Therefore, the profile of the response population from mass media tends to be less creditworthy and contain more fraudulent cases than that which results from targeted direct marketing.

In general, what one tends to see is that response and conversation rates vary widely across different media, but the average cost incurred to generate one new customer from a marketing campaign tends to be relatively similar regardless of the media employed. As rough guide, one can expect to incur promotional costs of between \$50 and \$120[6] for each new customer (Tapp 2008 p. 303).

3.3.4   Campaign management and the prospects database

A complete promotional strategy will consist of several different campaigns, some running in parallel, using a variety of media. It is important that campaigns are not undertaken in isolation, otherwise individuals may receive conflicting messages from different campaigns or people may be sent the same communication many times.

Each new campaign undertaken as part of the wider promotional strategy should build upon previous campaigns, taking on board what has been learnt about people's behaviour in the past. In practice, this means that a prospects database should be maintained. A prospects database holds information that is known about prospects (prospective customers) including a record of the activities undertaken with respect to each prospect. Any responses received from a prospect, even if this has not led to a conversion, should be recorded. Other types of information may also be maintained. For example, if individuals have previously been customers, their behaviour when using the product and the contribution to profit that they generated should be included. The way in which different individuals behave in response to different types of promotional literature can then be analysed and the results applied to future campaigns. In particular, a comprehensive prospects database will allow an organization to undertake the following activities:

* Apply additional list screening to exclude people from new direct marketing activity. For example, people who have already been contacted more than twice in the last 30 days and prospects that have already been converted into customers.

- Use alternative communication channels to communicate with people who it is believed are very likely to want the product, but did not respond to the original contact. For example, by making a follow-up phone call a few days after a mailing has been sent.
- Make improved offers to people who have been contacted previously, but did not respond to the original communication. For example, reducing the interest rate, offering a free gift if they take up the product or providing some other incentive that was not offered originally.
- Customize direct marketing activity to match an individual's known behaviours. For example, if it is known that a prospect regularly used their credit card to buy cinema tickets, the prospect might be offered some free tickets as an incentive to take out a loan.
- Build accurate segmentation and scoring models (to be discussed in Chapter 4) to predict which individuals are most likely to respond to direct marketing activity, or other aspects of their behaviour when using the product. These models can then be applied to individuals who have not been mailed before, to determine whether or not it's worth contacting them.
- Generate contact lists for new products that are developed in the future.

A prospects database should be a single 'data warehouse' providing a central repository of information, containing details about all transactions and communications that have taken place between prospects and the organization, in relation to any of the organization's products and services. This facilitates an integrated communication strategy at the customer, rather than the product level. What this means is that rather than a promotional strategy being used to promote a single product, the prospects database is a tool that can be used to identify the basket of products that someone may be interested in. Therefore, a direct marketing strategy can be devised that aims to maximize the revenue from each customer, rather than the revenue from individual products. If an individual is targeted with a mortgage offer, it should be possible to estimate the individual's desire for a motor finance loan or an additional credit card, and take appropriate action to cross sell these products.

3.3.5 Inbound communications

The consequence of promotional activity is to generate response from potential customers. Some responses will be applications for the product.

Others will be product enquiries, and hopefully these can be converted into credit applications and then customers. The type of response and the way in which a customer is dealt with will be dependent upon the channel of communication. If the customer sends a completed application form by post or internet then it can be placed in a holding state for a number of hours or days, and processed whenever resources are available. If response is by phone a very different approach is required because the communication must be dealt with quickly. Although the call will initially be placed in a queue, if the waiting time is more than a few seconds the customer is likely to put the phone down or be in a disgruntled state by the time someone answers – making it an uphill struggle to convert them. Additionally, communication is interactive, and different outcomes will result depending upon the way in which the conversation develops. In most cases conversations will be scripted so as to guide the customer towards agreeing to take up the credit offer and to cross sell them anything else that appears suitable. The operator within the call centre will be briefed to respond to customer calls in certain ways, and they will be prompted via their computer terminal to ask certain questions. Based on the person's answers the computer will decide what the next question will be. So an operator may begin by asking someone for their income and how much they were thinking of borrowing. If the computer determines that the amount they wish to borrow is less than they can afford, then the operator may be prompted to suggest to the customer that they borrow more, perhaps to have a holiday or to help with Christmas. Alternatively, if a customer wants one product, but is deemed suitable for others, then this cross selling opportunity will be introduced into the operator's script. Usually there will be some scope for the operator to customize the call, but at all of the key decision points the most appropriate actions will be suggested by the call management system.

The design of scripts will be a joint responsibility of marketing and the operational areas. Marketing will be responsible for identifying the key decisional components, as well as ensuring that the overall contact with the customer is brand aligned; that is, any brand specific features that have appeared in promotional literature are included within the scripts. Call centre expertise will be required to implement scripts in a way that minimizes call times, and ensure that staff are suitably trained. IT resources may be required to ensure that information about the outcomes of the call are recorded and uploaded to the prospects database, thus allowing alternative scripting strategies to be compared and improved upon.

3.3.6 Resource issues

In order to deal with the demand generated from each campaign, operational resource requirements need to be considered within the marketing plan. The two issues that are always in the mind of the managers of customer contact centres are:

1. Meeting or exceeding customer service level targets. This will be measured in terms of call waiting times, length of telephone calls, number of queries resolved, customer satisfaction with the service they receive, and so on. For example, it may be required that on average 99 percent of telephone calls must be answered within ten seconds, or 95 percent postal applications should be processed within three working days.
2. Minimizing the cost of meeting the customer service level targets that have been set.

The biggest obstacle to maximizing service levels and minimizing costs are fluctuations in the demand for various resources – which occur with the surge in customer enquiries that are generated whenever a promotional campaign is undertaken. At best, if changes in demand are known well in advance, resource levels can be adjusted so that the desired service levels can still be met. For example, if new staff are needed then there is sufficient time to recruit and train them – a process that could take several weeks or months. At worst, if there is a sudden large and unexpected change in demand, then customer service levels will decline and significant costs may be incurred in overtime payments or by contracting out work to a third party supplier. In either case, any increase in demand will result in some increase in cost, a reduction in customer service levels or both. Therefore, one objective is to keep the demand for customer contact centre resources as constant as possible over time. This means that promotional activity should be staggered. If a mailing is being undertaken, then rather than dispatching all mailings in one go, resulting in a sharp peak in customer applications a few days later, the mail shot should be dispatched over a number of days or weeks so that the response is more balanced. Alternatively, if a telephone campaign is undertaken, it may be possible to make use of slack times within customer contact centres. At these times, staff not working at full capacity can be used to make phone calls to prospective customers.

3.4   Chapter summary

Marketing covers all aspects of credit management that influence consumer decisions about whether or not to apply for a product, and how the product is then used by successful applicants who are converted into customers. This means that marketing has a responsibility for determining what the features of a credit offer should be, which individuals should be targeted, and how information about the credit offer should be communicated to the target audience. Operational issues such as the expected number of responses from promotional campaigns and IT requirements also need to be considered and communicated to the relevant areas of the business.

When designing a credit offer, several features of the product need to be determined. Primary features define the functional aspects of a product that determine the terms under which credit is provided and repaid. These include the amount of credit, the term over which credit will be provided, and most importantly, the pricing structure that will be applied. In consumer credit markets competing products tend to have very similar primary features. Therefore, one or more secondary features may be included to provide consumers with additional incentives to take up the product rather than a competitor's. Typical secondary features are loyalty schemes linked to credit card usage and cash back offers on mortgages. Affinity schemes – where a discount is offered on some good or service provided by a third party, are also common. Brand features are the less tangible things that imbue a product with a unique image that consumers feel represent their values and lifestyle.

To determine which features should be used for a particular credit offer, market research needs to be undertaken to establish the size and nature of the market, and to gain an understanding of the product features that will appeal to different segments of the target population. There are a variety of ways that market intelligence can be obtained. These include: carrying out customer surveys, holding focus groups, examining existing customer databases, reviewing public information and obtaining expert opinions. An understanding of the competition within the market should also be obtained.

Determining the final credit offer is something of a mixture between a science and an art. Analysis of market data will indicate general consumer preferences for different product features, but the subjective opinions expressed by individuals within the marketing department will always have some bearing on the final decision as to what the credit offer should be.

Having decided upon a credit offer, a promotional strategy needs to be put in place to target individuals. A variety of communication channels can be used to communicate with potential customers. However, while mass media such as TV and press advertising are widely used to generate brand awareness, by far the most widely used method for recruiting new customers is direct marketing, via mail shots, e-mails and phone calls.

4
Predicting Consumer Behaviour

As discussed in Chapter 1, a large part of credit management is about predicting how people are likely to behave and acting in response to these predictions.

One of the most important behaviours that credit professionals want to predict is response to direct marketing activity; that is, the likelihood that someone reacts by applying for the product they have been targeted with. Predicting response is important because the response rate to untargeted one-to-one direct marketing activity is extremely low. If a marketing department decided to dispatch mail shots completely at random, without any consideration of how likely the people mailed were to respond or how creditworthy they were, then it would be necessary to mail hundreds of people to get just one new customer. This is not cost effective and such a strategy would prove very unprofitable in most cases. To reduce costs and make direct marketing a viable proposition, various techniques are used to predict response behaviour. Only individuals where the likelihood that they will respond makes them a cost effective prospect will be targeted as part of a direct marketing campaign.

In this chapter two of the most popular techniques used by credit professionals to predict consumer behaviour are introduced – scoring and segmentation. As well as predicting how likely someone is to respond to direct marketing activity, scoring and segmentation are also used across many other areas of credit management to predict different types of behaviours. For example, how likely someone is to default on a credit agreement or defect to a competitor's product. It is therefore, prudent to introduce scoring and segmentation at this point, and we begin by explaining their use within the context of direct marketing.

Its worth pointing out (before anyone panics) that yes, most scoring and segmentation techniques are based on mathematical processes that require someone with a university education in mathematics or statistics to fully understand. However, just as you don't need to know anything about engineering to drive a car, you don't need to know anything about mathematics or statistics to understand how scoring and segmentation are applied in practice. As long as you are numerate, can carryout basic arithmetic and are comfortable looking at simple graphs and tables, then that is all that is required.

For those interested in the technical details of how the most popular scoring and segmentation techniques are applied, further details are provided in Appendix A.

4.1 Scoring

Scoring is a process that uses information about someone to produce a single number (a score) representing the probability that they will do something or behave in a certain way. For example, the probability that someone will respond to a mailing or the likelihood that a credit applicant will repay what they borrow. The higher the score the more likely the individual is to behave in this way, the lower the score the less likely they are. The first application of scoring to credit management dates from the early 1940s (Durand 1941; Wonderlic 1952). However, it was not until the late 1970s and early 1980s that scoring became widely adopted, as computer systems were developed that could automatically calculate scores for large numbers of consumers very quickly and very cheaply.

The basic principle of scoring is that it is possible to take information about a group of individuals and use it to construct a mathematical representation of the relationships between individuals' characteristics and their behaviour. This mathematical representation is referred to as a scorecard, a scoring model or simply, a model. Once a model has been developed it can be applied to someone whose behaviour is unknown, to produce a score that estimates the probability of them exhibiting the behaviour of interest. Decisions about how someone should be treated are then based on the score that they receive.

The most popular type of scoring used in direct marketing is response scoring. When someone is sent promotional material offering them a product they can behave in one of two ways. They can respond to the offer and apply for the product or they can ignore the material they have been sent and do nothing. The goal of response scoring is to construct a model that predicts how likely someone is to respond to a direct marketing communication by applying for the credit being offered. Direct marketing is then targeted only at potential applicants that the model predicts are likely to respond; that is, people with a high response score. Those with a low response score will not be targeted. The dividing line between the two groups; that is, the score that determines whether or not someone should be targeted, is referred to as the cut-off score (or score cut-off.)

It is important to stress that scoring deals only in terms of probability, not certainty. It is impossible to be absolutely sure how someone will behave given their score. Instead, what I am saying is that if a large number of people have the same score, then on average, a given proportion of them will behave in the same way. If a response score of 950 means that the probability of someone responding to a mailing is 0.03, then if 1,000 people with a score of 950 are mailed then 30 responses can be expected.

Perhaps the best way to illustrate the application of response scoring is to use an example. Consider a finance house that is planning a direct marketing campaign for a personal loan that they are about to launch. The situation is as follows:

- In the marketing plan a budget of $1.545 million has been allocated to spend on direct marketing activity. It has been decided to spend this money on personalized mailings to potential customers.
- The cost of a mailing is $0.90 (in addition to postage this includes the cost of printed materials, reply envelopes and so on).
- The finance house has created a prospects database using a database purchased from a list provider, together with existing customer data from the account management system. The database contains contact details and geo-demographic data of about six million prospective customers.
- Within the marketing plan it has been estimated that the average contribution from each new customer, excluding direct marketing costs, will be $72. For the sake of simplicity it is assumed that the response cost and the conversion cost are the same; that is, every customer that responds subsequently coverts and becomes a customer. As discussed in Chapter 3, in practice not all of those that

apply will be granted credit and therefore the conversion cost will, in practice, be higher than the response cost.[1]

From the above information, each mailing costs $0.90, and for the recruitment strategy to be profitable the finance house can afford a response cost of no more than $72; that is, spend no more than $72 on direct marketing to recruit each new customer. It follows that to break even there must be an average of one response from every 80 mailings ($72/$0.9). So the response rate must be at least 1.25 percent (1/80). Therefore, a key goal that the marketing department wants to achieve is to identify those individuals on the prospects database where the response rate is likely to be greater than 1.25 percent, and only send mailings to people within this group.

The first task is to acquire information about response behaviour. To do this the marketing team decides to undertake a test mailing. Fifty thousand individuals are selected at random from the prospects database and sent a promotional mailing. This incurs a cost of $45,000 (50,000 * $0.9), leaving a remaining budget of $1.5 million for the full mailing campaign. The team then waits four weeks,[2] after which time 600 responses have been received. This equates to a response rate of 1.20 percent (100*600/50,000). This tells the marketing department two important things. First, the maximum number of responses that could be expected to be received if the entire prospects database was mailed is 72,000 (1.20% * 6m). Second, if the entire prospects database was mailed with no pre-selection process, then the proposition will be unprofitable. This is because with a response rate of 1.20 percent the cost of acquiring each customer will be $75 (1/ (1.2%* $0.9)). Therefore, the expected contribution would be $-3 per customer ($72–$75).

The marketing team's statistician then takes the sample of 50,000 cases, together with information about which individuals responded and which did not, and develops a response scorecard that generates scores ranging from 0 to 1,000. The relationship between score and response rate for the test mailing is illustrated in Figure 4.1.

The main purpose of the graph shown in Figure 4.1 is to estimate the response cost based on the response score. So, for example, people with a score of 200 have a response rate of 0.4 percent. This means that on average, 250 (1/0.4%) mailings need to be sent to generate one response. The average response cost is therefore $225 ($0.9 * 250). The conclusion is that individuals with a score of 200 should not be mailed because the response cost of $225 is higher than the $72 contribution

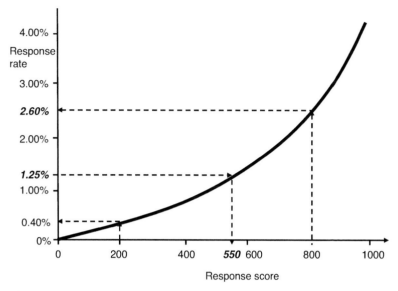

Figure 4.1   Response rate by score

that each responder is expected to make. On the other hand, individuals with a score of 800 have a response rate of 2.6 percent. The corresponding response cost is $34.61 ($0.9/2.6%). So mailing people with a response score of 800 is worthwhile.

Given that it has previously been determined that the minimum acceptable response rate is 1.25 percent, we can use Figure 4.1 to determine that an individual should only be mailed if they have a response score of 550 or more. Therefore, one possible strategy would be to define a cut-off score of 550 and mail everyone scoring 550 or above.

Figure 4.1 has been produced using the 50,000 cases used for the test mailing and provides information about expected response rates by score. What it tells us is whether or not it will be profitable to mail people on the basis of their score. What Figure 4.1 does not provide is any information about the number of individuals with each score. Therefore, it is not possible to use Figure 4.1 on its own to say anything about how much it would cost to mail everyone scoring above 550 or the total number of responses that could be expected. To overcome this problem, the scorecard developed using the test mailing is applied to all six million records on the prospects database. It is then a relatively simple matter to rank individuals by score and calculate the total

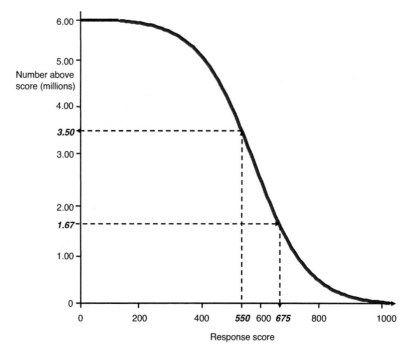

Figure 4.2 Cumulative mailing volumes by response score

(cumulative) number of individuals at or above each score, as illustrated in Figure 4.2.

Figure 4.2 shows the number of people on the prospects database scoring at or above each score. So from Figure 4.2 it can be seen that if everyone who scored 550 or more was mailed, a total of 3.5 million mailings would be required. The cost of this mailing would be $3.15 million ($0.9 * 3.5m). Obviously this is a problem because the remaining budget for direct marketing activity is only $1.5 million, limiting the maximum number of mailings to 1.67 million ($1.5m/$0.9). Therefore, what the marketing department needs to do is identify the highest scoring 1.67 million people and mail these. From Figure 4.2 it can be seen that this is achieved by mailing those scoring 675 or more.

The final question that has yet to be answered is how many responses can be expected from the mailing? This can be calculated by multiplying the response rate at each score from Figure 4.1 by the number of people with each score to produce the graph shown in Figure 4.3.

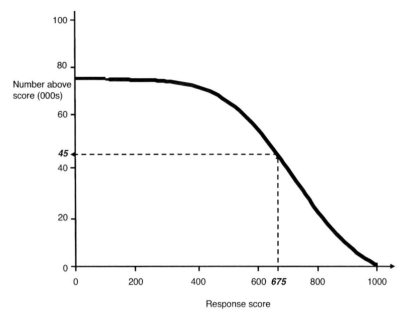

Figure 4.3   Cumulative response volumes

Figure 4.3 again shows the total number scoring above each score, but this time the figures are only for responders. It can be seen that if the cut-off score of 675 is applied, and only the 1.67 million individuals scoring 675 or more are mailed, then 45,000 responses can be expected. This represents an average response rate of 2.69 percent and an average response cost of $33.33 ($1.5m/45,000). To put it another way, by developing a response model the marketing department has been able to target 62 percent of all potential responders (100 * 45,000/72,000) by mailing less than 28 percent of the prospects database (100* 1.67m/6m).

4.2   Segmentation

The principles underpinning segmentation have some similarities to those for scoring, and the data collected for building a response score can also be used to develop a segmentation model and vice-versa. The main difference between scoring and segmentation is that whereas scoring looks to generate a numerical measure for each individual in the population, segmentation divides the population into a number of discrete groups or segments. Individuals within each segment will have similar characteristics and usually come from similar socio-economic groups, and can therefore be expected to exhibit similar behaviour. The response rate within each segment is then calculated and a decision made whether or not to target people within a segment, rather than specific individuals. Let us continue with the example introduced in section 4.1. Assume that instead of using the test mailing to develop a scorecard, a segmentation process is applied instead. For the sake of argument, assume that 11 different population segments are identified, as illustrated in Table 4.1.

Table 4.1 shows the analysis of the test mailing and figures for the 11 significant segments that were found. It shows the number of people in each segment, the percentage of the test population this represents and the number of responses received. These figures have then been used to calculate the response rate for each segment. The segments have then been ranked in response rate order from highest to lowest. Segment 1 contains people aged 18–34 with an income less than $65,000 who are home owners. The response rate is 4.19 percent and the response cost is $21.48. Conversely, people aged over 70 in segment 11 have a response rate of just 0.08 percent. This means that to generate just one customer response from this segment 1,250 mailings would be required at a cost of $1,125. Given that the minimum acceptable response rate is 1.25 percent any individuals within segments 1 through 5 could be mailed profitably.

The segmentation is then applied to the entire prospects database of six million individuals, resulting in each individual being assigned to one of the 11 segments. The expected number of responders in each segment is then calculated by multiplying the expected response rates for each segment (as shown in Table 4.1) by the number of individuals in each segment. The results of this exercise are shown in Table 4.2.

The final task is to choose which segments to mail. Although anyone in segments 1 to 5 could be mailed profitably, it is important to remember that the marketing budget remaining after the test mailing is $1.5 million, allowing a maximum of 1.67 million mailings to be dispatched. From the cumulative figures in the rightmost columns of Table 4.2 it can be seen that there is sufficient budget to mail all of the individuals within the first four segments, but not the fifth. By looking at the cumulative response column we can see that this is expected to generate 44,880 responses – very similar to the 45,000 predicted by the scoring model.

Table 4.1 Mailing response rates

Segment	Description	Number mailed	Percent of population	Number of responders	Response rate	Average cost per response
1	Age 18–34, income <$65,000, home owner	2,434	4.87%	102	4.19%	$21.48
2	Age 35–69, married, 2+ children	3,552	7.10%	115	3.24%	$27.80
3	Age 18–34, income ≥$65,000, 1+ children	5,022	10.04%	105	2.09%	$43.05
4	Age 18–34, income <$65,000, tenant	2,881	5.76%	52	1.81%	$49.86
5	Age 18–34, income <$65,000, living with parents	6,732	13.46%	88	1.31%	$68.85
6	Age 35–69, married/cohabiting, 1 child	8,107	16.21%	69	0.85%	$105.74
7	Age 18–34, income ≥$65,000, no children	5,000	10.00%	27	0.54%	$166.67
8	Age 35–69, single, home owner	4,875	9.75%	21	0.43%	$208.93
9	Age 35–69, married/cohabiting, no children	3,678	7.36%	13	0.35%	$254.63
10	Age 35–69, single, renter	5,218	10.44%	6	0.12%	$782.70
11	Age 70+ years	2,501	5.00%	2	0.08%	$1,125.45
	Total	**50,000**	**1.20%**	**600**	**1.20%**	**$75.00**

Table 4.2 Expected response for total population

Segment	Description	Number mailed	Mailing cost for segment @ $0.90 per mailing	Estimated number of responders	Mailing cost (cumulative)	Estimated number of responders (cumulative)	% mailed (cumulative)
1	Age 18–34, income <$65,000, home owner	292,080	$262,872	12,240	$262,872	12,240	4.9%
2	Age 35–69, married, 2+ children	426,240	$383,616	13,800	$646,488	26,040	12.0%
3	Age 18–34, income ≥$65,000, 1+ children	602,640	$542,376	12,600	$1,188,864	38,640	22.0%
4	Age 18–34, income <$65,000, tenant	345,720	$311,148	6,240	$1,500,012	44,880	27.8%
5	Age 18–34, income <$65,000, living with parents	807,840	$727,056	10,560	$2,227,068	55,440	41.2%
6	Age 35–69, married/cohabiting, 1 child	972,840	$875,556	8,280	$3,102,624	63,720	57.5%
7	Age 18–34, income ≥$65,000, no children	600,000	$540,000	3,240	$3,642,624	66,960	67.5%
8	Age 35–69, single, home owner	585,000	$526,500	2,520	$4,169,124	69,480	77.2%
9	Age 35–69, married/cohabiting, no children	441,360	$397,224	1,560	$4,566,348	71,040	84.6%
10	Age 35–69, single, renter	626,160	$563,544	720	$5,129,892	71,760	95.0%
11	Age 70+ years	300,120	$270,108	240	$5,400,000	72,000	100.0%
	Total	6,000,000	5,400,000	72,000			

4.3 Which is best: scoring or segmentation?

Which is the best method for identify responders; scoring or segmentation? This question has been the subject of much debate, but there is really no right answer. In some situations scoring gives better results, in others segmentation, and it is not possible to say in advance which method will yield the best results. So, for the example presented earlier in this chapter, the results would seem to suggest that scoring is marginally better than segmentation because it was estimated that by using the scoring model, 45,000 responses would be received compared to 44,880 for the segmentation model. However, if the exercise was performed on a different population it is quite possible that the situation would be reversed. Given this ambiguity, it is quite normal for both scoring and segmentation models to be developed and then the best model chosen. There is also evidence that using different types of scoring and segmentation techniques in combination can yield better results than using any one method on its own (Kittler 1997). The most advanced list screening strategies make use of both segmentation and scoring techniques. For example, a segmentation approach may be used first to define a number of distinct groups within the population, and then a scoring model developed for each group.

4.4 Other dimensions of customer behaviour

In the examples used so far it has been assumed that response rate and conversion rate are the same. In many non-credit markets this is a valid assumption to make because when someone responds, they respond by buying the product. It is also true that for many products and services it is assumed that every customer who converts will generate the same contribution to profit.[3] If two people each buy a dishwasher in response to an e-mail promotion, then each sale will generate the same contribution (assuming they were both offered the dishwasher at the same price!) It follows that in such situations what is of prime importance is the response rate and the average cost incurred per response.

Credit is different for two reasons. First, the contribution to profit made by each customer is unknown at the time when promotional activity is undertaken. Two individuals who are given a credit card will not use the card in the same way, even if they are both given exactly the same credit limit, APR, annual fee and so on. Some individuals will even generate a loss; that is, be uncreditworthy. In most cases people are uncreditworthy because they default on their repayments, but people who do not make much use of their credit card or who repay a loan early will also be classified as uncreditworthy because insufficient revenue will be generated to cover costs. Second, in consumer credit markets customers respond by *applying* for the product. The receipt of a credit application in response to direct marketing activity does not necessarily translate into a signed credit agreement. A significant proportion of applicants will be declined because they are not deemed creditworthy, and others who are creditworthy may subsequently decide not to take up the credit offered and therefore do not sign a credit agreement – even though they responded initially.

What this means is that when developing a direct marketing strategy for a consumer credit product, aspects of behaviour other than response and conversion need to be considered. Some of the customer behaviours that are important in addition to response behaviour include:

- Repayment default. The probability that an individual will either repay or default on their credit agreement.
- Loss given default. This is the amount that can be expected to be written-off if someone defaults on their repayments.
- Fraud. The probability that a fraudulent credit application will be made.
- Attrition. The probability that someone will stop using your product and defect to a rival.
- Credit usage. For fixed sum credit this is how much an individual will borrow and over what term, which will determine the interest revenue generated. For revolving credit this is the amount of spend per month/quarter/year on retail/cash/balance transfers etc.
- Revolver/Transactor. The probability that a credit card customer will maintain a revolving credit balance – hence generating interest revenue.
- Cross sell. The probability that if someone buys one product they then purchase other products and services.

To maximize the overall return generated from a credit portfolio all of these behaviours need to be considered as part of the marketing strategy, but the behaviour that has the greatest impact on customer contribution, by a considerable margin, is repayment default. Therefore, an important goal of any direct marketing campaign should be to remove from the list of prospects anyone who is likely to default on any credit advanced to them. We discuss models of repayment default in the following section.

4.4.1   Risk pre-screening (credit scoring) models of repayment default

If a list contains up-to-date details about each person's credit history, then one strategy is to apply rules, based on expert opinion, to exclude people who are unlikely to be creditworthy. For example, those who have been declared bankrupt, people who are currently in arrears with other credit agreements or people with very large debts in relation to their income, who therefore, may not be able to support any new borrowing.[4] However this approach is crude. A more sophisticated approach is to use what is referred to as a risk pre-screening model (also referred to as a credit risk model or a credit scoring model[5]). This is a scoring or segmentation model that predicts the likelihood of someone defaulting on their repayments in the future, or being uncreditworthy due to some other criteria. Risk pre-screening models can be bought from a third party vendor such as a credit reference agency, or they can be developed in-house if sufficient information about credit repayment behaviour is available on the prospects database.

The principles underpinning the development and use of a risk pre-screening model are very similar to those that apply to a response model. Repayment behaviour (instead of response behaviour) is obtained for a sample of customers. The sample will contain details of 'good' customers who repaid to the terms of the agreement and 'bad' customers who defaulted. Statistical analysis is then undertaken to identify the relationships between individual characteristics and Good/Bad[6] repayment behaviour, and these relationships are captured in the form of a model. However, instead of predicting response rate the model predicts the bad rate; that is, the likelihood of someone defaulting. So if a risk pre-screening model predicts that someone has an expected bad rate of 5 percent, then there is a 1 in 20 chance of them defaulting, should they be granted credit.

A risk pre-screening model is used in a similar way to the response model discussed earlier in the chapter. Every lender has a view of the maximum bad rate (termed the marginal bad rate) that is acceptable for their business. The standard way of calculating the marginal bad rate is as follows:

Marginal bad rate[7] = 100 *Average profit from a good customer /
(Average loss from a bad customer +
Average profit from a good customer)

For example, assume that a lender has looked at a sample of recently completed credit agreements and calculated that the average profit generated from a good customer who kept to the term of the agreement was $100 and the average loss from bad customer who defaulted was $2,400. The marginal bad rate is 4 percent ($100 / ($2,400+$100)). So in this example, if a risk pre-screening model estimates that the likelihood of an individual being bad is more than 4 percent then the individual should not be offered credit. Another way to think about this is; in order for the lender to make a profit from a group of potential customers, the ratio of good to bad customers (termed the good:bad odds) must be no more than 24:1; that is, there must be no more than one bad customer who defaults for every 24 good customers who repay.

4.4.2   Using response and risk pre-screening models in combination

Using a risk pre-screening model to exclude all individuals where the expected bad rate is higher than the marginal bad rate is a common strategy. However, an important feature of consumer credit markets is the risk/response paradox, which was introduced in section 2.1.1. Individuals who are most likely to respond to a mailing for a credit product tend to be those with the highest bad rates. Conversely, people whose response rates are very poor generally have very low bad rates in the unlikely event that they respond. This means that defining one cut-off based on response rates and another cut-off based on bad rates is not necessarily the best strategy to follow to select individuals for direct marketing. Instead, the exclusion strategy should take into account the combined cost of response and bad debt. If people are very likely to respond the response cost will be low. Therefore, the lender can accept someone with a higher estimated bad rate because they can offset some of increased bad debt cost against the lower response cost. Conversely, for people who are unlikely to respond the average response costs will be high. Therefore, the lender can only accept people for whom the bad rate is very low. To illustrate this point, let us continue with the example that was introduced earlier in the chapter that considered a finance house that is planning to launch a new personal loan product.

If you recall, the expected contribution from each loan was estimated to be $72 (remember – this is the contribution before any marketing costs have been taken into account). This means that in order to achieve a positive contribution to profit, the average conversion cost must be less than $72. Now let's break down this figure further and see how it was arrived at. Suppose that some further market research was carried out to come up with the following estimates about the expected financial behaviour of loan customers:

A. The average loan amount will be $10,000.
B. The average contribution to profit generated from a loan that is repaid will be $300.
C. The average loss incurred in the case of default will be $5,000. The average loss is less than $10,000 because a borrower can be expected to make some repayments before default and some funds will be recovered through debt recovery action.
D. The average bad rate of prospective customers will be 4.30 percent. The lender has estimated this figure by applying a risk pre-screen model to calculate a bad rate for each prospect, and then taking an average across all prospects.
E. The average good rate of prospective customers is estimated to be 95.70 percent (100 – average bad rate).

So what can be learnt from these figures? First, the average contribution to profits from each loan (excluding conversion costs) can be calculated as:

Average contribution = (B * E) – (C * D)

That is, the average contribution from a good prospect multiplied by the average good rate, minus the average loss from a bad payer multiplied by the average bad rate. So for the average bad rate of 4.3 percent the expected contribution will be:

$$\text{Average contribution} = (\$300 * 95.7\%) - (\$5,000 * 4.3\%)$$
$$= \$72$$

Second, the marginal bad rate can be calculated:

Marginal bad rate = B / (C+ B)

$$\text{Marginal bad rate} = \$300 / (\$5,000 + \$300)$$
$$= 5.66\%$$

Third, the expected contribution (excluding conversion costs) can be calculated for each individual on the prospect database, taking into account the individual's expected bad rate, calculated using the risk pre-screen score. In the very best case, if the risk pre-screen model estimates an individual has a zero bad rate, the expected contribution will be equal to:

Expected contribution = ($300 * 100.0%) – ($5,000 * 0.0%)
= $300

What this means is that for these types of customers, with very low expected bad rates, it is worthwhile spending up to $300 to convert them. If the expected bad rate is 5.66 percent (the marginal bad rate) the expected contribution will be zero ($300 * 94.34% – 5.66% * $5,000). Therefore, it is not worth spending anything at all to convert these types. Another way to express this is that the most that the finance company can afford in conversion and bad debt costs together, is $300.

If a response and risk pre-screen score are both developed and applied to the prospects database, it is possible to produce a graph showing the combined effect of both scores, as illustrated in Figure 4.4.

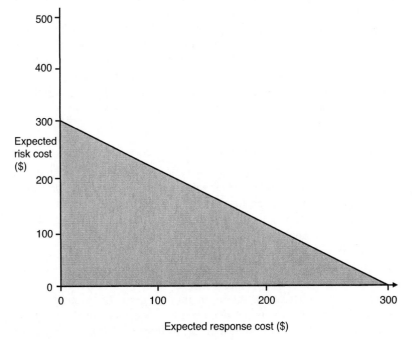

Figure 4.4   Response and risk costs in combination

Figure 4.4 shows the predicted response cost and bad debt costs, based on the scores from the relevant model. The area represented by the shaded triangle in Figure 4.4 shows the region where the combined conversion and bad debts costs are $300 or less. If estimated response and risk costs are plotted, then if the point where they meet is within the triangle, this indicates that these people could be converted profitably; that is, the response cost plus the bad debt costs is estimated to be less than $300. Given response and risk scores for every individual on the prospects database, it is possible to estimate everyone's expected cost. Individuals can then be ranked in cost order, and those with least cost targeted first.

4.4.3   Multi-dimensional models of behaviour

The principle behind using response and risk pre-screening models in combination can be extended to many different dimensions of customer behaviour. So, for example, if the profitability of a card product is partly determined by the probability that a customer defects to a rival's product (the customer is said to attrite) an attrition model can be created. The strategy discussed in section 4.4.2 can then be extended to include the costs associated with attrition.[8] All other things being equal, those with a high probability of attrition will tend towards being excluded from contact lists, while those with a lower probability of attrition will tend to be included on the list. Likewise, models could be developed to estimate the amount of credit someone is likely to want, whether or not they revolve their balance on a credit card (and hence generate interest revenues) or the chance that they can be cross sold another product or service.

4.4.4   Customer lifetime value

So far we have discussed a range of different behaviours people can exhibit during the course of their relationship with a credit provider. The strategy that has been described has been to construct models of one or more types of behaviour and then combine models together in order to select people who are likely to be profitable; for example, probability of response, probability of default and probability of attrition. However, the ultimate goal is not to predict individual behaviours, but the overall value of the customer over the lifetime of the relationship with them. Therefore, an alternative to constructing models of each behaviour, is to construct a single model that considers all the costs and revenues associated with an individual, in order to predict profitability over the long term. In practice however, very few lenders take this approach directly. Instead, most adopt the multi-model approach introduced in section 4.4.3. There are two main reasons for this. The first is lack of data. In order to be able to produce accurate models of customer lifetime value, large amounts of detailed transactional data is required over a period of many years (this is more the case for revolving products such as credit cards than fixed term products such as loans and mortgages). Some organizations do have this level of data, but many find that they have only partial or incomplete data for all or part of their prospects database. Second, even though organizations may in theory be looking to maximize profitability over a given time-frame, there are often constraints placed upon them, which means that individual behaviours are still important. For instance, it can some-times be very profitable to target people who are likely to default. This is because these types of people tend to be very credit hungry, cheap to convert and generate large amounts of revenue for the credit they receive (in the form of interest and penalty fees) before finally defaulting. However, ethical considerations may prevent an organization deliberately targeting people it believes won't repay their debts, or there may be limits on the bad debt levels that the organization is willing to support – even if maintaining such levels generate a considerable contribution to profit. Alternatively, credit granting institutions very often set their marketing departments monthly, quarterly or annual targets that include things such as the number of new customers that must be recruited or the percentage of existing customers that must be retained. Consequently, meeting these targets will take priority over longer term profitability objectives.

4.5 Chapter summary

Scoring and segmentation are used across many different areas of credit management. With a scoring model an individual's geo-demographic characteristics such as their age, income, residential status and employment status are used to generate a numerical measure (a score) representing the likelihood of them exhibiting one type of behaviour. The most common type of scoring used in direct marketing is response scoring. A response score represents the likelihood of an individual responding to a communication. It can therefore, be used to estimate the cost of recruiting customers with different scores by multiplying the probability of response by the cost of each communication. Only those individuals on the prospects database where the expected response cost makes the communication cost effective will be targeted.

The results of segmentation are in principle very similar to scoring. However, instead of generating estimates for each person, people with similar characteristics, who are likely to exhibit similar behaviours, are grouped together into a number of different segments. A decision about which segments to target is then made on the basis of the average response cost within each segment. All individuals within the chosen segments are targeted.

As well as response behaviour, scoring and segmentation can also be applied to other types of behaviour. Of particular interest in consumer credit markets are models of loan default, attrition, product usage and fraud. These models are then used in combination to identify the most desirable prospects to target with direct marketing activity.

5
Customer Acquisition

In this chapter we look at the second phase of credit management – customer acquisition. The customer acquisition process covers the events that occur between the time when someone applies for credit and the point when a credit agreement is created. This involves the following tasks:

- Assessing the creditworthiness of each applicant.
- Deciding whether to accept or reject applications on the basis of each applicant's creditworthiness.
- Deciding the terms that will be offered to accepted applicants.
- Undertaking the necessary logistical processes to create credit agreements, open accounts and make funds available to customers.

The main part of the acquisition process is focused around the assessment of each applicant's creditworthiness. At one time organizations employed large teams of underwriters to manually assess applications. When deciding if someone was creditworthy an underwriter would assess their application using a number of different criteria, often referred to as the 'Cs' of credit. These were the applicant's Capacity to repay debt (disposable income), their Character (intent to repay), current Conditions (of the economy) and any Capital or Collateral that the applicant could provide as security (Savery 1977). This was a time consuming and expensive process, that was difficult to control and relied heavily on underwriters' subjective view of each applicant's creditworthiness. In the modern lending environment only a small percentage of cases are assessed by underwriters. Most lending decisions are made using automated credit scoring systems (scoring and/or segmentation models as described in Chapter 4) to estimate each applicant's likelihood of default and other aspects of behaviour that contribute towards their creditworthiness.

The use of credit scoring (risk pre-screening) was discussed in section 4.4.1 as a way of screening contact lists so that they contained only individuals that were likely to be creditworthy. Therefore, an obvious question is, why is it necessary to go through the process again when someone applies for the credit they've been offered? There are a number of answers to this question:

- Risk pre-screening can only be applied to applications that result from direct marketing activity. If someone applies after seeing a TV ad or undertaking an internet search then no pre-screening will have occurred.
- New information may become available at the application point that was not available when the original contact list was compiled. The additional information will allow a better estimate of creditworthiness to be made. For example, it may not be possible to obtain a full credit report when a contact list is created.[1] Instead, a credit report will only be obtained from a credit reference agency when an application is received.
- The data originally used to select prospects for targeting may be several months out of date.[2] Therefore, it's worth obtaining up-to-date information to allow a revised estimate of creditworthiness to be made.
- Even if direct marketing has been used to target selected individuals, the person who applies may not be the person who was originally targeted. For example, a family member or another resident of the property may complete and return the application form.

The rest of this chapter is in three parts. The first part discusses the role of application processing systems in managing the customer acquisition process. The second part considers the different stages and decision points within the acquisition process. The final part discusses strategies for setting the terms of business of a credit agreement; that is, the product features that are defined for each customer, such as the amount of credit, the APR and the length of the agreement.

5.1   Application processing systems

A large credit granting institution will have an application processing system to manage the customer acquisition process. A typical application processing system is illustrated in Figure 5.1.

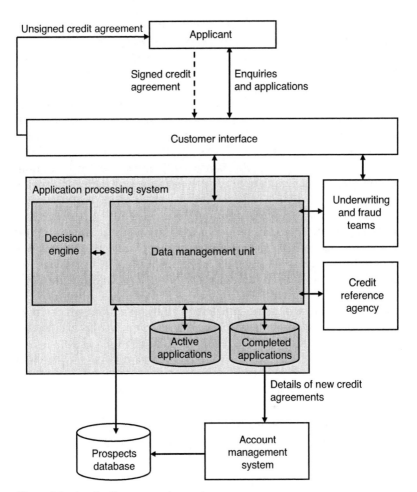

Figure 5.1 Application processing system

Figure 5.1 shows that the application processing system interfaces with a number of internal and external systems. When someone makes an application for credit their details will initially be captured by the customer interface; that is, staff at branches or in customer contact centres, or electronically via the lender's website. As information is gathered from the applicant it is entered into the application processing system. The application processing system then gathers additional information about the applicant from internal and external data sources such as the prospects database and credit reference agencies. When enough information is available a credit score can be calculated. A decision to accept or decline the application on the basis of the applicant's credit score can usually be taken automatically.

The application processing system also supports the operational areas responsible for manual underwriting and fraud prevention. In the minority of cases when a decision can't be made automatically, the application processing system will place these cases in a queue that is worked by a member of the relevant team. An underwriter will then make the decision whether the application should be accepted or rejected. The underwriter will then enter their decision into the application processing system to allow the customer acquisition process to continue.

As applications are processed, information about active and completed applications will be used to update the prospects database. This allows the marketing department to know who has applied and which applications have been accepted or rejected. So if someone has not responded to direct marketing activity, then follow-up communication can be initiated – perhaps offering them a further incentive, such as a lower interest rate or a free gift. Information about how much credit people asked for, how much they were granted, application details and information from credit reports can also be used as a source of information when planning new products and cross sale opportunities in the future.

For successful applicants, once a credit agreement has been created, details of the agreement will be passed to the account management system where an account record will be created. The account record will be used to record events, such as repayments, further advances, accrued interest and penalty charges, that occur during the lifetime of the agreement.

5.1.1　The data management unit

As shown in Figure 5.1, an application processing system contains two major components, a data management unit and a decision engine. The data management unit provides a centralized control function, managing the flow of information between different areas of the business during the acquisition process.

When an application for credit is made, the first task is to capture basic personal information that enables the applicant to be uniquely identified – thus allowing data from other sources to be linked to the application. This will usually be the applicant's full name, address and date of birth.[3] The applicant's personal details are then used to create a record of the application that is stored within the active applications database. As the application progresses the application record will be updated with relevant details as new information becomes available and decisions are taken. The application will only move from an active to completed state[4] when one of the following events has occurred:

- A credit agreement has been created. Even after the decision to grant credit has been taken in principle, an agreement will not exist until the borrower has signed the relevant paperwork. Therefore, if the application is being made remotely, via post, phone or internet, it could take several days or weeks before the agreement is finalized and the application is classified as complete.
- The application has timed-out. In cases where a credit agreement needs to be signed by the applicant a decision needs to be made about how long to wait for them to sign it before withdrawing the offer. Usually a credit offer is left open for a limited period of time, often between 30 and 60 days. After this time the application will be marked as a 'Not taken up' and the application process completed. If the applicant subsequently changes their mind then they will need to reapply.
- The application is declined. In which case the reason(s) for decline are recorded for future analysis.

Once personal details have been captured, the application processing system will collate the information required to finish processing an application from a number of sources. The first port of call will be the organization's internal databases. The prospects database will supply information about people who were targeted as part of the current promotional campaign and any other individuals the organization may already know something about; such as previous customers and people targeted in earlier campaigns. Typically, the prospects database will contain geo-demographic information, previous contact history and/or limited credit reference data. Information about existing customers and how they manage their accounts will be obtained from the account management system.

After interrogating the organization's internal databases, the data management unit will identify any additional data items that need to be obtained. If necessary, the application will be passed back to the customer interface where the applicant will be asked to provide further information. For example, they may initially have been asked to provide their current address and the time they have lived there. If they say that they have lived at their current address for a short period of time,[5] then it is standard practice to obtain details of their previous addresses(s). If the applicant is a previous customer, or has been targeted via direct mail, then previous address information may exist on the prospects database or the account management system, and therefore need not be asked.

Sometimes a decision about an application can be made purely on the basis of the information gathered from the applicant and/or data supplied from the organization's own systems. However, in most cases a credit search will also be undertaken (at a cost) with one (and sometimes several) credit reference agencies to obtain a credit report detailing the applicant's repayment behaviour with other lenders in the past.

5.1.2   The decision engine

The data management unit is responsible for gathering and maintaining data throughout the application process, but it does not make any assessments of the applicant's creditworthiness or make any decisions about how applications should be treated. A decision engine is a piece of software that can be thought of as the 'brain' of the application processing system, which makes decisions about how each application should be dealt with. At key points in the customer acquisition process the decision engine receives information from the data management unit. The decision engine processes the information and decides what action should be taken. Decisions and actions are then fed back to the data management unit where they are passed to the relevant system or person to be acted upon. The decision engine will, for example, decide if a credit report is required before an applicant's creditworthiness can be assessed. If a credit report is required, the decision engine will inform the data management unit that it needs this information and will then wait for the data management unit to provide it. When the required information is available, the decision engine will calculate one or more scores that collectively provide an estimate of the applicant's creditworthiness. This will primarily be a score that estimates the probability that an applicant will default if provided with credit, but as discussed in section 4.4, scores will also be used to predict other aspects of applicant behaviour such as the likelihood that someone will maintain a revolving balance, the likelihood that they can be cross sold other products and services, and ultimately, the overall contribution toward profits that they are likely to make. The decision engine will then apply score cut-off(s) and decide to provisionally accept an application if the applicant's score(s) pass the cut-off(s) that have been set. Policy rules (override rules) will also be applied to override score-based decisions in certain circumstances. Policy rules exist for a number of reasons:

- System override rules. All credit granting institutions maintain a list of rules defining criteria when they will not provide credit under any circumstances. These types of policy rules tend to be derived from expert opinion and past experience, and will have evolved over a considerable period of time. Many lenders will not provide credit to the unemployed on ethical/responsible lending grounds, and will decline applications from anyone who has been declared bankrupt within the last six years. Some lenders will not provide credit to students, while others decline anyone who is under or over a certain age.
- Data sufficiency rules. These exist where insufficient data is available for a final decision to be made, or the applicant's identity has not been confirmed. This means that some form of paper documentation (such as a passport, payslip or utility bill) may be required. Therefore, the application needs to be referred back to the customer interface so that further information can be obtained from the applicant before processing continues.
- Legal rules. There may be a legal requirement to deal with an application in a certain way. For example, in the UK if fraud is suspected (but not proven) an application should not be declined automatically and must be referred for manual review by an underwriter. Likewise, if someone places a 'Notice of Correction' on their credit report,[6] an organization is legally required to manually review the application before a final decision is made.
- Marginal cases. Some organizations manually review cases where an applicant's credit score is just above or just below the score cut-off. The usual argument put forward for doing this is that an underwriter can 'add value' to the automated decision recommended by the decision engine. However, if a good quality credit scoring model is in place the evidence to justify this approach is somewhat scant, particularly for low value/high volume products such as store cards and retail credit.

The use of policy rules varies enormously by organization and product. Some lenders may have no more than four or five policy rules, overriding the credit score in less than 5 percent of cases. Others have dozens of rules and override anything up to 50 percent or more of all score based decisions, with a large proportion of these cases being referred for manual review. The general advice offered here is that the use of policy rules should be kept to a minimum for three reasons. First, a good quality credit score will usually give the best overall measure of an individual's creditworthiness. Therefore, each new policy rule that is applied will lead to degradation in the overall quality of lending decisions being made. Second, large numbers of policy rules are almost impossible to manage because many people will satisfy more than one rule, making it very difficult to determine which rules are working well and which are not. Third, if cases are referred for manual review, it is very difficult to say objectively why someone is subsequently accepted or declined. Even if the application processing system allows an underwriter to enter a 'reason for rejection' interpreting what the underwriter meant by this at a later date often proves difficult.

5.1.3 The evolution of decision engines

Sometimes the decision engine and data management unit will be acquired/developed as a single integrated system, but it is quite common for the decision engine to be supplied as a 'bolt on' component by a third party software vendor. For example, Experian's Strategy Manager decision engine is sold as a component of its two application processing systems – Autoscore and Transact SM. However, Strategy Manager is also sold to organizations as a standalone product that can be integrated within their own application processing environment. Therefore, in many environments, software supplied by two or more different vendors will be employed together to deliver the functionality required by the application processing system.

Why have application processing systems evolved in this way rather than being delivered as one unified system? The reasons are mainly historic. The first application processing systems developed in the 1960s and 1970s did not contain decision engine functionality. Instead, the application processing system acted purely as mechanism by which information could be maintained and passed between the different areas of the organization that dealt with application processing. In the late 1970s and 1980s many organizations replaced underwriters with automated scoring and segmentation systems that were hard coded into the application processing system and controlled by the IT department. What soon became apparent was that when the credit or marketing functions wanted to change something, such as the credit limits given to new customers, it would be treated by the IT department just like any other system change request. The work would be prioritized and wait in the IT work queue until resource was available to make the change. The consequence was that it could take months for even small changes to lending policy to feed through to the operational lending environment, by which time they could be out of date and ready to be replaced by a new set of lending policies. To get around this problem decision engines were developed specifically to circumvent the requirement for IT involvement. A modern decision engine is based on the idea that all of the scores and rules required to make lending decisions can be captured as a set of parameters maintained by the people responsible for lending policy. The decision engine will include a piece of PC software that allows an analyst to type in scorecards, set cut-off scores, define policy rules and so on. To implement the scores and rules that have been entered, the analyst will simply choose a menu option to upload the changes to the application processing system without any recourse to IT resource. What this means in practice is that many organizations operate very dynamic lending policies that they fine-tune on a monthly or quarterly basis.

5.2 The customer acquisition process

A standard customer acquisition process implemented within the application processing system is shown in Figure 5.2.

Figure 5.2 shows that what an applicant may see as a straightforward yes/no decision to grant credit, involves a number of different stages and decision points. The stages of the acquisition process, as illustrated in Figure 5.2, are expanded upon in the sections that follow.

5.2.1 Obtaining application details

In Figure 5.2 the process begins with information being obtained about the applicant. Capturing application details can be a manually intensive activity. If an application is made by phone, an operator will need to liaise with the applicant to obtain the information required. If a paper based application has been received, details need to be transferred from the application form to the application processing system. Automated systems can be employed to read paper application forms and to interact with customers on the phone, but current state-of-the art systems are not perfect. Even if the most advanced systems are used to process applications, a significant percentage will still require manual processing of one sort or another. If credit is being applied for in a store/branch, then it is still common for the applicant to complete and sign an application form to confirm that the details they have provided are correct and that they accept the terms and conditions of the agreement. The applicant's details are then entered into the lender's application processing system via a

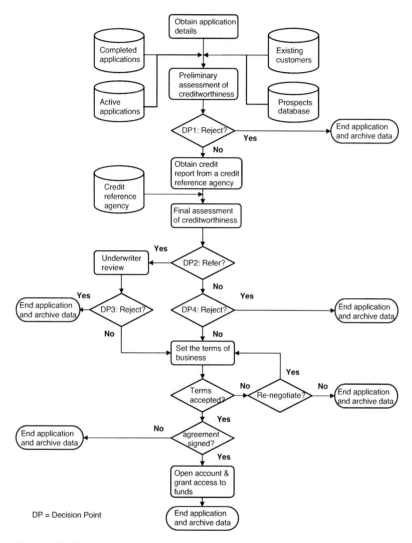

Figure 5.2   The application process

computer terminal. This may be done directly in the store/branch where the application is made, or a member of staff may make a call to a centralized processing centre and pass on the applicant's details to a data entry clerk over the phone. The cost of a centralized application processing centre is usually much cheaper than the cost of installing and maintaining terminals throughout a chain of stores. In addition, a centralized processing centre enables the lender to maintain control of the data capture process and facilitates improved security. This in turn reduces fraud and better enables data quality standards to be maintained.

With direct mailing, one strategy is to print a unique identifier, such as a barcode or string of characters at the top of each application form. This means that an application form can be scanned automatically and matched back to the prospects database (from which the mail shot originated) to retrieve relevant information about the applicant. However, some additional processing may be required to capture any new information that has been provided by the applicant; for example, a change to their employment details. For internet based applications the process can be more automated with applicants effectively typing their details directly into the application processing system via their home computer. Consequently, the processing overheads for internet based credit applications are typically far lower than for applications received from other sources. This is one reason why many financial services organizations offer discounts on their products if applications are made via the internet.

Whatever media channel is used to make an application, the applicant will usually be asked to provide the following types of information:

- **Personal details.** These are required to confirm the identity of the applicant, provide contact details and give information about the individual's bank account for repayment purposes. Usual data items will include title, forename, surname, date of birth, telephone number(s), postal address, e-mail address, name of bank, bank account number and sort code.
- **Product details.** For instalment lending this will be the amount and term of the credit applied for. Questions asking if the applicant would like to take additional products and services such as payment protection and fraud insurance, will also be asked.
- **Asset details.** For mortgages and other secured lending, information about the nature of the asset being used as security (usually house or car) will be required.
- **Geo-demographic details.** This is additional information, such as income, employment details and residential status, that the applicant is asked to provide.

Personal details, product details and asset details are essential items of information that all responsible lenders will need to obtain before advancing credit to a customer. The main reason for obtaining geo-demographic data is that it is one of the most important types of information used to calculate creditworthiness and the affordability of new borrowing. Therefore, the more geo-demographic data available, the better the assessment of creditworthiness will be. From a sales perspective however, the less questions asked the better because each additional question lengthens the time required to complete the application which acts as a disincentive to completing it. Therefore, there tends to be something of a compromise between asking enough questions to ensure that a good assessment of creditworthiness can be made, and not asking so many questions that the applicant is put off applying. Generally, the larger the amount of credit applied for, the more geo-demographic data will be sought before creditworthiness is assessed. This is because higher value agreements represent a greater level of commitment from both parties – most people are willing to spend a lot more time applying for a mortgage to secure their dream home than a store card to buy a few household items. What type of geo-demographic information should be sought from an applicant during the application process? A survey of UK unsecured personal loan and credit card application forms (Finlay 2006) showed that the following questions are asked by almost all credit providers regardless of the type of credit applied for:

- Applicant income.
- Employment status (full/part time, unemployed, homemaker, retired and so on.)
- Time living at current address.
- Residential status (owner, renter, living with parents and so on.)

A significant number of lenders also ask some or all of the following:

- Time bank account held.
- Occupation type (nature of employment, such as doctor, plumber, accountant, clerical worker and so on).
- Time in employment.
- Marital status.[7]
- Time at previous address.
- Credit card/store card details (number and type).
- Details of other credit commitments (on cards, loans, hire-purchase and so on.)[8]
- Number of dependents.
- Monthly mortgage/rent/board payment.
- Outstanding value of mortgage (home owners).

- Time in previous employment.
- Purpose of loan (loans only).

The results from the survey also showed that credit card providers asked an average of ten geo-demographic type questions, while personal loan providers asked an average of 15 questions. One surprising finding was that only 60 percent of loan providers asked applicants the intended purpose of the loan. Another interesting fact was that while all lenders asked about the applicant's income/expenditure, fewer than half asked questions about income from other members of the household or household expenditure. This is important because the way in which household expenditure is proportioned between individuals will have a very strong impact on an individual's disposable income, and hence the affordability of any new debt they are applying for.

5.2.2 Preliminary assessment of creditworthiness

Once personal information has been obtained via the customer interface, it is matched against the database of active and completed applications and the prospects database. The application will also be matched against the existing customer database to see if the applicant is already a customer, or has been a customer in the past. A preliminary assessment of the applicant's creditworthiness is then made. This may involve the calculation of a credit score based on the limited information available at this point in the application process and/or the application of policy rules. The decision engine is then in a position to make a preliminary accept/reject decision (DP1 in Figure 5.2.) Common reasons for classifying an applicant as uncreditworthy and rejecting them at this stage are that they have a low credit score and/or they fail one or more of the following policy rules:

- The applicant has been a customer of the organization before, but the customer's repayment record was unsatisfactory.
- The applicant has a low income. Therefore, they may not be in a position to meet the repayments for the credit they are applying for.
- The applicant lives overseas. This may mean that the applicant is not subject to the jurisdiction of the region in which the organization operates. Therefore, in the case of default, there is little action that can be taken to recover unpaid debt.
- The applicant already has the product. This could indicate fraud, but some organizations supply their credit products under a range of

different brand names. Therefore, it is quite possible for an individual to apply for the same product more than once without knowing it.

• The applicant is applying for the product again within a short space of time. This is often indicative of fraudulent intent. Therefore, many lenders will decline a new credit application if insufficient time, typically a minimum of 60–90 days, has elapsed since a previous application.

• The applicant is under the legal age of consent (18 years of age in many countries).

• The applicant is too old. Definitions of too old vary enormously. Some mortgage lenders won't lend to anyone if the completion date for the agreement is after the applicant's 65th birthday, meaning that a 40 year old could be considered to old for a 25 year mortgage. In credit card and personal loan markets, many lenders set an upper age limit somewhere between 70 and 80.

• The applicant is not in permanent employment.

If the application is rejected, the details will be archived for analysis at a later date.

5.2.3   Obtaining a credit report

If the application passes the preliminary assessment of creditworthiness, a credit report will be sought from a credit reference agency. A credit reference agency (also known as a credit bureau or a credit reporting agency) is an organization that collects, owns or controls access to information about the financial status of individuals or other entities. Credit reference agencies exist in all developed countries, and in many countries there are two or more competing agencies. Most credit reference agencies are owned by Equifax, Experian and TransUnion. These organizations originally operated in the US and/or UK, but can now be viewed as the three main players in the world credit referencing market. In some regions credit reference agencies have also been set up by governments or central banks as publicly managed services to which commercial lending institutions can subscribe.

The central principle underpinning the operation of a credit reference agency is reciprocity. Credit providers have always known that anyone with a history of defaulting on credit in the past is very likely to default again in the future. The converse is also true: people who repay their debts tend to be good customers if granted credit again. So if a lender was approached by a previous customer who had not repaid their debt the last time they borrowed money, the lender would refuse to provide further credit. For uncreditworthy individuals who could no longer obtain credit from one lender, the easiest way of obtaining funds would be to approach a different lender who didn't know about their repayment history. The cycle would often be repeated many times, with an individual leaving a trail of unpaid debts behind them. It therefore made sense for lenders to pool their knowledge and share information about their customers' repayment records – particularly those with a history of non-payment. So when someone with whom a lender has never had any previous contact comes seeking credit, information about the person's other credit agreements is considered to be of considerable value.

Providing competitors with information about your customers is generally not a clever thing to do, but the accepted position across the credit industry is that the benefit of gaining knowledge about customers from many other lenders far outweighs the costs of giving up information about your own. Research into the effect of credit reference agencies on consumer credit markets lends support to this position, suggesting that the more data that is shared between lenders the larger the overall size of the credit market (Barron and Staten 2000; Miller 2003 p. 52). Circumstantial evidence also supports this view. The two countries that have the largest and most developed consumer credit markets in the world; that is, the US and UK, also have the most comprehensive arrangements for data sharing.

A credit reference agency acts as an intermediary in the data sharing process, providing a repository for data and managing the exchange of information between different lending institutions. On a regular basis (usually once a month), lenders provide credit reference agencies with information about their customers and details about which ones are in arrears with their repayments. In return, credit reference agencies provide credit reports containing information about peoples' credit history with other lenders.

In recent years, credit reference agencies have expanded their operations to include other types of personal data that is useful for credit assessment and other commercial purposes. Therefore, most credit reports now contain a range of additional personal information about individuals as well as their credit history. The precise information contained in someone's credit report is country specific. This is due to differences in national legislation, local industry agreements as to what data lenders agree to share and the maturity of the financial services industry. However, the general types of information provided in a credit report tend to be very similar the world over and can be classified into the following types.

- Credit account information: This is information lenders provide about their customers. The information on the credit report will include the type of debt (mortgage, credit card, loan and so on), when the agreement began, when the agreement is due to terminate, the customer's outstanding debt, the monthly repayment and whether the account is up-to-date or in arrears. It will also include a record of past arrears; that is, the arrears status one month ago, two months ago and so on. Flags will also be included to indicate any special circumstances. For example, where fraudulent behaviour is suspected, the customer has died, or where there is some sort of dispute with the customer. Information will also be provided about completed credit agreements and whether they were fully repaid or written-off.

- Credit search information: Every time a lender requests a credit report (a process referred to as a credit search) a record of the search is made. A credit report will contain details of how many credit searches have been undertaken in the past and for what types of credit.
- Public information: This is data that is freely available to the general public. The most common types of public information are details of successful legal action to recover debt, such as bankruptcy orders and court judgements, and electoral (voter) roll information, that confirms that an individual is registered to vote at their stated address and how long they have been registered there.
- Summarized information: Much of the data in a credit report is provided in a summarized form. So, as well as providing information about each individual credit agreement, a credit report will contain details of how many credit agreements someone has, the total value of all their debts, the worst arrears status across all their accounts and so on. This type of summarized information is often more useful than raw data for assessing creditworthiness.[9]
- Derived information: Credit reference agencies maintain large amounts of diverse data, which they have used to construct scoring and segmentation models to predict many different types of consumer behaviour. Perhaps the best known are the FICO scores developed by the FICO Corporation for the US market and the Delphi scores supplied by Experian in the UK. Credit reference agency supplied scores may be used instead of, or in conjunction with, any scoring and segmentation that has been developed in-house by a lending institution.

In some countries, including France, Germany and Australia, organizations only share credit information about customers who are in arrears with their repayments or whose debts have been written-off for non-payment. In the US and UK lenders share more data, which includes information about good paying customers who are up-to-date with their repayments.

In addition to information about the applicant, a credit report may also contain information about 'associated individuals'. An associated individual is a family member who lives at the applicant's address, or another person with who the applicant has a known financial association.[10] Most commonly, this will be the applicant's spouse or partner, or someone with whom they share a mortgage.

An important point is that only month end account information is provided on a credit report. Detailed information about customer transactions is not provided. A credit report may show someone's outstanding balance on a credit card, but it will not contain any information about where the credit card has been used or what purchases have been made using the card.

The process of obtaining a credit report is automatic and is usually completed within a few seconds. The data management unit will initiate the search process by transmitting the applicant's name, address and date of birth to the credit reference agency via the internet or a dedicated computer link. The credit reference agency will then search its databases and provide a credit report containing all relevant information about the applicant.

5.2.4   Final assessment of creditworthiness

After a credit report has been obtained, an application will be credit scored again, resulting in a revised assessment of creditworthiness that takes into consideration the information on the credit report. Additional policy rules will also be applied at this point, and if necessary the application will be referred for manual review (DP2 in Figure 5.2). For credit cards, retail credit and low value unsecured personal loans, a typical lender may refer anywhere between 1 and 10 percent of cases for manual review by an underwriter. For higher value lending, and in particularly mortgages, the proportion of referred cases tends to be higher. A referral rate of 10–40 percent is not uncommon. Reasons for referring an application at this stage include:

- Suspected fraud. This will usually be because of some irregularity in the information provided by the applicant (such as a non-existent contact number) or because the individual's personal details can be matched to previous cases of known or suspected fraud.

- Identity/address confirmation. If a credit reference agency is able to produce a credit report for someone, then this is often taken as evidence that the person is who they say they are[11] and live at their stated address. If no credit report is found, then the applicant may be asked for further proof of identity and residence.
- Credit report information. Specific items on the applicant's credit report may trigger a referral. For example, if someone has a lot of existing credit commitments, then this may raise questions about the affordability of new debt.
- Marginal credit score. The applicant is only just deemed creditworthy/ uncreditworthy by the automated system. Therefore, the final decision will be made manually.

As part of the manual review process an underwriter will consider all of the information available. If necessary, the applicant will be contacted to discuss their situation and asked to provide any additional information that is required. For example, if the applicant has been referred because of concerns about the level of their existing credit commitments, the underwriter may want to discuss the applicant's income and outgoings to establish if the repayments are affordable.

If the application is not referred, a final decision to accept or reject the application will be made automatically by the decision engine (DP4 in Figure 5.2). This is the main decision point in the application process, with the majority of decisions about someone's creditworthiness (usually 75 percent or more) being made at this point. The main reason for rejecting an application at this stage will be because of a low credit score, based on the applicant's full details including their credit report. However, an application may also be automatically declined for a number of other reasons defined by policy rules. These include:

- The presence of specific items of derogatory data within a credit report. For example, bankruptcy or a case of serious delinquency with another lender within the last 36 months.
- The credit report is empty. The credit reference agency was unable to find any information about the applicant and there is no record of them being registered on the electoral (voters) roll at their stated address. Some organizations refer these cases for manual review, but many believe it is not cost effective to deal with such cases and automatically decline them.
- The applicant is seriously over-indebted. Therefore, they would not be able to afford to repay any new credit they were granted.

- A large number of credit searches are reported on the credit report; that is, the applicant has made many other applications for credit in a short period of time. This is often indicative of someone who is desperate for credit and who has a very high risk of payment default.
- The application is suspected of being fraudulent. In some regions there is a requirement to refer such cases before declining them, but in many countries cases of suspected fraud are declined automatically.

In theory the decision to reject an application should be made purely on the basis of the applicant's creditworthiness. However, in some situations uncreditworthy applicants may be offered credit in order to meet organizational objectives. Providers of retail credit often enter into agreements with retailers that specify a minimum acceptance rate. A finance house may agree to supply credit to customers of a furniture retailer, where a clause in the contract specifies that each month at least 90 percent of customers who want goods on credit terms are accepted. If 20 percent of applicants are uncreditworthy then the finance house must accept half of these in order to comply with their contractual obligation. This is one reason why retail credit has a reputation for charging higher interest rates than other forms of credit. The revenue generated from creditworthy customers needs to cover the additional loss incurred from accepting some people who are known to be uncreditworthy.[12]

It is also common for organizations to set themselves acquisition targets which, for various reasons, pay little regard to the creditworthiness of applicants. This can sometimes be justified for a new product if the primary goal is to establish significant market share quickly. In other situations the rationale for accepting uncreditworthy customers is questionable at best. During my time working in the credit industry I witnessed several situations where unrealistic acquisition targets were set by senior management, to appease the short term concerns of shareholders about how well the business was doing. The result is that for a short period of time the business appears to be doing very well due to the increase in the number of new customers. However, within a few months significant losses start to be incurred as uncreditworthy customers default on their debts in large numbers. This is exactly what happened to precipitate the meltdown in the US sub-prime market in 2006/7. In a saturated market, lenders felt that in order to grow their mortgage portfolios they had to offer loans to people on low incomes and/or with poor credit histories. A number of ingenious repayment plans were employed to make mortgages seem more affordable to those on low incomes, based on the assumption that house prices would continue to rise. When the housing market began to stagnate, repayments on these mortgage agreements increased considerably. The end result was that many people could no longer afford to repay their mortgages and the banks foreclosed. Subsequently, several mortgage providers declared bankruptcy due to the volume of bad debt that resulted, and many others only survived due to the financial support provided by governments and central banks.

5.2.5   Setting the terms of business (product features)

If an application is accepted in principle, the next stage is to finalize the terms of the credit offer; that is, what product features such as the interest rate, credit line, maximum loan amount and so on should be – which are commonly referred to as the 'terms of business'. At this point, those who are likely to be good candidates for cross sell and up sell opportunities for other products and services will also be identified. The final terms of business are then communicated back to the customer. It is important to note there may be a difference between the terms of business someone is offered and the terms that the person seeking credit originally asked for or has encountered previously within promotional material. For example, the typical APR for a mortgage product may be 5.9 percent and this is the rate that was advertised. However, if an applicant has a less than perfect credit record the lender won't offer them this rate, but a higher rate of say, 7.5 percent. Therefore, it will be necessary to explain to the applicant why they are being asked to pay the higher rate.

For fixed term products such as loans and mortgages, it may be that the applicant has applied for more credit than the lender is willing to grant, or has requested that the term of the agreement is for a period that is shorter or longer than is acceptable. In these cases it may be necessary for the lender and the applicant to renegotiate the amount and/or term of the credit to be advanced.

If the applicant accepts the terms of the credit offer then they must confirm their acceptance by physically signing a copy of the agreement,[13] or in countries where it is permitted, providing an electronic signature. The signed agreement is then returned to the lender. If an application has been made remotely there is often a requirement to send a paper copy of the agreement to the applicant to sign and return. If no response is received within a reasonable period of time, follow-up activity, such as a reminder letter, may be initiated to encourage the applicant to sign and return the agreement. Only when a signed credit agreement has been received should an account be opened and funds advanced; otherwise, there is no legal recourse should the borrower default.

5.2.6 Account opening and access to funds

Once a credit agreement has been created an account record will be created within the account management system to facilitate the management of the credit agreement on an ongoing basis. Funds will then be made available to the borrower. For a cash loan this will usually be an automatic transfer of funds to the borrower's bank account, but in some cases a cheque may be provided. For card products the process is more complex. A card will need to be dispatched to the customer, along with any passwords/PIN numbers. This raises a number of security issues. For example, there is a risk of the card being lost or stolen in transit, or a fraudster may receive a card and use it, but then claim that they never received it. For this reason card issuers use one or more of the following procedures to reduce the incidence of card fraud.

- Separate dispatch of card and PIN numbers/passwords.
- Registered delivery. The applicant must sign for the card when it arrives.
- Card activation. To use the card, the customer must contact the lender and activate the card. Usually, the customer will be asked a number of security questions, based on information they provided when they applied. These questions must be answered correctly before activation occurs.
- Branch collection/alternate address. Some organizations maintain lists of 'high risk' postal areas where the incidence of fraud is particularly high. If a customer lives in one of these areas they will be asked to collect their card from their local branch. Alternatively, the customer may be asked to supply another address to send the card to, located in a different postal area.

Fraud issues are discussed in more detail in Chapter 9.

5.3 Variations on the standard process

Figure 5.2 shows a fairly typical application process. In practice, several variations can be adopted. Some organizations do not undertake a preliminary credit assessment; that is, they do not make a preliminary accept/reject decision at DP1 in Figure 5.2. Instead, they obtain a full credit report for every applicant and then undertake a single assessment of each applicant's creditworthiness. Obtaining a credit report for everyone incurs additional cost, but having a credit report for all applicants does have benefits. It is valuable for assessing the profile of customers in future, particularly if the organization decides to move 'down market' and start accepting some applicants that were previously considered to be uncreditworthy. In addition, if an applicant's creditworthiness is only assessed once, then the application process is simpler, and hence easier and cheaper to manage.

Another view is that the information provided on a credit report is more important than personal data provided by the applicant. A lender that adopts this view will begin by asking only the most basic identity information such as name, address and date of birth in order to allow them to undertake a credit search. If the credit score and policy rules based on the credit report are satisfactory, they may then proceed to solicit further information such as the applicant's income, residential status and occupation, before (optionally) undertaking a second and final assessment of creditworthiness. The advantage of this approach is that it can speed up the application process and reduce costs. If an applicant has a very poor credit history and is clearly uncreditworthy, then the application can be rejected on the basis of the credit report alone. No further time need be wasted dealing with the application. Likewise, if an applicant's credit report is very good, then it may be possible to classify them as creditworthy without needing to ask them any more questions.

Different recruitment channels may require different processes to be applied to some applications. For example, if an application results from a direct mail campaign, where the majority of the applicant's personal details are already known, there is little point in having a two stage process because those who would be declined due to their income, age, having an overseas address and so on, would have already been excluded from the mail shot. The lender will proceed directly with a credit report and then make their decision. However, this logic may not be suitable for applications received from the internet or in response to a mass media campaign where relatively little is known about the applicant before they apply, requiring a two stage process to be undertaken.

5.4   Pre-approval

A pre-approval credit offer is where someone is told that if they apply, then they will automatically be accepted. Most pre-approval credit offers are targeted at existing customers who already have one of the organization's credit products. Therefore, in one sense these cases fall outside the bounds of the customer acquisition process. Rather, the pre-approval offer is an account management tool that is used to cross sell products and services to the existing customer base. Common examples are personal loans offered to existing credit card customers and credit cards offered to current account customers.

For the reasons discussed at the very start of the chapter, true pre-approved credit offers to people who are not existing customers, are rare. In most cases what may appear to be an unconditional pre-approve offer is subject to a number of restrictions contained in the small print. Typically, there will be a condition along the lines of 'credit subject to your circumstances not having changed' which means that when an application is received; if the applicant is no longer creditworthy they will be declined. Alternatively, the credit line or the APR that the individual will be charged will only be set when the individual applies. Therefore, very high APRs and/or very low credit limits can be set for those that are deemed to be very uncreditworthy.

5.5 Multi-product processing

Most large financial services organizations offer a range of credit products. Some maintain separate application processing systems for each product, but most have a single application processing system that can deal with all of the different products on offer. So, if an organization provides credit cards and personal loans, the application processing system will be configured to establish at the start of the application process which product is being applied for. Different processes will then be applied depending on the product type. Usually, this means that the applicant is asked a slightly different set of questions and different credit scores, policy rules and terms of business will be applied by the decision engine.

Multi-product processing capability is also commonly found within other systems, such as those for account management and debt recovery.

5.6 Multi-applicant processing

For credit cards and retail credit, most credit agreements are entered into individually.[14] One person applies for credit and that person is responsible for meeting the terms of the credit agreement. For mortgages and personal loans, applications are often made in joint names by two (or sometimes three or four) individuals, all of whom have joint responsibility for repaying the debt. There is therefore, a question as to how such applications should be treated and the criteria under which creditworthiness is assessed. Most lenders adopt one of two approaches:

1. Worst case. Each applicant's creditworthiness is assessed individually. The lending decision is based on the applicant who is least creditworthy.

2. Pooled data. The information from all applicants is pooled,[15] and a single credit assessment is made using the pooled data.

Other strategies could be adopted. For example, considering the best applicant's creditworthiness or taking an average. However, these options are not popular because the general industry view is that it is the worst applicant that is likely to exert the greatest influence over future repayment behaviour.[16]

5.7   Strategies for setting terms of business

For some types of credit only a single set of terms may be applicable. Consider a retailer advertising furniture on three year interest free repayment terms. If the applicant is creditworthy they will be offered a three year interest free agreement for the value of the goods they wish to purchase. No additional terms need to be set. However, for cards, loans and mortgages, once someone's application has been accepted as creditworthy in principle, decisions then need to be made about the following product features:

- The interest rate(s) that the customer will be charged.
- For revolving credit agreements:
  o The type of card account offered (for example platinum or black).
  o The credit line and shadow limit.
  o The time until account renewal.
  o Whether or not to charge an annual fee, and the amount of fee to charge.
- For fixed term credit agreements:
  o The amount of any arrangement (documentation) fee charged for processing the credit application.
  o The maximum loan amount.
  o The minimum acceptable deposit (for mortgages, retail loans and hire-purchase).
  o The minimum possible repayment period.
  o The maximum possible repayment period.

The main driver for setting the terms of business is the applicant's credit score (the assessment of their creditworthiness) and a common strategy is to apply a pricing for risk strategy where the interest rate is derived as a function of credit score; that is, those with low credit scores are charged a higher than average rate of interest, so that the increased levels of bad debt associated with lower credit scores are offset by higher interest revenue. However, a number of other aspects of a credit application will also be considered when deciding the terms of an agreement. These include:

- The customer's personal income.
- Household income.
- Current credit commitments. In regions where it is available, the total amount of outstanding debt and/or the applicant's current monthly repayments will be included on their credit report. In countries where this information is not provided on a credit report, questions about existing credit commitments may be asked during the application process.
- Whether the individual is an existing or new customer.
- Where the customer is classified as a special case or 'VIP', for example, employees of the lending organization and their families.
- The customer's assets – principally, whether or not they own their own home, the value of the property and any outstanding mortgage on the property.

This data will then be used to segment the population using a number of rules and/or tables that can be represented in the form of a decision tree. An example of a decision tree for an unsecured personal loan product is shown in Figure 5.3.

So, if in Figure 5.3 the applicant:

- Has a credit score of between 760 and 875 and
- has an income of more than $100,000 and
- is not an existing customer

$30,000 is the maximum loan amount and the interest rate on the loan would be 10.9 percent. The minimum and maximum possible term for the loan would be 12 and 84 months respectively.

For large organizations with several different credit products, it is not uncommon to have dozens of population segments, all with different terms of business assigned. In Figure 5.3 a single set of terms have been allocated for each segment within the tree, but the terms of business can be set using formulae. So in cases where income multipliers are used these can also be applied. So if it had been decided that the maximum loan advance should be equal to 30 percent of gross income, the maximum $30,000 loan figure

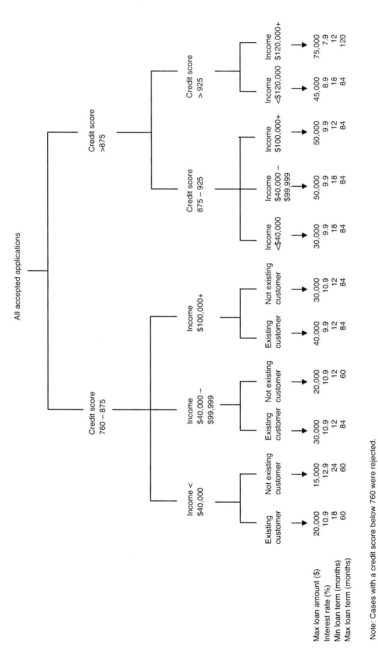

Figure 5.3 Personal loan terms of business

discussed earlier in relation to Figure 5.3 could be replaced by the formula:

Maximum loan amount = Applicant's gross income * 0.3.

If the applicant earned $100,000 the maximum loan would be $30,000, but if they earned $150,000 they would be permitted a loan of up to $45,000. More complex formulae can also be used that consider several different aspect of an applicant's profile. For example, a measure of disposable income could be calculated for each applicant based on their income, other (their partner's) income, existing credit commitments, utility bills, local taxes, general household expenditure and so on. The maximum loan amount would then be determined based on the amount of disposable income available to meet repayments.

5.7.1 Shadow limits

For revolving credit products a common strategy is to allocate shadow limits. Two credit limits will be assigned to each customer. The lower credit limit is the formal limit up to which the customer can spend, and this is the amount that is communicated to the customer when their account is opened. The second, higher limit (the shadow limit), is the maximum credit line that the lender is willing to provide, and is not usually revealed to customers. Shadow limits tend to be set in one of two ways, either as percentage of the lower limit (often somewhere between 110 and 120 percent of the lower limit) or as a fixed amount above the lower limit say, $500. Shadow limits are used in two ways:

1. If a customer requests an increase to their credit limit, the credit limit may be increased by an amount up to the shadow limit.
2. If the customer spends beyond their allotted credit limit, they are permitted to continue spending up to their shadow limit, although they may incur penalty fees for exceeding their official credit limit.

The main reason for having shadow limits is that it simplifies the account management process and reduces the IT resources required to update customer accounts. As discussed in more detail in Chapter 6, most providers of revolving credit recalculate customers' creditworthiness on a monthly basis at the account cycle point, and will also review the terms of business at this time. By having a pre-allocated shadow limit the need to recalculate the credit limit at times other than the cycle point is much reduced.

5.7.2   Affordability

The use of consumer credit increased dramatically in many regions of the world in the late 1990s and 2000s, with a corresponding rise in customer defaults and bankruptcies. Many concerns were raised by governments, consumer groups and the media about the affordability of debt and the increasing number of people who were struggling to meet their debt repayments. In the UK this led to the establishment of a government taskforce on over-indebtedness. The taskforce produced a number of reports and recommendations advising how affordability and over-indebtedness should be dealt with. Consequently, pressure was exerted on the consumer credit industry in the UK to adopt a more responsible attitude to lending policy and to put in place procedures that prevented people borrowing beyond their means (Consumer Affairs Directorate 2001; Consumer Affairs Directorate 2003; Department for Constitutional Affairs 2004).

To be absolutely sure that credit is not being provided to people who can not afford it, a lender could go to great lengths during the application process to establish an applicant's income and outgoings and demand to see certain proofs such as pay slips, utility bills and shopping bills. In practice, this level of investigation is often infeasible due to cost, customer inconvenience and the competitive disadvantage that results from such a lengthy and intrusive process – particularly for low value retail credit that may be for no more than a few hundred dollars. A more achievable goal, and one which regulatory authorities seem to accept, is to be able to demonstrate that reasonable steps have been taken to inform potential customers about the cost of credit and not to lend in situations where there is clear evidence that advancing new credit will cause someone to become over-indebted. Two steps are recommended for avoiding over-indebtedness. The first is to provide applicants with simple information that enables them to assess affordability for themselves. This is in addition to any statutory information about the terms of the credit agreement that may be required by law. Many loan and mortgage companies provide an 'affordability calculator' on their websites or within product brochures, to help people to work out their disposable income and what they can afford in terms of new credit commitments. The second is to implement policy rules within the application processing system. These are based on data the applicant provides about their income and outgoings, in conjunction with information about their existing credit commitments provided as part of their credit report. People who have very large credit commitments in relation to their income and are clearly over-indebted are automatically declined. More borderline cases are referred to an underwriter who can discuss the affordability of the credit with the applicant before a lending decision is made.

The UK taskforce on over-indebtedness (Consumer Affairs Directorate 2003) suggested that a household where any one of the following conditions is found to be true is highly likely to be over-indebted:

- Having four or more non-mortgage credit commitments (this excludes debt on credit and store cards that is paid in full each month and utility bills).
- Spending more than 25 percent of gross income on credit, excluding mortgages.
- Spending more than 50 percent of gross income on credit, including mortgages.

These three conditions will not identify all those who are over-indebted, but they will identify the most serious cases, and if implemented within a lender's application processing system will prevent credit being advanced to a considerable proportion of people who can't afford it. Its also worth noting that implementing these or similar rules demonstrates that an organization takes the issue of over-indebtedness seriously, and if positioned correctly, can be used positively to demonstrate the organizations ethical credentials in this area.

5.7.3 Optimizing the terms of business – champion/challenger

An obvious question arising from the previous sections is, how is the applicant population segmented and how are the terms of business defined for each segment? In Figure 5.3, for example, how would a lender know that those with a credit score greater than 925 and with an income of more than $120,000 should be able to borrow a maximum of $75,000? Why not $70,000 or $80,000? For a new product, the answer is to set the terms of business based on expert opinion and current market conditions. To put it another way, an educated guess will be made on the basis of a credit manager's experience of dealing with similar products in the past, what is known about what competitors are currently offering their customers and the state of the economy.

After a new credit product has been launched the terms of business will be repeatedly refined to maximize the contribution to profit generated from each population segment. The most popular strategy for refining the terms of business is the 'champion/challenger' approach. Within any given customer segment, a small percentage of customers will be randomly assigned to a challenger sub-group that is used to test some new terms of business. The majority of accounts – the champion group – continue to have the existing terms of business applied. After the new challenger terms of business have been applied for a period of time, the performance of the champion and challenger groups are compared. If the challenger outperforms the champion, the challenger terms of business are adopted by the champion group. The process is then repeated with a new challenger. To illustrate the champion/challenger approach, consider a credit card where people with a moderate income and who are very creditworthy are granted a $3,000 limit on their credit card. Two challenger groups are assigned. Five percent of new customers are randomly assigned to the first challenger group with a credit limit of $2,900. Another 5 percent are randomly assigned to the second challenger group with a credit limit of $3,100. The remaining 90 percent continue to receive a $3,000 limit. After 12 months, revenue, bad debt and other costs for each group are used to calculate the average profit contributed by each account within the group. In the $2,900 challenger group the average contribution was $45, and in the $3,100 challenger group the average contribution was $39. In the champion group the average contribution was $41. Therefore, it would appear the best strategy would be to reduce the credit limit for moderate income, but very creditworthy, customers from $3,000 to $2,900.

The champion/challenger approach is popular and has proven to be very successful in practice. However, it suffers from two main drawbacks. The first is the time taken to evaluate performance – many months need to elapse before enough information is available to determine whether the champion or the challenger is best. One solution to this problem, if a lender has sufficient volume of new applicants, is to run many challengers in parallel. One strategy might be to assign 90 percent of cases to the champion and 1 percent to each of ten challengers. Another option is to measures the performance of competing champion/challenger groups over short outcome periods. If the challenger outperforms the champion in the short term, it is assumed that this will also be true in the long term.

The second drawback of using champion/challenger is that some, or even most, of the time the challenger group(s) will perform less well than the champion. Therefore, the best terms found to date are not being applied to all accounts. Consequently, there is a desire to keep challenger groups as small as possible.

5.7.4 Beyond champion/challenger

The major alternatives to champion/challenger are forecasting methods based on simulation and statistical optimization. Inferences are drawn about how accounts might have behaved if their terms and conditions were changed. Given the scope of this book it is not possible to go into detail about how these forecasting techniques are applied, but the basic principle is that if an organization has experimented with a number of different champion/challenger strategies in the past, then it is possible to use this information to estimate what the performance of new and untried challengers would be. Therefore, it is possible to determine the best terms of business that will maximize the profit contribution from each account. The main advantage of the forecasting solutions currently available is that they promise to optimize the terms of business quickly, based on information that is already known about account behaviour. There is no need to wait many months to see how well different challengers perform. The main drawback with forecasting approaches is that they require very large and diverse portfolios to work well, where many different champion/challenger strategies have been tried before, so there is lots of information to work with. If few alterative terms of business have been tried in the past, then forecasting methods do not tend to perform very well. Another problem with many of the forecasting solutions currently available is that they are 'black box' in nature. Many vendors of forecasting solutions provide their clients with very little information about how their forecasts are derived in order to protect their intellectual property. Another point is that the results produced by forecasting methods are estimates, not actual figures. It can be difficult to verify that the forecasts are correct, and there is significant scope for error and hence loss. The champion/challenger approach on the other hand is easy to understand and is based on actual figures. This gives management a certain level of confidence in the results that are produced.

The best overall method for refining terms of business is to combine forecasting/optimization methods with champion/challenger. Forecasting and optimization are used to generate a list of potential challengers, which are then tested against the champion.

5.8   Chapter summary

The customer acquisition process is about evaluating the creditworthiness of potential customers and deciding the terms to offer to those that are creditworthy.

Customer acquisition is managed using a computerized application processing system, consisting of two main components – a data management unit and a decision engine. The data management unit collates data from different sources, and distributes it to the relevant business areas at appropriate times. The decision engine uses information supplied to it by the account management system to make decisions about how applications should be treated. For example, deciding which applicants are creditworthy and how much credit accepted applicants should be allowed to have.

The customer acquisition process contains a number of steps and decision points that must be traversed before a credit agreement is created and funds made available to the customer. Most organizations undertake a two stage process. In the first stage, a preliminary credit assessment will be made, based on personal information provided by the applicant combined with any existing information that the organization may know about them. If the applicant passes the preliminary credit assessment, then additional information will be sought from a credit report, supplied by a credit reference agency. A credit report provides details of the applicant's repayment behaviour in the past and the status of existing credit commitments with other credit providers. A more complete assessment of creditworthiness will then be made, based on all of the information that has been obtained. If the application is deemed to be creditworthy and accepted, then further decisions need to be made about the terms of business; that is, the amount of credit to allow the customer, the term of the agreement, the APR to charge and so on. If the applicant accepts the terms of business they will then be granted access to funds and a customer account record created within the organization's account management system.

6
Customer Management

This third phase of credit management – customer management – begins once a credit agreement has been created. It continues until the customer has repaid their debt according to the terms of the agreement or they become delinquent, requiring collections action to be taken (the fourth phase of credit management). The goals of customer management are twofold. First, to ensure that relationships with customers function as intended and an acceptable level of customer service is provided. Second, to maximize the return generated from customers over the lifetime of the relationship. These goals are achieved by undertaking:

1. Operational management: This is about providing and managing the infrastructure required to maintain customer relationships. For example, dealing with customer enquires, updating account records when transactions occur and issuing statements of account.
2. Relationship management: This is about understanding and meeting customer requirements for products and services over the long term. For example, regularly reviewing the credit limit and APR for a credit card customer, and identifying which mortgage customers are suitable targets for cross selling credit cards, personal loans and insurance.

This chapter deals mainly with the management of revolving credit, and in particular, credit cards. This is because the nature and type of activities involved in managing card agreements are more complex than those for fixed term credit agreements such as personal loans and mortgages. Card transactions can occur many times a day, and decisions regularly need to be taken about how to manage accounts in response to patterns in customer behaviour. For fixed term credit agreements relatively little needs to be done to manage accounts once an agreement has been created. The main tasks are to ensure that regular repayments are made and customers are sold additional products they need or desire. Where appropriate, actions relating to the management of fixed term agreements are highlighted.

6.1   Operational management

Operational management is about providing the infrastructure to allow credit agreements to function as specified in the terms and conditions. This covers two main areas. The first is providing an account management system that allows transactions such as retail purchases, cash withdrawals and customer repayments, to occur. The account management system will also provide data storage facilities holding information about customers, their accounts and account transactions, so that it is possible to provide customers with regular statements and to produce management information about the behaviour of the customer base over time. Second, a customer interface needs to be provided (usually via a call centre/customer contact centre and/or website) to enable communication between the credit provider and the customer.

6.1.1   The account management system

The backbone of operational management is the customer's account record, maintained within the account management system. The account record contains details of all transactions that have occurred over the lifetime of the credit agreement, and information about the current status of the agreement.[1] The account record should contain all of the following information:

- Details of the customer acquisition process that led to the creation of the credit agreement. This includes:
  - o Original contact details; that is, name, address, phone numbers and e-mail addresses when the account was first created.
  - o Personal details, such as age, income and employment status.
  - o The customer's credit report, as obtained from a credit reference agency at the point of application.
  - o The date the customer applied for the product.
  - o The date the credit agreement was created.[2]

o The initial terms of business; that is, the credit limit, APR and so on.

o A measure of the customer's original credit worthiness; that is, their credit score.

• The date, time, location and value of each financial transaction that has occurred since the agreement was created. This will include details of:

o Retail purchases.

o Balance transfers.

o Cash withdrawals.

o Charge-backs. This is when a completed transaction is revoked. For example, if someone buys something from a store using their credit card, but later returns the item and obtains a refund.

o Repayments made by the customer.

o Charges and fees that have been levied.

• Statement summary data. This will include:

o A summary of payments that have been made each statement period.

o A summary of the different types of credit advances that have been made. For example, the value of cash withdrawals, purchases, balance transfers and interest charges.

o The delinquency status at the end of each statement period (up-to-date, one month in arrears, two months in arrears and so on).

• Current account status. This covers:

o Up-to-date contact details, including address, phone number(s) and e-mail address(es).

o The account balance split by retail purchases, cash withdrawals, balance transfers and so on.

o The credit limit.

o The interest rate(s) currently being applied to the account.

o The card expiry date (or the expected completion date for fixed term products).

o The current delinquency status of the account.

o Account status indicators. For example, indicating whether the account is open, closed, dormant, in debt recovery, or that the account holder has died.

It is important that this information is maintained in an efficient and timely manner. If not, then customer service will suffer and the ability to analyse and understand trends in customer behaviour over time will be limited. For a large organization with millions of customers this represents a huge amount of data and considerable computer power is required to process it. A typical account management system will cost upwards of $10 million dollars to install and several million dollars a year to maintain.

Transaction processing to update account records with details of retail purchases, cash withdrawals, customer payments and so on, may occur in real time or as a batch process run each day. If transactions are processed in batch, then a temporary transactions file will be created during the day, and then at night customer account records are updated with details of the transactions that have occurred since the last update. Batch processing usually occurs at night because this is when demand for IT resources from other parts of the business are low.

6.1.2   Account cycling and statement production

Three key principles underpinning the management of credit agreements are:

- The statement period.
- The payment due date.
- The cycle point (also referred to as the statement date).

At the end of each statement period a statement of account is produced. The statement contains details of financial transactions that have occurred, together with a summary of the account's current status; that is, the outstanding balance (referred to as the statement balance), the payment due and any arrears owing. For many credit agreements the statement period is one calendar month – and this will be assumed during the course of the discussion that follows. However, it should be noted that some mortgage and loan products have an annual statement period, and there are a few revolving credit products that have a four week statement period.[3]

The payment due date is the date in the next statement period by which a customer must make a repayment or enter a state of default. This is usually somewhere between 14 and 28 days after the statement date.[4] The cycle point is the date that defines the end of one statement period and the beginning of the next. Accounts are said to cycle from one statement period to the next at the cycle point. A common sense approach would be to set the cycle point to be the last day of the month for all accounts. However, usual practice is to set the cycle point to be the day of the month when the account was first opened, or chosen at random,[5] so that on average a similar number of accounts cycle each day. The reason for this is to improve efficiency and reduce costs. If all account holders cycled on the last day of the month, then a large amount of computer processing capacity would be needed and all customer statements would need to be produced in one go. By spreading the cycle dates throughout the month, statement production is a much more efficient process requiring fewer resources.

When accounts cycle a number of steps are taken prior to statements being printed and dispatched to customers. The first stage of the process is to gather raw transaction data from throughout the statement period. This is used to produce summary information such as the total value of retail transactions, the total value of cash transactions and the sum of any payments made by the customer. The second step is to calculate fees and charges to be applied. This will mainly involve the calculation of interest, but if the customer did not make a payment by the previous due date or has exceeded their credit limit then penalty fees will also be applied. In parallel with this process, customer details may also be provided to a credit reference agency so that an up-to-date credit report can be obtained. Summarized account information, together with credit reference data will then be passed to a decision engine. The decision engine will assess any actions that need to be taken to optimize the relationship with the customer, for instance, changing their credit limit or the APR on the account. Relevant information will then be selected for use in statement production.

When cycling accounts have been processed, details are passed to the print unit so that customers' statements can be printed. Prior to statement dispatch, any promotional materials for cross sold products and services will also be produced, as well as notice of late payment and other communications. These can then be dispatched with statements, thus saving the cost that would be incurred if they were mailed separately.

6.1.3 Card networks

Organizations that issue credit cards bearing the VISA or MasterCard logos do not have a direct relationship with the merchants who accept their cards as a means of payment. Instead, a third party bank, called a merchant acquirer, acts as an intermediary. The relationship between card issuers, their customers, merchants and merchant acquirers is shown in Figure 6.1.

When a customer presents a merchant with their credit card to pay for something, the customer's account details and information about

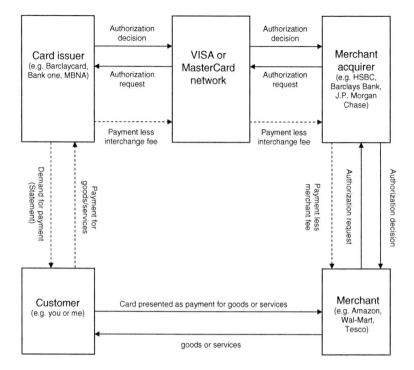

Note: Full arrows represent activities that occur during a credit card transaction.
Dotted arrows represent activities that occur sometime after the transaction has occurred.

Figure 6.1   The relationship between customers, merchants and card issuers

the proposed transaction will be passed to the merchant acquirer. The merchant acquirer then passes this information to the card issuer via the VISA or MasterCard computer network. The card issuer then decides whether or not the transaction should be authorized.[6] The authorization decision will primarily be based on the amount of headroom between the customer's current balance and their credit limit, with most transactions being authorized if the customer has sufficient funds available. If the transaction is unusually large, appears to be fraudulent or causes the customer to exceed their credit limit, then the transaction may be declined automatically based on the rules that are in place within the account management system. Alternatively, the transaction may be referred for manual review. In this case, an underwriter may attempt to contact the customer, either directly or via the merchant, to confirm that the transaction is genuine.

Once the issuer has made a decision to authorize or decline a transaction, the decision is passed back through the network to the merchant. The VISA and MasterCard computer networks act as intermediaries for these processes, managing the flow of information between merchant acquirers and card issuers, as well as the transfer of funds once transactions have occurred.

In order for a merchant to be able to accept credit cards from VISA and MasterCard customers, they must first enter into an agreement with a merchant acquirer. The merchant acquirer provides the equipment required to process card payments and manages the relationship between the card network and individual card issuers.

Accepting credit cards as a means of payment provides merchants with a number of benefits over cash or cheque:

- The merchant acquirer guarantees payment for all purchases that customers have made using their cards. If a credit card is used fraudulently, or the customer doesn't pay their credit card bill, the merchant will still receive payment for the goods they have sold.
- By accepting credit cards the amount of cash that a merchant will have on their premises is reduced. This in turn reduces the losses that may result from theft and reduces the number/value of cash deposits that a merchant needs to make at their bank.
- The merchant receives payment promptly, usually within one or two days of a transaction occurring. The card issuer bears the cost of funding the transaction while waiting for a customer to pay their credit card bill.

In return for receiving these benefits, the merchant pays a merchant fee (often called the merchant discount) on each transaction. The merchant fee comprises a fixed component of between $0.05 and $0.25, plus a percentage of each transaction's value (Evans and Schmalensee 2005 p. 260). Merchant fees are negotiated between individual merchants and merchant acquirers. Large retailers dealing with millions of dollars worth of card transactions each month can negotiate merchant fees as low as 1 percent because of the volume of business they deal with. Small retailers on the other hand may pay 4 percent or more.

A proportion of the merchant fee is retained by the merchant acquirer and a small percentage is paid to VISA or MasterCard to pay for the upkeep of their networks. The remainder – referred to as the interchange fee – is retained by the card issuer. Interchange fees are set by VISA and MasterCard. They are country specific and vary depending on the type of transaction. Higher interchange fees are charged where the cardholder is not present (over the internet or via the phone) because of the higher incidence of fraud with such transactions. On average, interchange fees are between 0.5 and 1.5 percent of the value of each transaction. Both VISA and MasterCard publish details of their interchange fees on their websites (www.mastercard.com and www.visa.com)

The VISA and MasterCard organizations are run as industry joint ventures, owned by member organizations; that is, organizations that are either merchant acquirers or card issuers.[7] For single card networks, such as American Express and Discover, the card issuer negotiates the merchant fee directly with merchants. The main benefit of this more direct approach is that costs should be lower because there is no need for merchant acquirers. The main drawback is lack of competition because merchants negotiate directly with the card issuer; therefore, there is no scope for entering into a better deal with an alternative provider.

Interchange fees have proven controversial because the majority shareholders who control the VISA and MasterCard organizations are the card issuers and merchant acquirers who benefit from the fees that are charged. It is therefore in their interest for interchange fees to be as high as possible, and it can be argued that this is a form of cartel that limits competition and inflates prices. Consequently, interchange fees have been subject to regulatory scrutiny in a number of regions. In the UK, interchange fees have been subject to review by the Office of Fair Trading (Office of Fair Trading 2003) who subsequently found that MasterCard had breached anti-competition laws (Office of Fair Trading 2005). The Reserve Bank of Australia concluded that the charging structure for interchange fees stifled competition and acted against the public interest (Reserve Bank of Australia 2001 pp. 115–16). This subsequently resulted in legislation limiting interchange fees that card companies can charge in Australia (Reserve Bank of Australia 2006).[8] In 2009 both VISA and MasterCard reduced cross border interchange fees in response to pressure from the European Commission (Gow 2009). In the US many trade bodies and state legislatures are also seeking the reduction of interchange fees.

6.1.4   The customer interface

In support of the operational functions an interface with the customer needs to be provided to allow communication with them. Three types of customer interaction need to be catered for:

1. Inbound customer communications. Customers may wish to contact the credit provider by a variety of different channels including phone,

internet and letter. Typically, a customer will contact their credit provider to enquire about the status of their account, to report their card as lost/stolen, or to request an increase to their credit limit.

2. Outbound communications. There will be times when the credit provider will want to communicate with customers other than via their statement. This may be to chase up late payers, obtain authorization for transactions that are suspected of being fraudulent, or to cross sell additional products and services.

3. Payments. A payment processing function will be required. Although a growing number of people now pay their credit card bills automatically via their bank accounts or on-line, a significant proportion still pay monthly by cheque. A large credit card provider can expect to receive thousands of postal payments every day.

Inbound and outbound communications will be managed via a dedicated customer contact centre linked to the account management system, so that when a customer contacts them they can be matched to their account record(s) and full information about the customer can be accessed by the customer services representative dealing with them. Payment processing will usually be managed as a separate function, and may be located in a different physical location from the customer contact centre. This is because payment processing is often contracted out to a third party supplier.

6.2 Relationship management

Operational management is concerned with providing the infrastructure within which customer relationships are managed. In contrast, relationship management is about making the most of relationships going forward. An analogy is that operational management is akin to building and maintaining a car, with decisions being made about the size of the engine, the number of seats, the colour and so on. Relationship management is about how you drive the car, where you go and who comes along for the ride.

Organizations operate at three levels when managing customer relationships:

• Account level. Each credit agreement is managed separately. It is assumed that by managing each credit agreement effectively the overall benefit from customer relationships will be maximized. Within a modern lending environment account level management is usually driven by product and customer level management strategies.

- Product level. Strategies are designed to maximize the return from a customer's product holdings across products of the same type. The product level strategy is then used to drive account level strategies. For example, a total card limit may be set, which is then proportioned between each of the customer's cards.
- Customer level. Customer level management strategies are designed to maximize the return from across all of the products that an individual currently has and might have in the future. This will include other financial products such as pensions and insurance, as well as credit products. The customer level strategy will then drive product level strategies which in turn drives account levels strategies.

It is now common for financial services organizations to offer a wide range of products and services. Therefore, there is a need to manage customer relationships at a product and customer level, rather than just an account level. Consumers have also become more diverse in their appetite for financial products and services and it is common for someone to have several different products at any one time, including several of the same type. It is quite normal for someone to have both a MasterCard and VISA credit card, a couple of store cards, an unsecured loan and a mortgage, as well as savings accounts, share holdings and various types of insurance.

6.2.1 Account level management

Most account management activities are coordinated with statement production at the account cycle point, as discussed in section 6.1.2. This means that as soon as a statement period ends, information from the statement period, such as the number, value and type of transactions, can be used for decision making. Any changes to the terms and conditions of the credit agreement can then be communicated to the customer via their statement. For example, if the decision is taken to increase the credit limit on an account, the new credit limit and an explanatory message can be printed on the account holder's statement. This is cost effective because no additional materials need to be produced and no additional mailing costs incurred.

The general approach to account management is to re-evaluate each customer's creditworthiness and other aspects of their behaviour at the cycle point.[9] An up-to-date credit report may also be sought from a credit reference agency to enable the most current view of the customer's credit commitments with other lenders to be incorporated into the re-evaluation process.

Re-evaluating customer behaviour on a frequent basis is important for two reasons. First, customer behaviour changes over time. A customer who has recently lost their job or is going through a divorce is likely to be less creditworthy than when they were originally acquired, and this is likely to be reflected in the way they use their credit card(s). Likewise, if someone has received a promotion and a salary rise, there is scope for providing further credit as they increase their spending in line with their new income. Second, once someone has used a credit product for a period of time, a considerable amount of information about spending and repayment patterns becomes available. This allows a more accurate estimate of creditworthiness and other behaviours to be made. For example, customers with a history of paying off their card balance in full each month tend to be much less likely to default in the future than people who revolve their balances, but generate far less interest revenue.

The types of decision that usually result from the re-evaluation of customer behaviour are:

- To change the credit line and/or shadow limit.
- To change the interest rate(s)charged for different types of transactions.
- To issue one or more credit card cheques.
- To offer a payment holiday, free gift, loyalty scheme or other incentive to encourage product usage.
- To provide a new card when an existing card is about to expire.
- To close accounts that have been dormant for a period of time (often around 24 months without the card having been used)
- To offer other products or services provided by the lender.
- To offer products and services provided by another organization, upon which the lender will receive a commission.

The derivation of these decisions is similar to the way in which the original terms of business were assigned during the application process. Different strategies evolve over time using a mixture of expert opinion, champion/challenger testing and forecasting techniques to determine which strategies are best for which types of account. Consider a customer who has had a credit card for say, 12 months, and whose credit score (their risk of default) has improved, but whose spending has declined. Previous analysis of the customer base may have established that customers displaying this type of behaviour are likely to have acquired an additional credit card from a competitor and are highly likely to close their account in the near future. Therefore, a strategy to incentivize the customer to continue using their card might be to raise their credit limit and offer a three month payment holiday.

6.2.2 Product level management

In card markets a customer can have two or more card accounts with the same card issuer. One reason this can occur is because the card issuer offers more than one type of card (MasterCard and VISA credit cards for example) and the customer is permitted to hold one or more of each. Another reason is if the card issuer provides a number of differently branded affinity cards, all of which are processed within the same account management system. The customer may, for example, have a Manchester United VISA card, a Greenpeace VISA card and a Virgin MasterCard, and be unaware that the same financial organization is providing all three cards. There may also be a small number of customers who have been granted an additional card because they applied for it after changing their name or moving house, resulting in the organization's IT systems failing to recognize that the applicant was an existing customer.[10]

If an organization operates a purely account level relationship management strategy, then having customers with multiple products creates a number of problems. One major issue is that each time an account is re-evaluated at the cycle point, decisions about changes to the credit line or other features of the account are made purely on the basis of information about that account. Information about the customer's other accounts will be ignored. This can lead to contradictory actions being taken – the APR on one account could be increased, while the APR on another account is reduced. Another problem is duplication of customer communications. Imagine that a credit card provider decides to target all of its customers with a personal loan offer. If only an account level view is taken, customers with two or more cards will receive a personal loan offer for each of their accounts. This is a waste of a mailing and an annoyance for the customer. The customer could also apply for each loan they have been targeted for. It is likely that only the first loan application would be accepted, with subsequent applications being rejected, creating further customer dissatisfaction.

To deal with this problem an organization that manages customer relationships at a product level will maintain a product level customer record in addition to individual account records. The product level record will contain summarized information about all of the customer's cards. If the customer has one credit card with a $10,000 limit and a $5,000 balance, and another with a $6,000 limit and a $3,000 balance, the product level record would record the customer as having two card accounts, a total card limit of $16,000 and a total card balance of $8,000. When each account cycles, the customer will be revaluated using a combination of the account and product level information held about them. Decisions are then made about how the terms of business should be managed across a customer's total product holding. Continuing with the previous example, if the customer's credit worthiness has improved, then a decision may be taken to increase the total credit limit from $16,000 to $20,000. A further decision will then be taken as to how best to proportion the new product level limit between each of the customer's accounts.

6.2.3 Customer level management

In divisionally orientated organizations the customer management functions tend to be product focused. Each product (cards, loans, mortgages and so on) is managed by a different division, with separate account management systems for each type of product.[11] The problem with this is that each division tends to focus on optimizing the customer relationship from their own perspective. The division responsible for managing card products will aim to maximize card revenue from customers, while the personal loan division will aim to sell as many personal loans as possible, even if this impacts card revenue. It is not unheard of for the personal loan division to be offering customers unsecured 'consolidation loans' with a relatively low APR of say, 8.9 percent per annum, that are targeted at the organizations card customers paying a much higher rate of say, 19.9 percent. So although the take up of the organization's products and services increases, the overall contribution from the customer will fall if all they do is transfer their high interest card balance to a low interest loan.

Not surprisingly, many organizations have evolved from applying product level strategies to customer level ones. This means that the full basket of a customer's credit requirements (and associated requirements for investment and insurance products) are considered together when making decisions about how individual accounts are managed, and when it's suitable to target customers with additional products and services. Is it, for example, worth offering cheap home insurance to entice an existing personal loan customer to take out a mortgage? Having said this, few financial institutions can be described as having a fully integrated customer level strategy. In practice, many organizations operate mainly at product level, with some limited customer level decisioning that is designed to prevent interdivisional conflict and minimize duplication across divisions. This is combined with operational functionality that allows customer service staff to view all of a customer's account records from their terminals simultaneously. The reasons for not moving to a full customer level management strategy are mainly due to organizational structure and the cost/benefit case for customer management. Divisional structures naturally lend themselves to account and product level management strategies. This means that to fully adopt a customer level management perspective requires a strategic and costly change to the organization's structure. Customer level management also requires more complex, well integrated and hence more costly systems because each time a customer level decision is made information needs to be accumulated from across all of the customer's individual accounts. This complexity follows through to the design and management of customer strategies, as well as the databases used for management reporting. The net result is that much more analytical effort is required to determine how the entire customer offering can be optimized. Unless an organization provides a relatively wide range of products to a significant proportion of its customer base, then the cost of moving from a product focused management strategy to a customer orientated one can not always be cost justified.

6.2.4   Retention and attrition

Whether an organization operates at an account level, product level or customer level, a key concern is the retention of profitable customers. There is little benefit in expending considerable time and effort recruiting large numbers of new customers if after a relatively short period of time they close their accounts and defect to a rival.

Improving customer retention is important because it can have a very significant impact on profitability. Reichheld (2001 p. 36) reports figures for the credit card industry where increasing retention rates by 5 percent, from say 90 to 95 percent per annum, leads to a 75 percent increase in contribution over the lifetime of the customer relationship. Why does increased retention have such a marked effect on profit contribution? One reason is that a relationship has already been established. This means that a wealth of information is available about how the customer uses their account that simply doesn't exist for new customers. As a result, marketing effort can be tailored very effectively towards specific behavioural traits. If a customer frequently buys books using their credit card, customer loyalty could be encouraged by sending them promotional material that explicitly mentions how their card is welcome at certain book stores. Alternatively, they could be sent a free gift such as a discount voucher, or even a book – perhaps a recent best seller. A second reason why retention is important is that the cost of customer acquisition has already been sunk, and the cost of retaining a customer is usually lower than the cost of acquiring a new one. A third reason is that, as a rule, customers with whom a relationship has existed for a considerable period of time are less likely to default on their credit repayments than new customers. They have a proven track record of repayment, and therefore, the costs associated with bad debt are much reduced. Finally, long serving customers often generate a greater contribution to profits than new customers because they have large interest-bearing balances that have been transferred to standard terms. This is a much more profitable source of revenues than the introductory terms often provided to new customers.

Before developing a retention strategy, efforts should be made to understand which customers are defecting and why, and it is a good idea to solicit from former customers their reasons for defecting. Statistical analysis can also be applied, to detect changes in customer behaviour that indicate that a customer is likely to defect. However, most reasons for defection come down to one of two issues. The first is when a competitor is perceived as offering better terms and conditions than the customer's current product. The second is customer dissatisfaction arising from poor customer service or an unresolved issue about their account. It should be noted that defection requires effort on the part of the customer. A rational customer is not going to defect if they believe they will get the same benefits from the rival product. They must believe that the new product is significantly better than their current offering to the extent that it justifies the effort involved in closing one account and opening another.

To improve customer retention, a strategy needs to be developed to address the reasons for attrition. Some retention strategies are designed to apply when a customer is first recruited, to encourage them to remain a customer over the long term. This may be by offering them some benefit after a period of time, or to offer continually better product terms as the relationship with them matures. A credit card customer could be promised that if they remained an active customer for two years, then the annual fee would be waived in the third year (or even the fees paid in the first two years refunded). For mortgage customers cash back offers – where a lump sum is paid to the customer when the mortgage is taken out, is often provided if the customer guarantees to keep their mortgage with the lender for a minimum period of time. Another strategy is to offer a product bundle – so that as customers take out an increasing number of an organization's products and services, the benefits of doing so get better and better. The result is that even if the customer doesn't think they've got the best possible deal on one (or even several) products, they feel that overall they are getting a good deal. Often these bundles will be tied into affinity offers with third party organizations, offering products and services in other market sectors. The reason for doing this is the realization that most financial products are not particularly exciting in themselves. Therefore, financial organizations identify the products that customers find more interesting and enter into arrangements with the providers of these products (Harrison 1999 p. 258).

Other types of retention strategies are applied to the existing customer base on a regular basis, usually in conjunction with account cycling and statement production. Scoring and/or segmentation models will be applied to predict the likelihood that a customer will attrite within a given period (usually within the next 6–12 months). Models will also be applied to predict the worth of the customer should they be retained. Therefore, the expected loss from attrition for each customer can be estimated by multiplying the likelihood of attrition by the customer's expected future lifetime value. If there is a 20 percent chance of a customer attriting and the estimated worth to the business, should the customer be retained, is $200 then the expected cost of attrition will be $40 ($200 * 20%). One interpretation of this figure is that it's worth spending up to $40 to retain the customer. In practice however, the effect of any retention activity is to reduce the likelihood of attrition, not eliminate it. Assume that in the past one strategy for increasing customer retention has been to send customers birthday cards. The cost of sending a card is $2 and the effect is to reduce attrition by 3 percent; that is, the attrition rate falls from 20 percent to 17 percent if a card is sent. The expected loss from attrition would therefore reduce from $40 to $34 ($200 * 17%) and the benefit from sending a card is $4 ($40 – $34 – $2). However, for customers where the benefit of retaining them was lower, say $25, then the expected cost of attrition, all other things being equal, will be $5 ($25 * 20%). The benefit from sending a card would be ($5 – $25 * 17%) = $0.75. Given a card costs $2, it is not worthwhile trying to retain this type of customer using such a strategy.

6.3 Chapter summary

Customer management covers the day-to-day activities required to manage customer relationships once a credit agreement has been created. There are two main areas of customer management; operational management and relationship management. Operational management is about making sure that the infrastructure to manage relationships is in place. This includes providing communication channels between customers and the organization, delivering an acceptable level of customer service and maintaining accurate and up-to-date information about customers' accounts. Relationship management is about ensuring that the organization's business objectives are met by maximizing the contribution from each customer relationship. This is achieved by altering the terms and conditions of existing accounts and identifying prospects for cross sell and up sell opportunities in response to changes in customer behaviour.

If an organization operates an account level relationship management strategy, then relationships are managed on an agreement by agreement basis. In modern lending environments account level relationship management has become rare: most organizations operate either a product level, or increasingly a customer level relationship management strategy. With a product level strategy a single management strategy will be applied across all of a customer's product holdings of the same type. So when a customer has two credit cards a single customer card limit will be determined and then proportioned between each card. However, if the customer also has other product holdings, such as a mortgage or personal loan, these will not be considered when reviewing card limits.

A customer level strategy extends the product level strategy principle to cover all of the different products and services that a customer needs or desires. The goal is to optimize the overall benefit from the total product offering, rather than seeking to obtain the best return from individual products and services on a piecemeal basis.

7
Collections (Early Stage Delinquency)

One of the biggest costs of running a consumer credit business is the loss from debts that are written-off due to customers failing to repay what they owe. For a typical credit card business, write-off accounts for about one third of all costs (Evans and Schmalensee 2005 p. 224).

Average write-off rates for credit cards are around 3–4 percent of outstanding balances per annum, and for personal loans around 1–2 percent. However, write-off rates vary considerably throughout the economic cycle, rising considerably in downturn conditions. At the height of the economic downturn of 2008/9, annualized write-off rates for American credit cards and personal loans were running at 9.8 and 3.1 percent of outstanding balances respectively (The Federal Reserve Board 2009) – around twice the long run average. In the UK, annualized write-off rates were 6.4 percent and 1.7 percent of outstanding balances for credit cards and personal loans respectively for the same period (Bank of England 2009).

When someone fails to make a repayment to the terms of their credit agreement their account is described as being delinquent, in arrears or past due (past the payment due date). Decisions then need to be taken about how to manage the delinquency so that the likelihood of the account recovering is maximized and potential future losses due to write-off are minimized. Given the huge amounts involved, even small improvements to the way that delinquent customers are managed can significantly reduce the cost of write-off and provide significant improvements to bottom line profitability.

Most lenders adopt a two phase approach to the management of delinquent accounts. The collections phase (the fourth phase of credit management) covers early stage delinquency, during the period immediately following a missed payment. The general view during the collections phase is that the customer relationship is salvageable. The goal is to encourage payment of the arrears without alienating the customer. Should the customer fail to respond to collections activity, the lender will eventually conclude that the customer relationship has broken down. If this occurs, the account will enter the debt recovery phase (the fifth phase of credit management) where action is taken to recover as much of the debt as possible before the relationship is terminated. When to transfer an account to debt recovery depends on the lender, but usually occurs somewhere between 30 and 120 days after an account first becomes delinquent.

The remainder of this chapter deals with the management of accounts during the collections phase. Late stage delinquency and debt recovery are discussed in Chapter 8.

7.1 Preliminary assessment of delinquency

The first task when an account becomes delinquent is to undertake a preliminary assessment of the current status of the account. A typical assessment process is illustrated in Figure 7.1.

As shown in Figure 7.1, the account will first be assessed to see if any exception conditions exist, indicating that the account should not proceed through the normal collections process. This is decision point 1 in Figure 7.1. If the customer is in dispute over transactions that have occurred on their account, an agreement may be in place to suspend repayments until the dispute has been resolved. Alternatively, if a customer has died, then the account will be frozen and a claim registered against the deceased estate. Members of staff may also receive special treatment if their accounts are in arrears.

If no special indicators are set, the account will be assessed for its likelihood of being fraudulent (decision point 2). If fraud is suspected, a block will be placed on the account to prevent further credit transactions[1] and it will be transferred to the fraud team for further investigation. Common reasons for suspecting fraud are if one or more of the following conditions are met:

- The customer has failed to make the first payment that is due.
- High volume of cash withdrawals or balance transfers occurred immediately prior to default.
- A fraud indicator was present on the credit report received when the account last cycled, indicating that another lender has strong reasons to suspect that the customer has acted fraudulently.

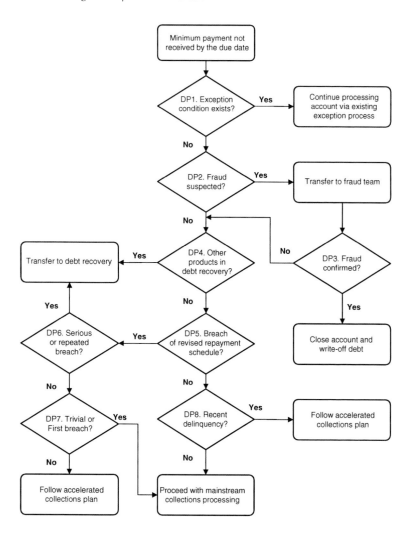

DP = Decision Point

Figure 7.1 Preliminary assessment of account status

- Prior to default, internal fraud detection systems may have flagged the account as having a high likelihood of being fraudulent, but not high enough to justify putting a block on the account or undertaking any detailed investigation at that time. The missed payment is the additional information required to confirm that the account is probably fraudulent.

If the fraud team decides the account is fraudulent, the account will be closed and the debt will be written-off. Otherwise, the account will be returned to the main collections process. After the fraud check any other accounts that the customer has with the organization will be reviewed.[2] If the customer is already subject to debt recovery action on another account, then the decision may be taken to transfer the account directly to debt recovery and manage the delinquency at a customer level.

In some situations a customer may already have been through the collections process, resulting in a revised repayment schedule having been agreed. If the customer subsequently misses a further repayment, then the lender has a choice of actions (decision points 5 & 6):

1. If prior to a revised repayment plan being agreed the customer was in serious arrears, and the repayment plan was agreed quite recently, then the missed payment is a strong indicator that the customer had little intention of adhering to the revised plan; that is, they only agreed to the revised plan to get the lender off their back for a while. Therefore, a decision will be made to transfer the account straight to debt recovery (decision point 6).
2. If the customer has made one or more payments to the terms of the revised schedule, or was only mildly delinquent when the revised repayment schedule was agreed, then the account may be assigned an accelerated collections strategy. This means that the account enters the mainstream collections process, but some of the pre-liminary stages may be skipped. Remaining collections actions will be taken more quickly than for customers entering collections for the first time.
3. If the revised repayment schedule was agreed before delinquency occurred (perhaps because the customer contacted the lender because they knew they would be unable to meet their next repayment), and the customer has shown an ability and willingness to repay by making a number of repayments, then the decision may be taken to let the account enter mainstream collections processing (decision point 7).

Finally, if the customer has a recent history of delinquency (decision point 8) then they may also be assigned to an accelerated collections path, or in cases of repeated delinquency be transferred to debt recovery. If the customer has not been identified as an exception case, a case of fraud or been transferred to debt recovery, then they will enter the mainstream collections process.

7.2   Mainstream collections processing

Customers fail to make loan repayments for a number of reasons, ranging from simple forgetfulness through to deliberate attempts to avoid payment, but whatever the reason, delinquent customers can always be classified into one of three groups:

1. Customers with good intent and the financial means to meet their repayments. These customers will have become delinquent for some trivial reason such as forgetting to pay before going on holiday, an administrative error by their bank or their payment was lost/delayed in the post.
2. Customers with good intent, but not the financial means to meet their repayment obligations. Customers in this situation have usually been subject to financial hardship due to illness, loss of employment or divorce. Only a relatively small proportion will be in this category because they have behaved irresponsibly when obtaining/using credit facilities.
3. Customers with the financial means to meet their repayments, but have no intention of doing so.

Those in group one represent the majority of cases that a lender will encounter. Customers in this group are likely to rectify the delinquency of their own accord, or require only a gentle reminder that they need to make a payment. In industry terms a "soft" collections strategy is required. For customers in group three, a "hard" collections strategy is more appropriate. This puts pressure on them to pay and threatens legal action if they fail to do so. Group two presents the most challenging problem, because there is often a desire to repay, but an inability to do so. In some cases the inability to pay will be temporary. This means that if the period of delinquency can be well managed, there is a good chance that they will continue to be profitable customers again in the future. It is also true that the late fees charged when an account becomes delinquent are an important source of revenue (although many lenders will deny this claiming they seek only to recover costs). Some of the most profitable customers are those who repeatedly become delinquent, recover their account and then become delinquent again, thus incurring multiple penalty fees. The cost of a computer generated reminder letter, for example, is of the order of $1–2 but a typical late payment fee is $25–$50.[3]

The main problem when deciding how to treat customers is that it is very difficult in practice to say into which group a customer falls before there has been any communication with them about their delinquent account. Therefore, when a customer misses a payment, standard practice is to assess the likelihood of the account recovering to an up-to-date status, based on the customer's repayment record and other aspects of their behaviour prior to delinquency. Soft collections strategies are applied when the likelihood of recovery is high, and harder strategies when recovery is less likely. The assessment of how likely an account is to recover will usually be made using a collections score. A typical collections score provides a measure of how likely the account is to fully recover within a period of about 3–6 months. Various policy rules may also be applied in conjunction with a collections score in certain situations. For example, for a first payment defaulter there will be little data upon which a collections score can be built. Therefore, these cases will be treated differently from more established customers for who there is an established record of product usage. An example of a collections strategy in which customers are classified into one of five segments is shown in Figure 7.2.

The different communications with customers in relation to Figure 7.2 are as follows:

- **Letter 1.** A firmly worded letter, re-stating the terms of the agreement and requesting prompt payment. The letter invites the customer to discuss any problems or issues they may have with their account.
- **Letter 2.** A firm but polite letter, expressing concern over non-payment, stating further action will be taken if payment is not received promptly.
- **Letter 3.** A strongly worded letter requesting payment within 14 days or the account will be transferred to debt recovery where legal action will be taken to recover the debt.
- **Letter 4.** A polite reminder letter, notifying the customer of the arrears on their account and requesting the customer makes a payment.
- **Statement message 1.** A reminder, printed on the customer's statement, notifying them that the payment due date has been missed.

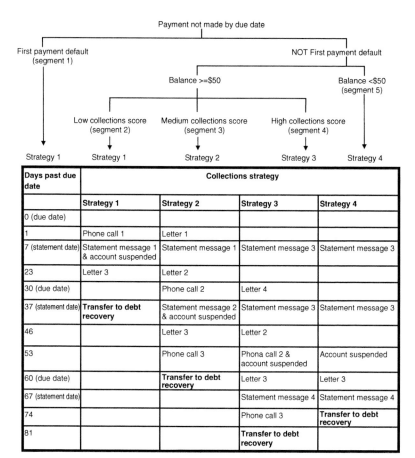

Figure and table:

Payment not made by due date

First payment default (segment 1)

NOT First payment default

Balance >=$50

Balance <$50 (segment 5)

Low collections score (segment 2)

Medium collections score (segment 3)

High collections score (segment 4)

Strategy 1   Strategy 1   Strategy 2   Strategy 3   Strategy 4

Days past due date	Collections strategy			
	Strategy 1	**Strategy 2**	**Strategy 3**	**Strategy 4**
0 (due date)				
1	Phone call 1	Letter 1		
7 (statement date)	Statement message 1 & account suspended	Statement message 1	Statement message 3	Statement message 3
23	Letter 3	Letter 2		
30 (due date)		Phone call 2	Letter 4	
37 (statement date)	**Transfer to debt recovery**	Statement message 2 & account suspended	Statement message 3	Statement message 3
46		Letter 3	Letter 2	
53		Phone call 3	Phona call 2 & account suspended	Account suspended
60 (due date)		**Transfer to debt recovery**	Letter 3	Letter 3
67 (statement date)			Statement message 4	Statement message 4
74			Phone call 3	**Transfer to debt recovery**
81			**Transfer to debt recovery**	

Note: The statement date is seven days after the payment due date. Statements are issued every 30 days. Therefore, statement messages can be printed on statements on day 7, 37, 67 and so on.

Figure 7.2   Example collections strategy

The customer is asked to contact the lender if they are experiencing repayment difficulties or other problems with their account.

- **Statement message 2.** Another reminder, using a different form of words from statement message 1, and warning of possible further action if payment is not received promptly.
- **Statement message 3.** A polite reminder, notifying the customer that their payment is overdue.
- **Statement message 4.** A final reminder warning of legal action if action is not taken to rectify the arrears on the account within 14 days.

- **Phone call 1.** A specially scripted call where the customer services representative tries to establish if there is a genuine problem with the first statement, or if the account should be transferred to fraud or debt recovery.
- **Phone call 2.** A call designed to establish contact with the customer, determine the customer's situation and to discuss options for bringing the account back into line.
- **Phone call 3.** A final phone call made with the view of threatening legal action if the account is not brought back up-to-date within seven days.

In Figure 7.2, if a delinquent customer falls into segment 4 they will be assigned to strategy 3. This is a "soft" strategy for low risk customers with a high collections score, who have made at least one payment (so they are not a first payment defaulter) and who have a significant balance on their account. Consequently, there is a desire to continue to maintain a good relationship with them. The first action in strategy 3 is to do nothing; that is, the customer is given an additional seven days to pay before any action is taken. Given that customers in segment 4 are low risk, payment from a significant majority can be expected within this period. If payment has not been received after seven days then a politely worded reminder is printed on the customer's statement (statement message 3). This is followed by a letter (letter 4) on day 30, by which time the customer will be two payments in arrears. On day 37, the statement message is repeated, and a further letter (letter 2) sent on day 46. If after 53 days payment has still not been made, things move up a gear. The account is suspended, preventing further transactions occurring, and an attempt is made to contact the customer by phone. A more strongly worded letter (letter 3) is sent on day 60 by which time the customer will be three payments in arrears. This is followed by a statement message on day 67 and a phone call a week later on day 74. If by day 81 the account remains delinquent, it is transferred to debt recovery.

The approach taken for customers in segments 1 and 2 is very different. They are assigned to strategy 1 where action is taken as soon as their payment is past due, with transfer to debt recovery occurring after only 37 days. For defaulting customers with a balance of less than $50 another soft strategy is adopted, regardless of collections score. No phone calls are made prior to transfer to debt recovery and a letter is only dispatched on day 60. The main reason for adopting this approach is economic. The uplift in recoveries from multiple letters and phones calls is difficult to justify, given the low value of the balance at risk.

7.2.1   Over limit accounts

With card accounts it is possible for a customer to exceed their credit limit. Sometimes this occurs because the card issuer has decided to authorize a transaction which takes the customer over their limit, or because the fees and charges applied to an account cause the limit to be exceeded. In other situations an account may become over limit because transactions have occurred where authorization has not been sought from the card issuer. This can occur if a merchant has been allocated a 'floor limit' that permits them to accept a card as payment without authorization if it is below a certain value.

Over-limit accounts are often treated in a similar manner to delinquent accounts, even if the customer has been making the required payments. They are therefore dealt with within the collections process. The objective is to obtain sufficient payment from the customer such that the balance on their account falls below their credit limit. As with collections activity, statement messages, letters and phone calls will be used to persuade the customer to comply.

7.2.2   Pre-delinquency

As a rule, people don't want to get behind with repayments on their credit agreements. They do so because their financial situation has changed, resulting in a loss of income. When such a situation occurs, people's patterns of credit usage change. Whereas someone might have previously only used their credit card to buy things over the internet, they start using their credit card to buy groceries at their local store and other essential items that they can no longer afford. Sometimes it takes many months or even years before debts become unmanageable following a loss of income. Therefore, there is an opportunity to spot the problem long before delinquency occurs. The changes in the patterns of credit usage that are seen when someone's financial situation changes can be detected using scoring systems that calculate a pre-delinquency score, similar to those used for fraud detection, which are discussed in more detail in Chapter 9. This means it is possible to identify people who have previously had a very good repayment record, but are highly likely to default at some point in the future.

There are generally two actions that can be taken in response to an account that has a high pre-delinquency score. Where there is some headroom between the customer's balance and their credit limit, action can be taken to lower the credit limit on the account to limit the exposure to future write-off. The second response is to make pre-emptive contact with customers to determine if there is any mitigating action that can be taken. For example, repayments may be suspended for a period of time to allow the customer to regain their financial footing.

Pre-delinquency scoring is relatively new, and at the time of writing is not applied by the majority of lenders, but its use is growing and the management of pre-delinquent accounts is likely to be an area that sees steady growth within collections and account management departments in the future.

7.2.3 The use of credit reports in collections

A recent credit report from a credit reference agency is an important piece of information that can be used within collections and debt recovery processing, and will form a key component of any collections score(s) used to predict the likelihood of account recovery. Credit reference data is important for a number of reasons. First, if the borrower is in default with other lenders, this indicates the delinquency is not the result of forgetfulness or administrative error, but is due to some problem with their financial situation. Second, in some countries a person's credit report will detail their balance on other credit products and their monthly repayments, and this can be used to help gauge how much disposable income a customer has for debt repayments. Third, and perhaps most importantly, if the borrower is in arrears with one or more credit commitments with other lenders, then it can be assumed that these lenders will also be pursuing the customer for payment. Therefore, careful thought needs to go into the design of the collections strategy so that the customer has a greater incentive to repay the debt owing to you, rather than their debts to other creditors. If you are taking a hard line with the customer and threatening legal action while at the same time a competitor is sending pleasantly worded reminder messages, then the customer will almost inevitably repay the debt to you first.

7.3 Managing customer contact and payment negotiation

The most common response to collections activity is for customers to pay the arrears owing on their account in full within a few days, without any need to discuss the situation with the lender. The account then leaves collections and returns to the customer management phase of the credit cycle. A second type of customer behaviour is non-response. The arrears are not paid and no contact can be established with the customer. Therefore, the account is transferred to debt recovery at the end of its allotted collections strategy. The third type of customer behaviour is to enter into dialogue with the lender. A dialogue might start when the lender notifies the customer of their delinquency. Alternatively, the customer (or their representative) might make the first move and contact the lender when they realize they are going to find it difficult to make their next repayment. When communication is established the aim is to arrive at a negotiated agreement over how the delinquency should be managed, so that the arrears are recovered.

The first task when contact is established is to determine why the arrears have occurred. The second task, assuming the arrears are not the result of some administrative error, is to establish the means, if any, the customer has to repay and the best mechanism for facilitating payment. For some customers an immediate payment in full may be most appropriate. For others, a revised repayment schedule may be better. Experienced collections staff will be able to add significantly to the negotiation process by interpreting the way in which the customer responds, by their tone and their willingness to cooperate. They will be able to identify situations where the customer is perhaps holding back on making a commitment to pay and persuade them to do so. In cases where they believe the customer is in genuine financial difficulty an understanding approach can be taken, especially where a customer is seriously ill or has died. The process also works the other way. If there is something suspicious about the customer's behaviour, they could refer the case to the fraud department. Alternatively, if the customer is being uncooperative or is deliberately attempting to deceive, the account could be transferred directly to debt recovery. Successful negotiation with the customer will result in one of the following outcomes:

- Full payment of the arrears at the end of negotiation. This may be via a credit card that the customer has with another lender.[4]
- A 'promise to pay'. An agreement will be reached where the customer agrees to make one or more of payments by certain dates to clear the arrears. If the promise to pay is broken, collections activity will resume, or the account transferred to debt recovery.
- Partial payment of the arrears at the end of the negotiation. Given that some of the arrears will remain outstanding, the customer's account will usually remain in collections. However, further activity may be postponed for a period of time to allow further payments to be made. As a general rule, even a small payment from a delinquent customer is a positive indicator of the customer's intent to repay.
- A revised repayment schedule is agreed. The repayment schedule will be amended so that lower payments are made over a longer term.

This is common where people have some disposable income, but not enough to meet their original loan repayments.

- Re-aging the debt. If the customer has missed one or more payments, but has subsequently resumed paying, then they will continue to be in arrears unless additional payment is made to cover the payments they missed. If it is believed that the customer will continue to make repayments, then the debt may be re-aged. This means that the arrears on the account are removed, but the number of payments extended to cover those that were missed.
- A payment holiday. Payments are suspended for a number of months. Interest charges may also be suspended, but it is more common for them to continue to accrue. This is a common strategy for people in temporary financial difficulty. For example, when someone has had unpaid time off work due to illness or maternity leave.
- An acknowledgement that the customer is unable to make any significant contribution towards their debt, now or in the foreseeable future. The account will be suspended and transferred to debt recovery where a decision about further action will be taken. This avoids unnecessary delay and saves the cost of further collections action prior to debt recovery.

7.4 Designing, assessing and optimizing collections strategies

There are a number of considerations when designing collections strategies. These include:

- The segmentation of customers into different groups representing their account status and expected recovery behaviour. So in Figure 7.2, there were five segments in total, with customers in each segment subject to one of four possible collections strategies. Segmentation can occur using various credit scoring or segmentation techniques, or be based on expert opinion.
- The type of collections activity that will occur within each customer segment (letter, statement message, e-mail, phone call and so on). Statement messages tend to be the cheapest form of communication, but are restricted to occur only when statements are produced. e-mails are another cheap means of communication, but are less effective than letters and phone calls. Phone calls tend to be the most effective method for encouraging payment and facilitating dialogue with customers, but are several times more expensive than a standard letter.[5]

- The content and style of each activity. This covers the wording used in printed materials and the scripts used in telephone conversations.
- The timing of each activity; that is, how long after the previous action the next action occurs.
- The fees to charge delinquent customers. Most credit agreements allow for penalty charges to be applied as soon an account becomes delinquent or goes over limit. However, in some circumstances it may be prudent to waive penalty charges. For a long standing customer who has never been delinquent before, and who generates hundreds of dollars of revenue a year, imposing a $50 late fee on the first day after the payment due date is not likely to encourage customer loyalty.
- For revolving credit accounts, when to suspend normal account activity, preventing further credit transactions occurring.
- When to transfer the account to debt recovery.

Collections strategies can be considered analogous to the terms of business, as discussed in section 5.7, in the way in which they are created, implemented and assessed over time. Collections strategies are usually implemented in the form of a decision tree within a decision engine that is linked to the account management system, or sometimes a specialized collections sub-system. The collections system is then supplied with details of delinquent accounts on a daily basis. Each collections strategy contains a different set of actions that will have evolved over long experience of testing many different champion/challenger strategies to find out which ones have the greatest impact on customer behaviour.

A key question is the basis under which competing collections (and debt recovery) strategies should be compared. The simplest option is to consider recovery rates; that is, the proportion of delinquent balances that recover within say, three months, of entering collections. This is a popular measure because it enables simple targets to be set for operational staff dealing with individual cases, with incentives for staff that deliver the highest recovery rates. The problem with this is that it does not take into account the fact that different collections strategies will have different costs, depending on the number of letters, phone calls and so on that are made. Therefore, another option is to calculate the cost of write-off plus the cost of collections activity. After a period of time, say six months, the write-off from customers that followed a particular collections strategy is measured and added to the cost of the collections actions that were applied. When two strategies are compared, the one with the lower overall cost is considered the best.

Measuring the performance of collections strategies on the basis of recovery rates or write-off plus collections costs is common practice. However, they are somewhat simplistic measures because they do not take into how collections activity affects the future behaviour of recovered accounts. In particular, a hard collections strategy may well lead to greater account recovery and lower write-off than a softer strategy, but the customer may feel that they have been roughly treated and defect to a competitor. A better alternative is to measure the effect of collections activity in terms of customer contribution; that is, see how much revenue and write-off is generated by customers in the 6–12 months after a given collections strategy has been applied to them.

7.5   Event driven collections strategies

The collection strategies discussed in relation to Figure 7.2 are based on a preliminary assessment of account performance at the point where the account becomes delinquent. While popular, the limitation with this approach is that the initial forecast of customer behaviour made when an account entered collections (as represented by the customer's collections score) may become out of date after the account has been in collections for some time. Consequently, the collections strategy assigned to a customer when they entered collections may no longer be the most appropriate one for them. An event driven collections strategy looks to reassess the likelihood that the account can be recovered each time a significant event occurs. Significant events include:

- Inbound communication from the customer.
- A partial payment of the arrears.
- A customer payment is refused (for example a bounced cheque).
- A promise to pay is made by the customer.
- A change to the customer's credit report, indicating a change in the status of their credit agreements with other lenders.
- Retail or cash transactions are made on the account (assuming the account has not yet been suspended).
- Transactions that occur in relation to a customer's other accounts. In particular, if the customer has a current account, then a large deposit made to this account will be a good indicator that the customer is able to pay.

- An application for additional credit or another of the organization's products is received.

When one of these events occurs, the customer's status will be reevaluated, incorporating the information about the event that has occurred. So, returning to the example of Figure 7.2, an account may enter collections on day 1 and be assigned to segment 4 because a high collections score indicates there is a very good chance that the account will recover. Therefore, no action is taken at that point. However, the next day the customer uses their card to make large cash withdrawal, which is known to be a strong indicator of financial distress, and hence the chance of recovery falls. The collections score is recalculated, resulting in the account being reassigned to segment 2 where a more aggressive strategy is pursued.

7.6   Chapter summary

When a customer fails to make a repayment to the terms of their credit agreement, their account is described as being past due, delinquent or in arrears, and is subject to collections action. When an account first becomes delinquent it will be assessed for its propensity to recover – usually using a collections score that predicts the likelihood of recovery within a few weeks or months. Those for which the propensity to recover is high will be subject to a more gentle collections strategy that gives them time to repay before any collection activity occurs, and begins with customer friendly reminders that are designed not to upset the customer. Those who it is believed are less likely to recover are subject to stronger action that puts greater pressure on them to pay what they owe more quickly.

As long as the customer relationship is believed to be recoverable, collections action will continue. This typically involves communicating with the customer through various channels that include letter, statement messages, e-mails and phone calls. The goal is to maintain a positive relationship with the customer and to encourage them to pay the arrears on their account. However, at some point the lender will decide that the likelihood of the customer clearing the arrears is slight, and therefore the customer relationship is no longer worth maintaining. At this point the account will leave collections and be passed to the organization's debt recovery function where further action will be taken to recover the debt.

8
Debt Recovery (Late Stage Delinquency)

When collections action has failed to persuade a customer to pay the arrears on their account, or the relationship with a customer has broken down, then the account will be transferred to debt recovery (sometimes referred to as late stage delinquency, late stage collections or recoveries). Transfer to debt recovery usually occurs when an account is between 60 and 120 days past its due date (2–4 months in arrears), but each lender has its own policy about when accounts should be transferred. Once in debt recovery the goal is to recover as much of the outstanding debt as possible in order to minimize the losses due to bad debt write-off. If a good rapport with the customer can be maintained then that is all well and good, but it is not a priority.

In the remainder of this chapter the role of the debt recovery department is discussed, together with the actions that the department can employ to manage delinquent debts that have been passed to it.

8.1 The debt recovery department

A typical debt recovery department is run as a specialist operational function staffed by people trained to deal with accounts in the mid-late stages of delinquency. One strategy is to make the debt recovery department a separate legal entity, with its own letter headings, contact details and so on. This gives the impression the debt has been passed to a third party debt collector, which provides two benefits. First, it sends a clear message to the debtor that their delinquency has reached a new stage and that it is being dealt with as a serious matter by a specialist team. Second, positioning debt recovery as a separate organization distances the lender from the negative connotations that some people have about debt recovery practices.

The main tools used in debt recovery departments are similar to those used in collections – as are many of the outcomes that result. Letters, phone calls, texts and e-mails are used to try and persuade customers to pay what they owe. One difference between collections and debt recovery is in the tone and content of the communication with customers. There is a move away from conciliatory messages that are not intended to offend more than absolutely necessary, towards stronger language and threats of legal action. Some debt recovery departments may also employ debt collectors to visit individuals' homes, but this is a costly and time consuming business. Therefore, home visits tend to be more widely employed by specialist debt collection agencies that are able to utilize economies of scale to make home visits a cost effective proposition.

The other main difference between collections and debt recovery is that in debt recovery decisions are made about what to do with the debt (rather than just how to collect the arrears). This could be to:

* Continue trying to collect the debt using the in-house debt recovery team.
* Refer the debt to an external debt collector. The debt collector will collect the debt on behalf of the lender, and in return will receive a commission on what they recover.
* Sell the debt to a third party for a proportion of the debt's value. The difference between the value of the debt and the amount it is sold for is then written-off.
* Move to repossess property if the debt is secured. In some situations the permission of the courts may be required before repossession can occur. For example, in the UK repossession[1] of someone's home can only occur after a court order has been obtained and a final chance to pay the debt has been given to the customer.
* Take legal action via the courts in an attempt to force the customer to pay. There are usually several different types of legal action that can be taken to recover debt, including various forms of bankruptcy.
* Accept a partial payment to settle the debt in full and write-off the difference. Partial payment of the debt may be accepted if it is believed that the customer has only limited assets and that the likelihood of further recoveries is low.
* Write-off the entire debt, taking no further action. This is a common strategy where debts are small, or if there is little chance of the debt being recovered.

Debt recovery is a labour intensive area of credit management. Even with the most technologically advanced debt management systems there is a requirement for people to contact customers, negotiate repayments, repossess property and manage the legal process should it prove necessary. Many organizations have limited resources and therefore can not pursue all delinquent accounts as fully as possible. This means that one objective of debt recovery is to prioritize delinquent accounts, so that the greatest resources are applied to those cases where the most money is likely to be recovered with the minimum of effort. The most common way to do this is to rank debts in priority order, using various rules based on past experience. For example, giving people with assets (such as home owners) higher priority than those without (such as tenants), and people with a steady income higher priority than people who are unemployed. In recent years there has been increasing use of debt recovery scoring and segmentation systems to identify where the greatest opportunities for recovering debt lie. These systems have been developed using large numbers of historically delinquent accounts and their subsequent repayment behaviour, to determine how customers are likely to respond to different types of debt recovery action.

8.2 Power dialer based debt recovery systems

Several different mechanisms exist for contacting customers, with telephone contact being the preferred medium. This is because it enables real time two-way negotiation and is generally seen to generate greater levels of recovery than other forms of communication. Negotiation can be difficult and long winded if attempted by letter, and has not been proven to be very successful if attempted via e-mail or text.

A key tool employed within collections and debt recovery departments is the power dialer.[2] This is a telecommunications/work flow system that controls the contact strategy with customers so that contact plans can be implemented and monitored over time. The power dialer will be supported by a database of customer information, including contact details and account information supplied from the account management system. This may be supplemented by more recent information from a credit reference agency or a debt tracing agency, as well as any external debt recovery action that has taken place with a third party debt collection agency. The power dialer will be programmed to call customers in priority order – as determined by the organization's debt recovery score and/or prioritization rules. If the customer answers, the call will be transferred to a customer services representative who will negotiate with the customer. Details about the conversation will be captured, and any new information obtained will be available for use by the decision logic implemented within the power dialer. For example, a customer may agree to a revised repayment schedule to repay their debt. This information will be recorded, including the payment due dates for the revised schedule. If payments are not received from the customer by the agreed dates, then the power dialer will begin trying to make contact with the customer again. Alternatively, if in a previous conversation the customer has said they work night shifts, the dialer can be instructed to call the customer only in the afternoon, say between the hours of 2pm and 6pm. Likewise, if no contact has been made after a specific number of attempts, then the dialer could be programmed to produce a list of addresses to be provided to a debt collector to visit people at home.

8.3   Goneaways and address tracing

Many people who default on credit agreements attempt to escape their debts when they move address by not informing their creditors they have moved. If the customer has not provided an e-mail address or mobile phone number (or has changed them) then there will be no way to make contact with them and no way to know where to go to recover assets if goods are to be possessed in lieu of the debt. However, it is often possible to trace these 'gone away' customers by using third party tracing services. Some credit reference agencies offer address tracing services based on the address links they have established between individuals and the credit agreements they have with different lenders. What this means is that if an individual informs one of their creditors about a change of address, then the credit reference agency can pass this on to the individual's other creditors. Consider the case where someone has an unsecured loan and a credit card. When they move address they don't inform the loan provider and default on the debt. However, they do tell the card company that they have moved because they want to be able to continue using their card. The card provider automatically informs the credit reference agency of the change of address as part of their standard process for updating the credit reference agency with information about their customers each month. The new address is then passed to the loan provider.

Debt tracing agencies maintain similar databases to those of the credit reference agencies, based on their past knowledge of customer movements. They may also visit a person's previous residence to ask the new occupants if they have a forwarding address or if neighbours know where they have moved to. Other sources of information can also be utilized such as the voters roll and telephone directories to track peoples' movement. An internet search on someone's name/previous address may also provide contact details.

8.4 Legal action

If initial debt recovery action has failed to recover a debt, a lender needs to decide whether or not to take legal action to try and recover the debt through the courts. If the court rules in the lender's favour, the court may decide that the debt can be enforced via asset seizure and enforcement officers (bailiffs) appointed to recover goods in lieu of the debt. A court may also allow garnishment of an individual's wages (deductions from someone's wages at source). In some jurisdictions, a charging order may be placed on an individual's property. The individual is not forced to sell their home, but should they sell it at some point in the future, the proceeds must be used to repay their creditors. Alternatively, if the debt is large enough,[3] a bankruptcy petition may be made against the customer. In some jurisdictions court approval may also be required before goods bought on hire-purchase or conditional sale terms can be repossessed, or prior to foreclosure on a residential property.

If legal action is taken, the courts will almost always find in favour of the lender if all appropriate legal processes have been complied with; that is, the credit agreement was correctly drawn up and all relevant forms and procedures have been completed. However, this does not mean the debt will be recovered. In a large number of cases the debtor will not repay what they have been ordered by the court, and very little further action can be taken if the debtor has no assets to possess in lieu of the debt. In other cases the result may be for the court to define a new repayment schedule, based on the debtor's disposable income. This could result in little more than token payments being made, resulting in the debt being repaid over may years longer than the original term, possibly with all further interest charges being suspended. What this means is that legal action should only be considered if the amount recovered can reasonably be expected to exceed the organization's legal expenses. As with other areas of credit management, this decision is often based on scoring and/or segmentation models that estimate the likelihood of debt being recovered.

8.5 Debt collection agencies and debt sale

If internal debt recovery action has failed to recover a debt, then one option is to employ an external debt collection agency. The agency will be passed details of delinquent customers and will undertake debt recovery activity on behalf of the lender. This is often cost effective because a large agency will be collecting delinquent debts on behalf of many different clients. Economies of scale mean more complex debt recovery systems can be employed, providing better targeting and tracking of delinquent customers. In addition, specialist debt collection agencies can often resort to activities which are not cost effective for individual lenders, such as visiting someone's home in an attempt to persuade them to pay their debt. If several people with debts with different lenders all live on the same street or in close proximity, then a collector from an agency can visit one after another very quickly with little transit time between visits. This results in lower costs than would be incurred if each lender sent collectors to visit just their own customers. Debt collection agencies also have more experience of dealing with a diverse range of customer types, and therefore, can often recover more debt than an in-house debt recovery function. For their services, debt collection agencies will be paid a commission based on the proportion of the debts they collect.

The decision to use a debt collections agency will be based on a comparison of the performance of different debt collections agencies against the in-house recovery teams for different categories of debt. Various types of scoring and segmentation models can be applied to group debt into different categories, with debts in some categories being collected upon in-house and other types being contracted to collections agencies. For example, previous analysis of debt recovery activity may show that the in-house team is more effective at recovering debts where customers have been on the books for at least 24 months, while collections agencies are better at recovering debt from less established customers because they are able to draw upon information from other sources to assist them.

Another option is to sell the debt. In the US the bad debt market is valued at an estimated $100 billion dollars a year (Cyrus 2006). Credit card debt is sold for an average of between 7.5 and 10 percent of its face value, but can be anything up to 20 percent for good quality debt; that is, for high quality portfolios where there is a good chance of recovery. Trade values for retail and instalment lending are similar (Legrady 2006). There also exists a significant market in secondary debt sale, where one debt collection agency sells debt to another. However, the value of secondary debt is typically only 2–3 percent of the debt's original value because most of what can be recovered will already have been obtained.

Selling debt has a number of benefits. One is that it may be possible to sell the debt for more than the internal debt recovery team is likely to recover, less their costs. Another is that debt sale improves an organization's cash flow by realizing an asset very quickly, that might otherwise take many months or years to recover. A third benefit is that debt sale can be used as a mechanism for controlling capital requirements (as discussed in Chapter 11), by removing significant liabilities from the balance sheet (Shaw 2007).

8.6 Write-off

When an account has been delinquent for a considerable period of time, and action has failed to recover some or all of the debt, a decision will be taken to write-off the debt. This results in the debt being recorded as a loss within the organization's profit and loss account. In some organizations write-off can occur within six months of the first missed payment, while in others it may be 12 months or longer. Many months or years after write-off, monies may still be recovered on accounts via further debt recovery action or debt sale. In these cases, because the debt has been written-off, the additional revenue is treated as a positive contribution to profits.

8.7 Chapter summary

A customer's account will be transferred to debt recovery when there is no longer a reasonable possibility of recovering the arrears owing or the relationship with the customer has broken down. This is usually sometime between 60 and 120 days after an account first enters a state of delinquency. Once an account is in debt recovery a lender will seek to recover the entire outstanding debt, not just the arrears owing on the account.

During the early stages of debt recovery, similar actions will be taken as those applied in collections. Letters, phone calls e-mails and texts will be used to try and persuade customers to make contact and enter into an agreement to repay what they owe, albeit using stronger language and threats of legal action.

If there is little chance of recovering the debt then it will be written-off and no further action taken. Alternatively, if the debtor is believed to have assets or income, legal action may be taken to try and recover the debt through the courts. External debt collectors may also be employed in situations where it is believed they may be more successful at recovering debt than the in-house debt recovery team. Another option is to sell the debt outright. The main advantage of debt sale is that it realizes funds immediately, improving cash flow and increasing profitability in the short term.

9
Fraud

Fraud is an ongoing problem within the consumer credit industry. In the UK write-off due to credit card fraud is estimated to be $910 million[1] per year (APACS 2008). In the US the value of fraudulent card transactions is estimated to be in excess of $3.5 billion per year (Experian 2007). These figures represent only around 0.1 percent of all card transactions, but can account for more than 10 percent of all bad debt experienced by a card issuer. This is despite many lenders having sophisticated fraud detection systems – without which the cost of fraud would be many times higher. Card fraud is perhaps the most widespread form of fraud associated with consumer credit, but other types of credit are also targeted by fraudsters to varying degrees.

There are many types of fraud, and different approaches are required to deal with each. Some approaches are industry wide initiatives, such as the use of smart cards and the 'chip and pin' system used in many countries. Other fraud prevention strategies rely on individual lenders taking action to protect themselves against unacceptable fraud losses. In this chapter the focus is primarily on the latter, that is, internal action an organization can take to reduce its own losses resulting from fraud. In particular, we consider two specific areas:

- Acquisition fraud. This is fraud that occurs when someone tries to obtain funds by making a fraudulent credit application.
- Customer management (existing facility) fraud. This is fraud that occurs in relation to an existing credit agreement, where a fraudster makes unauthorized use of someone else's credit facility. Customer management fraud is mainly associated with credit cards and other

types of revolving credit, where funds can be drawn against an existing credit facility.

The first part of the chapter discusses acquisition fraud. The second part discusses customer management fraud.

9.1 Acquisition fraud

9.1.1 First party fraud

First party fraud occurs when someone knowingly provides incorrect information when applying for credit. Personal details such as name and address are correct, but other aspects of the credit application are falsified. In most cases the applicant intends to repay what they borrow, but provides misleading information so they appear more creditworthy. Typical first party fraud will involve someone stating they are older than they actually are, providing inflated salary details, lying about their employment status or how long they have lived at their current address.

First party fraud is arguably the most common type of fraud that occurs during the acquisition process, but it is difficult to ascertain its true extent or obtain precise figures for the losses that result. This is because many customers actually repay what they borrow, even though they lied about their circumstances when they applied. In cases where the customer defaults, it is often impossible to differentiate between customers who supplied correct personal details and those that did not.

First party fraud is detected in one of two ways. The first, is by using a rule based system that automatically refers suspect cases to the fraud team if an applicant hits one or more rules. Fraud referral rules are based on a number of different criteria which include:

- Differences in the data provided between subsequent credit applications made by the same individual. This works because a first party fraudster will often change the details they provide from one credit application to the next. If they said they were 19 years of age on one application and were declined, then they might decide to increase this to 35 on their next application in an effort to appear more creditworthy.[2] The greater the number of discrepancies and the bigger the discrepancies are, the more likely an application is to be fraudulent.
- Invalid data supplied during the application. For example, the applicant's phone number or bank account number do not exist.

- The presence of exceptional data items on the application form which are very unlikely to be true of a genuine applicant. If someone lives in a deprived area, it is very unlikely that they earn a six figure salary. Likewise, someone who claims they are 18 years old is unlikely to be a home owner in an exclusive neighbourhood.

The second type of fraud detection systems use scoring to predict the likelihood of someone being a fraudster; in just the same way as a credit scoring model predicts the likelihood of someone being creditworthy. Where the fraud score indicates that the likelihood an application being fraudulent is unacceptably high, then the application will be referred to the fraud team. A fraud score may be used in conjunction with or instead of a rule based system.

Scoring and rule based fraud detection systems work best when there is access to large databases of diverse information, provided by many different lenders. This enables data held by each organization to be cross referenced – allowing discrepancies between credit applications to be detected. Such systems are often supplied by credit reference agencies who maintain industry shared databases of previous credit applications. One example of such a system is Experian's Detect product. Detect is a rule based system that can be provided as part of an Experian credit report. Another example is FICO's Falcon ID. This is an advanced score based system that gains much of its power through the integration of multiple data sources, including the client's own data, credit reports and other external databases.

9.1.2   Identity theft

Identify theft occurs when a fraudster obtains sufficient information about an individual to be able to impersonate them when making a credit application. Information allowing identity theft to occur may come from a variety of sources including:

- Household utility bills, bank statements, payslips or other documents that have inadvertently been put out with the rubbish.
- The theft of items that contain personal information such as a credit card, passport or driver's licence.
- Illegal procurement of data from an internal source within an organization; that is, a member of staff obtains customer data and sells it to a fraudster or uses it fraudulently themselves.
- Phising. This is where someone is persuaded to provide information about themselves by impersonating an organization that the person

trusts, usually via some sort of website or internet service. Many Phising e-mails purport to be from the victim's bank, asking the individual to confirm their name, address, date of birth, bank account details and security information such as pin numbers and passwords.

Usually, the fraudster will first use the information they have obtained to set up a bank account. Any funds they obtain fraudulently can be paid into this account and then withdrawn. As the account has been set up using someone else's name and address, it is very difficult to trace the fraudster should the authorities decide to investigate.

There are three main tools for preventing identity theft. The first two are scoring and rule based systems similar to those used to spot first party fraud. These work because a fraudster will often obtain partial information about an individual, but not a complete picture. So, for example, the name, address, date of birth, phone number and bank details may be provided correctly on a fraudulent credit application, but salary details, time in employment, the length of time someone has lived at their address and so on will be invented by the fraudster. Therefore, the fraudulent application will show inconsistencies when compared to other genuine credit applications made by the person whose identity has been stolen. The third type of tool are national registers, containing details of previously confirmed or suspected cases of identity theft. An example is the CIFAS fraud database in the UK. When a lender undertakes a credit search with any of the three UK credit reference agencies, an indicator will be attached to the applicant's credit report if the applicant's details can be matched to the CIFAS database. This indicates that the applicant's details have been used by a fraudster before, and no further credit should be advanced without the true identity of the applicant being confirmed.

9.1.3 Falsified identity

A fraudster will sometimes make a completely bogus credit application using information they have invented. Cases of falsified identity are usually detected by cross referencing the name and address supplied by the applicant with national registers such as the voters roll or credit reference agency databases. If the applicant's name or address can not be confirmed, then the application is treated as a case of suspected fraud.

9.1.4 Card interception (mail inception)

Card interception is when a credit card is intercepted in transit, or when the card is received by the customer, who uses the card, but then denies having received it. Methods for reducing the incidence of card interception fraud were discussed in section 5.2.6.

9.1.5 Conversion fraud

Conversion fraud is when someone obtains goods, on hire-purchase or conditional sale terms, and then sells the goods to a third party. The biggest loser in this type of fraud is the third party, who believes that having paid their money they are now the owner of the goods. In actuality, the goods are still owned by the finance company because the title (ownership) does not pass to the borrower until all of the credit repayments have been made. Therefore, the finance company can recover the goods, even though the 'new owner' thought they were purchasing the item in good faith. Conversion fraud is relatively rare, accounting for only around 0.2 percent of all credit related fraud reported to CIFAS, the UK fraud prevention service (CIFAS 2009).

9.1.6 Dealing with suspect fraud

One of the main problems when dealing with fraud is that it is often impossible to say categorically whether someone is acting fraudulently or not when decisions to advance credit are made. Cases where fraud is *suspected* will be identified and referred to the fraud department for further investigation, but in most cases fraud will not have been proven at this point. Therefore, further investigation is required to establish if the application is genuine or fraudulent.

Undertaking detailed fraud investigation is a costly and time consuming exercise. Consequently, fraud teams are limited in the number of cases they can review, and the level of investigation they can undertake. This means that in most organizations there is a trade-off between the losses they are willing to accept and the amount of investigation they are willing to undertake. The result is that organizations operate a two tier strategy. For cases where the fraud detection tool (the fraud score or rule set for example) indicates a very high likelihood of the application being fraudulent, then these receive very cursory review by the fraud team and the application is declined. For those that the fraud detection tool indicates a marginal likelihood of fraud then these will receive more in-depth treatment. This will usually involve a member of the fraud team attempting to obtain proofs from the applicant that they are who they say they are and that the details they have provided are correct. For example, identity can be verified by the applicant providing documentation such as a passport or driving licence. Address is verified by provision of utility bills or other official documentation that contains both the applicant's name and address. Salary details are confirmed from payslips, bank statements or possibly via a letter from their employer (on company notepaper) confirming their income. Although a criminal offence, most credit related fraud is not reported to the authorities. This is because there is little financial incentive for organizations to do so. If a credit application has been declined, then no financial loss has been incurred. If a fraudulent credit application has been accepted and funds provided to a fraudster, then there is little chance that the debt will be recovered. Therefore, cases of suspected fraud are usually only referred to the authorities in cases where the fraud is believed to be part of a large organized crime ring, or where the fraud involves someone from within the organization, who has abused their position to obtain information that is then used fraudulently.

9.2 Customer management and transaction fraud

9.2.1 Compromised security

The most common type of customer management fraud occurs when a fraudster obtains credit card details, and then uses these to obtain goods or services without the card holder's consent. A card may be lost or stolen, or account details may be obtained by an employee who then sells on the customer's credit card details to a fraudster. Alternatively, a fraudster may employ a card reader, attached to an ATM or other legitimate card reading device, to "skim" the details from the user's card. These are then used to create a counterfeit card or to make transactions over the phone or on the internet, where the physical card is not required. In all of these scenarios it could be some time, possibly several weeks, before the legitimate card holder realizes that their account has been compromised and contacts their card issuer to have their account suspended.[3]

9.2.2 Account takeover

Account takeover occurs as a result of identity theft, when a fraudster obtains sufficient information to be able to pass themselves off as the genuine account holder and gain access to their account. They then change the details on the account so that they have ready access to funds. A common strategy is for the fraudster to change the address on a credit card account, and then request that they are provided with a new card, which will be dispatched to the new address. The fraudster can then use the new card to withdraw funds on the account. The main barrier to account takeover is the use of appropriate security questions. This is usually based on information only the applicant is likely to know. For example, a memorable date (other than their birthday), a password they have chosen, or details of the last transaction they made using their card (McNab and Wynn 2003 p. 192). However, if a fraudster manages to persuade a customer to divulge this information, via Phising for example, then there is little that can be done to prevent the fraudster gaining access to the customer's account.

9.2.3 Detecting and dealing with suspected fraud

Before a credit card transaction is completed, details are passed to the card issuer for authorization. To identify cases of suspected fraud, modern systems employ policy rules or fraud scores to identify transactions that are inconsistent with the customer's previous behaviour. If the likelihood of the transaction being fraudulent is higher than the threshold set by the card issuer, it will not be authorized and further investigation will be undertaken to establish the true status of the account.

Customer management fraud scores are based on information about the location of transactions, the frequency of card usage, the value of transactions and type of goods or services that have been purchased. If a credit card has only ever been used in the North East of England to buy groceries, then suddenly used to purchase high value electrical goods from stores in the far east, then this will result in a fraud rule being hit or a high fraud score. As a consequence, the transaction will be flagged as a case of suspected fraud and referred to a member of the fraud team. An attempt will then be made to contact the customer to see if the card is still in their possession. Alternatively, contact may be made with the merchant to ask them to solicit further proof of identity from the customer. If contact cannot be established immediately, the transaction will be declined and the account suspended, preventing further transactions until the status of the account has been established.

A big problem in preventing fraudulent transactions is the false positive rate. On many occasions cases of suspected fraud turn out to be valid transactions. I normally use one of my credit cards primarily to pay for work expenses, but I was recently targeted by the card issuer with a really good cash back deal. Therefore, I attempted to use the card to buy a computer and some furniture, via the internet, to take advantage of the cash back offer. However, the transactions were rejected and I was contacted by the issuer the following day to ask if I had authorized the transactions. On one hand I was reassured by the issuer having a fraud detection system in place to prevent fraudulent use of my card, but on the other hand I was disgruntled that I had been prevented from purchasing the items I wanted. The net result was that I ended up reordering the goods using a different credit card because I was concerned that if I tried to use the original card again, it would be declined again. This is the opposite effect to the one the card issuer intended when the cash back offer was made and resulted a rival card issuer getting my business for the two purchases. Due to customer experiences like this, relatively high thresholds tend to be set within transaction fraud systems, resulting in relatively few cases being referred for investigation. The consequence of this strategy is that many actual cases of fraud are not identified, because they are not sufficiently noteworthy or unusual, but customer satisfaction remains high. So if the stolen credit card discussed earlier was used to buy low value items within a few miles of the card holder's address in the North East of England, the fraud would probably go undetected. Card companies can not really be blamed for adopting this type of approach because most people object (and hence defect to a competitor product) if they find themselves subject to frequent checks and delays whenever they attempt a card transaction that deviates slightly from their normal patterns of behaviour.

9.3 Chapter summary

There are a number of different types of fraud that can occur during acquisition. These include:

- First party fraud.
- Identity theft.
- Falsified identity.
- Conversion fraud.

It is very difficult to say categorically that a credit application is fraudulent at the time when a credit application is made. Therefore, lenders use rule based systems and/or fraud scoring to identify cases where the likelihood of fraud is high. In some countries there also exist national registers, such as CIFAS in the UK, containing details of known fraud cases, against which new credit applications can be checked. If the personal details of the credit application match those on the CIFAS database, then the application is referred for further investigation by an experienced fraud investigator.

During the customer management phase there are two main types of fraud that can occur:

• Compromised account security.
• Account takeover.

As for acquisition fraud, customer management fraud is detected using rule based systems and/or fraud scores. These work by detecting transactions that deviate from the customer's normal pattern of behaviour. The main issue with these systems is that very often genuine transactions will be flagged as potentially fraudulent because someone uses their card for a one-off purchase that does not fit with their usual behaviour. To avoid customer's being continually subject to requests by their card issuer to confirm that they have authorized transactions, the thresholds within fraud detection systems tend to be set quite high. This means that in order to keep customer dissatisfaction at an acceptable level, and therefore reduce the incidence of customer's defecting to a rival product, a lender must be willing to write-off a certain amount of fraud as part of their day-to-day operational expenses.

10
Funding and Provision

In many ways consumer credit is the same as any other type of manufactured product; albeit a less tangible one. Lenders need to secure funds before they are transformed into neat packages of personal loans, credit cards, mortgages and so on, that are supplied to individual customers. The raw material is money, and like any raw material a supply needs to be established before it can be worked into the finished product (Finlay 2009, pp. 112–13). There are several ways that funds can be obtained to support an organization's lending activities, and the most popular of these are discussed in the first part of this chapter.

The second part of the chapter discusses provision. All credit granting institutions, no matter how creditworthy their customers, can expect some loans currently on their books to be written-off in the future due to customers defaulting on their debts. To ensure these losses do not come as an unexpected shock, organizations make an estimate of the amount of future write-off that they expect to incur. An amount of funds (a provision) will then be set aside to cover these expected losses when they occur.

10.1 Funding

There are many ways that lenders can obtain funds to support their lending activities. The main ones are:

- Deposit and saving accounts.
- The Interbank market (wholesale money markets).
- Securitization.

10.1.1 Deposit and saving accounts

Historically, the primary (and sometimes only) source of funds to support consumer lending came from deposits held in current accounts and savings accounts. Other sources of funding have become popular in recent years, but deposits and savings still provide the largest source of funding for most banks, credit unions and saving and loan companies (building societies). Organizations that relay heavily on deposits and savings to support their lending activities are often referred to as balance sheet lenders or asset based lenders. Deposits made by customers are assets that can be used to fund lending, and the obligation to repay money deposited by savers is classed as a liability.[1]

Obtaining money via deposits and savings incurs two significant costs. The first is the cost of maintaining the infrastructure necessary to manage a large number of customer accounts. This may include customer contact centres, a branch network and an account management system. Even for purely on-line banking services the costs of providing the necessary interface with customers to allow them to make deposits and withdrawals is considerable. The second cost is the interest that organization's must pay depositors to encourage them to deposit their funds. If interest rates are low relative to the market, then customers will be reluctant to make new deposits and existing customers will be inclined to transfer their accounts to a competitor.

10.1.2   The Interbank market (wholesale money markets)

The wholesale money market (also known as the Interbank market) facilitates commercial lending between banks and other large financial organizations. Historically, the cost of acquiring funds through the Interbank market has been at, or close to, the base rate of interest set by the central bank. So when a central bank cuts its interest rates, mortgage providers and other lenders often follow suit. However, the price of money, like any other commodity, depends on a number of factors. These include the term of the loan, the risk of borrower default, how the market believes the supply and demand for money will change over time and market liquidity (the total amount of money that organizations are offering to lend). If it is believed that the money supply will increase or decrease in relation to future demand, then lending rates will tend to change in line with this expectation. In the credit crunch of 2007/8 the supply of funds was severely limited as banks became unwilling to lend to one another. This was mainly due to a lack of confidence in the credit ratings of institutions seeking funds, making organizations unsure of the risk premiums that they should charge. The result was a sharp rise in the cost of funds, followed by central bank intervention to lower interest rates and pump huge amounts of tax payers' money into the banking system.

The main benchmark of the interest rates charged in the Interbank market for short term lending (12 months or less), which accounts for the majority of wholesale lending, is the London Interbank Offered Rate (LIBOR). LIBOR rates are calculated by the British Bankers' Association (BBA) on a daily basis. Separate LIBOR rates are calculated for loans of different terms, ranging from overnight borrowing to a maximum of 12 months, with the three month LIBOR rate acting as the main benchmark against which trends in borrowing rates are assessed. It is important to note that a LIBOR rate is not the specific interest rate that one institution charges another for a loan, but is an average rate compiled from a panel of major banking institutions. The BBA calculates LIBOR for several economic regions including Australia, Canada, the Euro Zone, Japan, the UK and the US. Details of historic LIBOR rates and the banks that are on the BBA panel within each economic region are provided on the BBA website (www.bba.com)

The interest paid on deposits is often lower than the interest charged for commercial loans obtained via the Interbank market. However, the administrative cost of dealing with a large number of individual customer accounts incurs a significant overhead which must be factored into the overall cost. In practice, many financial institutions acquire funds from both individual savers and the money markets to varying degrees.

The Interbank market focuses on short term lending for periods of up to 12 months. Given that many consumer credit products have terms in excess of 12 months, lending institutions that rely on the Interbank market for funds maintain a continuous cycle of new borrowing to cover their existing debts, taking out new loans as their existing ones mature – a process known as 'borrowing short lending long'. They do this because short term borrowing is cheaper than longer term borrowing. For example, one week UK LIBOR rates in the first half of 2009 were consistently around 1 percent lower than the 12 month UK LIBOR rate. However, short term borrowing carries an inherent risk (liquidity risk), because if for some reason a bank that has lent long can not obtain new loans when its current short term borrowing expires, it will have insufficient funds to pay back its creditors and will become insolvent if it can't raise funds via other sources (such as selling some of it's assets or issuing new shares via a rights issue). Liquidity risk can be reduced by taking out longer term loans – typically of between one and ten years. Alternatively, an organization may issue bonds that investors buy, paying a guaranteed rate of interest until the bond matures – which may be anything up to 30 years or more. However, the higher interest rates demanded for longer term borrowing makes it less attractive. Consequently, the type of funding a bank will seek via the money markets represents a balance between the increased cost of funds from long term loans and bond issues, against the liquidity risks that shorter term borrowing introduces.

10.1.3   Securitization

Securitization is a way of raising new capital from relatively illiquid, revenue generating assets. An asset is illiquid if it has value, but it is difficult to realize the value quickly; that is, it is difficult to sell the asset or borrow against it. Portfolios of mortgages, credit cards and personal loans are all examples of illiquid assets. It is possible for a lender to raise funds by selling all or part of a consumer credit portfolio. However, there is no pre-existing market for such assets. This means that to sell a consumer credit portfolio, a lender needs to seek potential buyers and enter into negotiation with them. This could take a considerable time to undertake, and there is no guarantee that at the end of the process a suitable buyer will be found.

Securitization of consumer credit portfolios became popular in the 1990s and 2000s. Today, many organizations regularly use securitization as a way to raise funds. The basic principle for securitizing an asset is as follows:

1. An organization (termed the originator) sets up a fund or trust that is a separate legal entity. This fund is referred to as a Special Purpose Vehicle (SPV). As separate legal entities, the originator has no liability for any losses that the SPV incurs.[2]
2. The originator sells the assets it wants to securitize to the SPV. This provides funds that the originator can lend to new customers.
3. The SPV obtains funds to buy the asset from the originator by selling bonds to investors. Net revenues generated by the asset are distributed amongst the bondholders. Therefore, the initial price of the bonds is determined by the expected revenues that they will generate.
4. The SPV pays the originator fees to maintain the securitized assets. In the case of consumer credit portfolios, this covers things like processing payments, issuing statements, chasing late payers and so on.

From a customer perspective, the securitization process is completely invisible. The customer continues to deal with the originator in the same manner as they have always done, and the SPV has no involvement in the day-to-day management of individual customer accounts.

The bonds issued by SPVs generate regular income for bondholders, but are themselves tradable instruments that rise and fall in value. So if the value of a securitized credit portfolio rises, maybe because the default rates within the portfolio are lower than expected, then bondholders may profit from selling the bonds to someone else. However, the converse is also true. If the value of securitized assets fall, then bondholders will be left nursing a loss. This is one of the key features of the US sub-prime mortgage collapse that occurred in the US in 2006/7 and the worldwide credit crunch that followed. Mortgage providers securitized large amounts of poor quality sub-prime mortgages, whose value was widely over-rated. When the US housing market collapsed the value of securitized assets fell dramatically, leaving bondholders with substantial losses.

Another potential benefit of securitization is that it can be used to remove potentially risky assets from the originator's balance sheet because the risk from defaulting accounts is transferred to the bondholders. The principle benefit to the originator is that by having less exposure to risk, they are required by banking regulators to hold less capital in reserve. Capital requirements are discussed in more detail in Chapter 11.

10.2   Provision

Every year some debtors will default on their loans. When the debt has remained unpaid for a considerable period of time, usually somewhere between 6 and 12 months, it will be classified as bad debt and written-off. Bad debts that have been written-off appear as a loss within the organization's accounts.

Losses incurred from bad debt represent only one half of the picture. Some customers, although not currently in arrears, will default in the future, resulting in some or all of their debt being written-off. Therefore, it is over-optimistic to base estimates of future profitability on the expectation that all outstanding debts will be repaid. Provision is an amount set aside against future bad debts, accounted for in the present. Making provision against future losses due to bad debt is recognition that the asset value of outstanding loans reported on an organization's balance sheet is less than the stated amount (McNab and Wynn 2003 p. 147). In some ways provision is analogous to depreciation, which represents the loss in value of an asset, such as a building or vehicle, over time (Wood and Sangster 1999 p. 213).

Any change in provision from one accounting period to the next will be included along with known write-offs within the profit and loss account, usually as 'provision for impaired loans'. An impaired loan is a debt where there is some reason to believe that some or all of the debt won't be repaid. To some extent all debts can be considered impaired because no matter how creditworthy someone is, there is always a small chance of non-payment. However, the vast bulk of the provision for impaired loans will be due to customers who are demonstrably more likely to default than average – for example, they have a history of missed payments and/or are currently in arrears.

At the start of each financial year an organization will estimate the level of provision that is appropriate for their portfolio of debts. This estimate is then used as an input to their profit and loss forecast for that year. Ultimate responsibility for the calculation of provision will lie with the finance and accounting function within the organization, but the credit management function will usually provide much of the portfolio analysis needed to produce the relevant information. The provision estimate will be revised on a regular basis (usually monthly or quarterly) and used to update the profit and loss forecast. The important thing to remember is that a provision reported in an organization's accounts is not a known quantity, but an estimate of a cost that is expected to be incurred at some point in the future.

If no new credit is advanced, the total value of debt written-off plus provisions should, all other things being equal, remain constant for a given cohort of debt. As time progresses the amount written-off will increase while provision decreases, so that eventually all debts will either have been repaid or written-off. However, credit granting institutions are continually advancing new credit and so the overall provision level will never decline to zero. Instead, the value of provisions will fluctuate depending on the size of the portfolio and the estimated likelihood that each risk (each loan) will default.

Provision is important because any change in provision has an impact on profit. Provision is treated as a loss and therefore, an overly pessimistic reporting of an increase in provision at year end will result in reduced profits. So, if provisions have increased from $75 million to $125 million, profits will be reduced by $50 million, even though no additional write-off will have occurred. Conversely, if the provision estimate is too low, profit figures will be seen to improve in the short term, but there will be an adverse impact on profits in subsequent years due to the unexpected increase in write-offs that occur, but which have not been accounted for.

Provision is only an estimate of future write-off. So whenever a debt that has been provided for is actually written-off, a corresponding amount of provision is released. This means that the total value of provisions is reduced by the amount of provision that was originally set aside for the debt. If the actual amount written-off is different from the value of provision originally allocated, then the difference is added into the profit and loss account. Take the case where a provision of $400 was made for a $1,000 loan because it was believed that there was a 40 percent chance that the loan would be written-off. If the entire $1,000 is written-off then the total amount of write-off will increase by $1,000, the value of provisions will decrease by $400 and the overall increase in the losses reported due to debt written-off will increase by $600 ($1,000–$400). If the loan is repaid in full, then the provision would also be reduced by $400, but there would be no increase in write-offs. Therefore, losses will decrease by $400.

10.2.1 Roll rate models of provision

In theory, the easiest way to estimate provision is simply to allocate a fixed percentage of the total portfolio, based on the bad debt written-off in previous years. If historically 3 percent of the credit advanced to customers ended up being written-off, then the provision estimate going forward will be set as 3 percent of current outstandings. This is a very simple way of calculating provision because it does not take into account changes that occur to the risk profile of the customer base over time.

A simple extension to the basic provision estimate is to calculate provision on the basis of the value of debt at different arrears status and the roll rates between arrears states; that is, the way in which accounts move (roll) between different delinquency states and eventual write-off, as shown in Table 10.1.

The leading diagonal (in bold) in Table 10.1 shows the proportion of accounts by value that moved (rolled) from one arrears status to the next in the course of a month. For example, for the $4,701 million of loans that were up-to-date last month, 91 percent ($4,278m) have remained up-to-date. The remaining 9 percent ($423m) have rolled to one payment in arrears. The roll rate from up-to-date to one month in arrears is said to be 9 percent. For loans that were already one payment in arrears, 65 percent recover to an up-to-date status, while the other 35 percent roll to two payments in arrears. The final row in Table 10.1 shows the roll rate for customers that are five or more payments in arrears. In this case 25 percent pay what they owe and recover. The other 75 percent don't pay and are written-off.

Table 10.1 Roll rate analysis ($m)

Arrears (delinquency) status last month	Current arrears (delinquency status this month)							
	Up-to- date	1	2	3	4	5+	Write-off	Total
0 (Up-to-date)	$4,278 91%	$423 9%						$4,701
1 (1–30 days past due)	$318 65%		$171 35%					$489
2 (31–60 days past due)	$84 58%			$61 42%				$145
3 (61–90) days past due	$26 40%				$38 60%			$64
4 (91–120 days past due)	$9 35%					$16 65%		$25
5+ (121+ days past due)	$3 25%						$9 75%	$12
Total	$4,718	$423	$171	$61	$38	$16	$9	$5,434

The roll rate figures in Table 10.1 are used to estimate the eventual value of accounts in each arrears status that will end up being written-off. This is achieved by multiplying the roll rates from each arrears status through to the final write-off stage. So for accounts that are up-to-date, the expected proportion that will eventually be written-off is calculated as the proportion that roll to arrears status one, then to arrears status two and so on, and is calculated as:

$$9\% * 35\% * 42\% * 60\% * 65\% * 75\% = 0.39\%$$

This means that whatever the balance of up-to-date accounts in the current month, the provision estimate will be equal to 0.39 percent of the balance. So for the $4,718 million of balances whose current arrears status is up-to-date, $18.26m ($4,718 * 0.39%) can be expected to be written-off. To generate a provision estimate for the whole portfolio the exercise is repeated for the balance at each arrears status. This gives a total provision estimate of $106.20 million, as shown in Table 10.2.

Table 10.2   Provision estimates based on roll rates

Current arrears (delinquency) status	Expected roll rate to write-off	Current outstandings $m	Provision estimate $m
0 (Up-to-date)	0.39%	4,718	18.26
1 (1–30 days past due)	4.30%	423	18.19
2 (31–60 days past due)	12.29%	171	21.03
3 (61–90) days past due	29.25%	61	17.81
4 (91–120 days past due)	48.75%	38	18.72
5+ (121+days past due)	75.00%	16	12.19
Total		5,427	106.20

In practice, more accurate provision estimates can be obtained by segmenting the portfolio into a number of groups that are believed to display different roll rate behaviour. For example, it is common to undertake separate roll rate analysis for accounts with different levels of credit limit utilization, or which have been on the books for different periods of time. A total provision estimate is arrived at by summing the provision estimates for each population segment.

10.2.2   Advanced models of provision

Provision estimation using roll rates is common practice and is reasonably accurate, but as McNab and Wynn (2003 pp. 154–5) point out, in the form presented so far, roll rate based estimates suffer from two limitations. The first problem is that standard roll rate models assume that accounts can only ever roll to one of two states; that is, they either recover to an up-to-date status or they roll to the next arrears state. In practice, it is quite common for a significant proportion of accounts to remain in the same arrears status from one month to the next. This occurs if someone misses their payment one month and resumes repayments the following month, but never makes up the payment they have missed – they will continue to be one month in arrears until the agreement ends. Accounts can also partially recover if a part payment of the overdue debt is made. For example, if a customer is three months in arrears, then makes two extra payments, then their account will recover to a one month in arrears status. The second problem is that roll rate models assume that states naturally follow on from one another: an account that is one month in arrears will naturally roll to two months in arrears, then three months in arrears and so on. If other states exist that don't naturally occur at a given point on the arrears path it is difficult to fully incorporate these cases into a roll rate model.

To overcome these two problems, some organizations use more advanced statistical modelling approaches; the most popular of which are Markov Chain models. Markov Chain models have some similarities with roll rate models, but their major advantage is that they can take into account situations where accounts can roll to many different unconnected states, and not just to the next arrears status. For more information about Markov Chain models see Thomas et al. (2002) and Thomas (2009). Some lenders also make use of scoring models, as discussed in Chapter 4, to generate their provision estimates. A model will be constructed using information that is known about a customer to predict how likely they are to default, when they are likely to default and the amount of any write-off that results.

10.2.3   International accounting standard IAS39

International accounting standard IAS39 lays down guidelines for how impaired loans should be accounted for within organizational accounts.[3] In particular, it requires that provisions for impaired loans are calculated on a net present value basis, using the contractual rate of interest. This means that provision calculations need to be adjusted to take into account the repayment schedule and the interest rate specified in the agreement.

Net present value is a measure of how much money received in the future is worth in today's terms. In general, the further in the future money is promised, the less it is worth today. A simple way to think about net present value is to ask yourself the following question: if someone promised to give you $100 in a year's time, how much would you be willing to accept if you were offered an alternative cash amount today? If we make this assessment based on inflation of say, 5 percent per annum, then the net present value of $100 in a year, would be $95.24 today, calculated as $100/(1+0.05) or working the other way $95.24 * 1.05 = $100. Another way of thinking about this is if inflation is 5 percent, then $100 in one year's time will have the same buying power as $95.24 today. If a longer time period is considered, say two years, then the process would be repeated: $95.24/(1+0.05) = $90.70.[4] So $100 in two years time is worth $90.70 today assuming inflation remains at 5 percent.

The implementation of IAS39 means that for the calculations described in section 10.1.1, an adjustment must be made to take into account the net present value of the debt. The calculation must be based on the contractual rate of interest specified in the credit agreement (rather than inflation as was used in the previous example). So if a company offers two different types of credit card, one with an interest rate of 17.9 percent and another with an interest rate of 21.9 percent, each rate must be used for customers with the respective card in the net present value calculation. As an example of net present value applied to provisions under IAS39, let us consider the case of a loan for which a provision estimate needs to be calculated. Imagine that a customer has taken out an unsecured loan for $20,000 to be repaid in 48 equal instalments over a term of 48 months. The contractual rate of interest on the loan is fixed at 9 percent. After making 24 payments, the customer misses a payment, enters a state of delinquency and the account is classified as impaired. Details of the customer's repayment schedule, interest charges and outstanding balance are shown in Table 10.3.

From Table 10.3, after the customer has made 24 repayments the outstanding balance at the start of month 25 is $11,683.03. From past experience, the bank estimates that it is likely to recover 90 percent of the outstanding debt, with 10 percent of the debt being written-off. Therefore, in this case the bank expects to receive 90 percent of the $11.683.03 owing; that is, $10,514.73. This amount is then subject to the net present value calculation over the two remaining years of the

Table 10.3 Customer repayment schedule

Month	Outstanding balance ($)	Interest added ($)	Payment ($)	Post payment balance ($)
1	20,000.00	144.16	494.38	19,649.78
2	19,649.78	141.64	494.38	19,297.04
3	19,297.04	139.09	494.38	18,941.75
...	...	...	...	...
...	...	...	...	...
23	12,494.58	90.06	494.38	12,090.26
24	12,090.26	87.15	494.38	11,683.03
25	11,683.03	84.21	494.38	11,272.86
...	...	...	...	...
...	...	...	...	...
47	978.17	7.05	494.38	490.84
48	490.84	3.54	494.38	0.00
Total		3,730.24	23,730.24	

Note: Interest added = outstanding balance * (1+contractual interest rate)$^{1/12}$

loan. $10,514.73/1.09 = $9,646.54 and $9,646.54/1.09 = $8,850.04. The provision is then calculated as the difference between the amount owing and the net present value of the expected loan repayments: $11,683.03–$8,850.04 = $2,832.99.

10.3 Chapter summary

This chapter has discussed funding and provision. Before an organization can provide credit to its customers, it must first obtain funds. Traditionally, the majority of consumer lending was funded by money held in deposit and saving accounts. Deposits and savings still account for the majority of funding for many organizations, but since the 1990s many have sought to obtain additional funding either through the Interbank market, or via securitization of their assets.

Provision is an amount put aside to cover losses that are expected to arise from loans that default at some point in the future, but have not yet been written-off. An estimate of provision is required because if it is assumed that all outstanding loans will be repaid, then the valuation of the organization's assets will be over-optimistic. Provision is calculated on an ongoing basis. Any change in provision from one accounting period to the next is reported within the profit and loss account alongside the actual write-off that has been experienced. If the amount of provision increases from one financial year to the next, indicating an expected increase in write-off in future years, then there will be a corresponding decrease in the profit reported – even if the actual amount written-off that year remains unchanged. Likewise, if the provision estimate is revised downward, then some of the provision that has been put aside can be released, leading to an increase in reported profits.

11
Capital Requirements

A feature of provision calculation, as discussed in Chapter 10, is that it covers expected loss. To put it another way, an organization will make a provision for bad and doubtful debts based on its 'best guess' as to the losses that it will incur in future. Provision estimates are not perfect. The actual amount written-off at the end of the financial year will always be different from the estimate that was made at the start of the year. In some years the provision estimate will be too high. This is fine, because it means that profits will be higher than originally forecast. However, if losses are higher than predicted, then this could be a problem. Consider a bank that makes a provision of say $100 million against bad and doubtful debts at the start of the financial year when the economy is booming. During the year the economy unexpectedly takes a downturn. At the end of the year the actual losses are $150 million because many of the bank's customers lose their jobs and are unable to meet their loan repayments. If the bank does not have sufficient funds (capital) to cover the $50 million shortfall in its provisions then it could face financial difficulty and become insolvent. A prudent strategy against such risks is to put some extra capital aside, in addition to provision, to cover any unexpected losses that might be incurred. This is especially important for deposit taking institutions that provide current accounts and savings accounts, to ensure that depositors don't lose their funds and to maintain the stability of the banking system.

Capital requirements are reserves, in addition to provision that deposit taking institutions maintain to cover unexpected losses. The BASEL II Capital Accord is an international agreement, drawn up by the Bank for International Settlements (BIS) based in Basel, Switzerland. The accord specifies how deposit taking institutions should go about calculating their capital requirements. The accord only applies to deposit taking institutions such as banks and saving and loan companies. Non-deposit taking institutions, such as finance houses and pawnbrokers are not covered by the accord and are not required to maintain capital reserves. The accord is based on three core principles or 'Pillars':

- Pillar 1. Minimum capital requirements. This is the capital an institution must maintain to cover unexpected losses to their assets. For the majority of retail banking institutions the most important assets used to calculate capital requirements are their credit portfolios. However, other risks are also covered. For example, devaluation of land and foreign currency holdings, and losses resulting from terrorist attack and natural disasters.
- Pillar 2. Regulatory response. This covers the role of banking regulators in ensuring that organizations maintain sufficient capital. Regulators are required to audit how organizations make their assessments of risk and hence their capital requirements. Regulators may specify that additional capital is needed to cover risks that an organization has not considered, or to address any shortcomings with the methods or data used in capital requirements calculations.
- Pillar 3. Disclosure. This is concerned with the information that an organization must release to the market about the risks it faces, and how it has calculated its capital requirement.

The full accord is extremely complex, contains hundreds of paragraphs, and comes with thousands of pages of supporting documentation. To further complicate matters, the accord is interpreted and implemented independently within national and international regulatory frameworks. There are probably only a handful of people worldwide who have full understanding of the entire accord and all of its nuances (and I don't count myself as one of them!) Therefore, for the purposes of this text the discussion is limited to cover only the most general principles of accord and should not be taken as a detailed or comprehensive guide. In particular, the discussion is limited to the calculation of capital requirements for retail credit risk within the first pillar, for lenders operating in the UK; that is, consumer credit portfolios such as mortgages, credit cards and personal loans which come under the regulation of the UK's Financial Services Authority (FSA).

11.1 What is capital?

Capital is the value of assets, less any liabilities (Smullan and Hand 2005). To put it another way, capital is the net worth of a business after all debts and obligations have been taken into account. Under the BASEL II accord, capital that can be used to meet capital requirements is categorized as the sum of Tier I (core) and Tier II (supplementary) capital. The most important of these is Tier I. Tier I capital covers assets that are readily available to cover losses, and consists of shareholder equity and retained profits (Howells and Bain 2004 p. 389). It is calculated as:

(The original value of shares issued) +
(Accumulated net profits after dividends have been paid) –
(Losses that have been incurred)

If an organization issued $5 million worth of shares, and then made net profits (after dividend payments) of $1 million and $1.5 million in the first two years of trading and a loss of $0.25 million in the third, then the overall Tier I capital would be $7.25 million. A very simple (and simplistic) way of thinking about Tier I capital is that it covers cash, plus any other assets that can be turned into cash very quickly (liquid assets). Tier II covers two other types of assets:

1. Assets that are not so readily accessible (less liquid) than Tier I.
2. Assets that are liquid, but which have been allocated to meet specific long term costs and obligations.

There are many different types of asset that can be classified as Tier II capital, but the most important ones are:

- Revaluated assets. A revaluated asset is something that has increased in value since its original purchase. A company's headquarters may have been built on a greenfield site many years ago and the land's value has subsequently risen. The increase in the value of the land would be classified as Tier II capital.
- Provisions. This is capital that has been put aside to cover expected losses, as discussed in Chapter 10. Allowing provision to be counted as capital within the context of capital requirements is controversial. This is because by allowing funds that have already been put aside to be counted as capital, there is an element of double counting. However, the losses covered by provisions may only be realized many years in the future and the money put aside represents a source of ready cash that is available to be used today, if an organization needs it. To deal with the concerns that have been raised, regulators

have capped the amount of provisions that can be included in capital requirement calculations.[1]

- Subordinated debt. Subordinated debt is low priority long term borrowing. Funds obtained from subordinated loans can be used in capital requirements because they are amongst the last debts to be paid should an organization become insolvent. In particular, they take lower priority than a bank's depositors.

For the purpose of calculating capital requirements, at least 50 percent of an organization's capital must be Tier I.

11.2 Assets, risk and risk weighted assets

Organizations have assets of various types. The portfolio of debts that a lender holds is an asset, as is property, cash, inventory, shares, foreign currency reserves, patent rights and so on. All of these assets are subject to risk; that is, there is a chance that something will happen to cause an asset to be devalued. The BASEL II Accord defines three types of asset risk that must be considered when calculating capital requirements.

1. Credit risk. This covers losses that might arise due to debts being written-off. Six different categories of credit risk are defined by the accord. These are corporate, banks, equity, retail, project finance and sovereigns (Gup 2004). Consumer credit, including mortgages, personal loans and credit cards are included within the retail credit category.[2]
2. Operational risk. Operational risk is the loss that could arise from internal or external events that may adversely affect an organization. An external event might be a natural disaster, lawsuit or an act of terrorism that disrupts business operations. An internal event could be a catastrophic failure of the organization's IT systems or industrial action taken by employees.
3. Market risk. This is the loss associated with changes in the value of financial instruments such as stock options, futures and foreign currency.

For some assets only a proportion of the asset may be at risk – whatever happens the asset will retain some of its value. Therefore, only a proportion of the asset's value needs to be considered when deciding how much capital needs to be put aside to cover losses that may be incurred.

The asset is said to be 'risk weighted'. Consider an office building worth $5 million, including the land it's built on. Assume that if the building didn't exist, then the land would be worth $2 million. For the sake of argument assume that the land itself is not subject to any risk of devaluation; that is, whatever happens the land will always be worth $2 million. Therefore, although the building as it stands is worth $5 million, if it was completely destroyed only 60 percent of the building's value would be lost; that is, $3 million. Therefore, an appropriate risk weight for the office building is 60 percent and the asset would be described as having a risk weighted value of $3 million.

Another example is someone who buys a barrel of oil for $100. The price of oil may go up or down, but if the market view is that even in the worst possible scenario the price of oil will never fall below $20, then only $80 of the investment is at risk. An appropriate risk weight for the oil would therefore be 80 percent.

11.3   The Capital Ratio

The Capital Ratio is the measure used to determine if an organization is maintaining sufficient capital. It is calculated as:

Capital Ratio = (Total Capital) / (Total Value of Risk Weighted Assets)

The Total Value of Risk Weighted Assets includes all assets that an organization has, subject to the relevant risk weights that apply. The accord specifies that organizations must maintain sufficient capital such that their Capital Ratio is 8 percent or more.[3] To put it another way, an organization's total capital must be greater than or equal to the total value of its risk weighted assets multiplied by 8 percent. At least half of an organization's capital (4 percent) must be in the form of Tier I capital. However, individual regulators have the power to set their own minimum. Following the credit crunch of 2007/8 a number of regulators temporally raised the minimum capital ratio for organizations that they supervise in response to fears about the overall stability of the banking system.

Many organizations deliberately maintain a Capital Ratio significantly higher than the regulatory minimum, perhaps equal to 14–16 percent or more of their Risk Weighted Assets. This is because having a large amount of capital gives them greater room to manoeuvre, and is seen by the financial markets as a measure of an institution's financial stability. This in turn means that organizations that hold a lot of capital can secure funds from the wholesale money markets more cheaply than organizations that maintain a lower Capital Ratio.

11.4 The standardized approach for retail credit

The Basel II Accord allows organizations to use one of two methods to calculate their capital requirements for retail credit portfolios. These are the Standardized approach and the Advanced Internal Rating Based approach (Termed Advanced IRB or IRB-A).[4] The simplest method is the standardized approach. The risk weights for each type of asset are set by the regulatory authorities. Different risk weights are set for mortgages and other types of retail credit.

11.4.1 Mortgages

For mortgage lending the risk weight for loans that are not seriously in arrears (less than 90 days past due with repayments) is dependent upon the Loan To Value ratio (LTV). If someone borrows $60,000 secured against a property valued at $200,000 then the LTV is 30 percent.

If the LTV is less than 80 percent then the risk weight is 35 percent, meaning that only 35 percent of the mortgage is considered to be at risk. This is because in the case of default there is little potential for loss given that the lender can repossess the property and sell it to recover the debt. A reasonable question to ask is, why are mortgages given a risk weight of 35 percent and not zero? There are two reasons. The first is because the risk weight reflects what the Basel committee believes is the 'worst case scenario' in which property values fall considerably. To put it another way, even if the economy suffers a serious downturn and house prices fall, it is very unlikely that they will fall by more than 35 percent. The second reason is the difference between the market value of a property that would be realized through a standard sale, and the discounted value of the property (called the haircut) that would be obtained should the property be repossessed and sold at auction. For example, a property worth $500,000 on the open market might only realize $400,000 at auction.

If the LTV is greater than 80 percent then the risk weight is set at 75 percent.

When mortgage loans are in serious arrears (≥90 days past due) then a different set of risk weights apply. These depend upon the amount of provisions that have already been set aside against the debt:

- A 100 percent risk weight is applied, if the provisions that have been set aside are less than 20 percent of the mortgage value.
- A 50 percent risk weight is applied, if the provisions that have been set aside are equal or greater than 20 percent of the mortgage value.

The value of Risk Weighted Assets for mortgage loans 90 days or more past due are calculated net of provisions. This reflects the fact that the accord is about unexpected loss, and provisions reflect a loss that one expects to incur. Consider a mortgage of $70,000 that is 90 days past due, for which a provision of $20,000 has already been made. The risk weighted asset value will be:

(70,000 – 20,000) * (Value of mortgage net of provision)
50%   (50% risk weight due to provision >20%)
= $25,000

Table 11.1 provides an example of the capital requirement calculation for a mortgage portfolio using the standardized approach.

In Table 11.1, the lender has a total mortgage book valued at $12,761 million. Of this, $12,600 million are not in serious arrears (<90 days past

Table 11.1   Standardized approach for mortgages

	Asset value $m	Provisions	Asset value less provision	Risk weight	Risk weighted asset value $m
Mortgages not in serious arrears (<90 days past due)					
LTV < 80%	10,500	N/A	N/A	35%	3,675
LTV ≥ 80%	2,100	N/A	N/A	75%	1,575
Total (A)	12,600				5,250
Mortgages in serious arrears (≥90 days past due)					
Provision <20%	0	0	0	100%	0
Provision ≥ 20%	161	35	126	50%	63
Total (B)	161	35	126		63
Grand Total (A+B)	12,761				5,313

Minimum capital requirement = 8% * 5,313 = 425.04

due) and $161 million are in serious arrears (≥90 days past due). Of those that are <90 days past due, 35 percent and 75 percent risk weights are applied to loans with LTV <80 percent and ≥80 percent respectively. For those ≥90 days past due, provisions account for more than 20 percent of the portfolio value, and therefore the 50 percent risk weight applies to the value of mortgages, less the provision. Adding these figures together gives a total risk weighted asset value of $5,313 million. Multiplying this by 8 percent gives a minimum capital requirement of $425.04 million.

11.4.2 Non-mortgage retail credit

Other types of consumer borrowing (credit cards, unsecured loans, overdrafts and so on) are allocated a risk weight of 75 percent if they are not impaired. Seventy-five percent reflects the fact that although there are no specific assets to possess in the event of default, there is reasonable expectation that some of the debt (at least 25 percent) will be recovered via debt recovery action and/or revenue raised from debt sale to third party debt collection agencies.

For impaired loans the risk weights are dependent upon the amount of provisions that have been made:

• A 150 percent risk weight is applied if the provision set aside is less than 20 percent of the outstanding debt. This is a conservative figure that is intended to cover any additional costs that an organization might incur trying to recover the debt.
• A 100 percent risk weight is applied if the provision set aside is equal or greater than 20 percent of the outstanding debt.

11.5 Advanced IRB approach

The standardized approach is something of a 'one size fits all' methodology. It is deliberately conservative in order to minimize the risk of banks having insufficient capital. If an organization has a good quality consumer credit portfolio, with very low risk of defaults, then the standardized approach will result in more capital than is actually needed. The advanced IRB approach provides a more flexible framework that allows organizations to generate their own assessment of credit risk. The requirement to have capital greater than 8 percent of risk weighted assets remains the same as for the standardized approach. However, the risk weightings used for the standardized approach are replaced by an organization's internal assessment of what the risk weights should be for its assets. The risk weighted asset value is calculated using the following four parameters.

1. The probability of default (*PD*). This is a value in the range 0–1 representing the probability that customers in a given risk grade will be in default (in serious arrears) with their repayments in 12 months time. The accord requires customer accounts to be grouped into a number of homogenous risk grades (pools) containing similarly performing accounts. The average probability of default is then calculated for each risk grade. All accounts within each grade are assumed to have the same probability of defaulting.
2. The exposure at default (*EAD*). This is the amount of the outstanding debt at the point when an account defaults.
3. The loss given default (*LGD*). This is the proportion of the exposure at default that is expected to be written-off, less any recoveries that occur after default has occurred.
4. The asset correlation (*R*). The asset correlation is a measure of how loans within each risk grades are related. A high asset correlation means that if one of the loans on an organization's books behaves in a certain way (in terms of repayment behaviour), then many of the others will display similar behaviour. A low asset correlation means that there is little relationship between the repayment behaviour of individual loans.

Each individual organization is responsible for calculating the first three parameters. That is, *PD*, *EAD* and *LGD*. The value of the asset correlation (*R*) is specified by the regulator. *R* is set to be 0.04 for qualifying revolving credit (credit/store cards) and 0.15 for mortgages. For personal loans *R* is calculated as function of *PD*:

$$R = 0.03 * \frac{(1 - e^{-35*PD})}{(1 - e^{-35})} + 0.16 * \left[1 - \frac{(1 - e^{-35*PD})}{(1 - e^{-35})} \right]$$

11.5.1 Expected loss

The expected loss is similar in principle to provision. It represents the 'average' loss an organization expects to incur, based on its estimates of *PD*, *EAD* and *LGD*. However, given the different methods of calculation, the values for provision and expected loss will not be the same. In particular, expected loss covers only a 12 month period. Provision on the other hand covers all expected losses over the remaining life of loans – which may be many years.

The expected loss (*EL*) for each risk grade over the coming 12 months is calculated as:

$$EL = PD * EAD * LGD$$

To put it another way, the expected loss is the probability that a loan defaults, multiplied by the value of the debt at the time when default occurs, multiplied by the proportion of the default value that is eventually written-off. Consider a credit card customer for whom the following estimates have been made:

- The expected probability of default within the next 12 months is 3 percent (*PD* = 3%).
- the expected balance on the card should the customer default is estimated to be $8,000 (*EAD* = $8,000).
- Should the customer default, the organization expects to recover 40 percent of the debt via debt recovery or debt sale. The remaining 60 percent is expected to be written-off (*LGD* = 60%).

the expected loss will be 3% * $8,000 * 60% = $144.

Expected loss is important because capital requirements only cover unexpected loss; that is, the calculations described in the following section generate a figure for an organization's capital requirement based on the risk of them incurring losses above the expected value.

11.5.2   Value at risk and the Vasicek formula

For the Advanced IRB approach the BASEL II Accord applies a Value at Risk (VaR) methodology for the calculation of capital requirements. The basic assumption of VaR methodologies is that for a homogenous pool of assets, the proportion of the pool that is likely to be lost follows a known loss distribution. The loss distribution can be used to determine the proportion of a portfolio's value that can be expected to be lost for a given level of risk. In general, the greater the proportion of the assets at risk of being lost, the less likely the loss is to be incurred. To illustrate the idea of value at risk, imagine that you have taken out a loan of $1 million and used it to buy a portfolio of shares. In 12 months time you must sell your portfolio in order to repay the loan. You have some additional funds (capital) sitting in a bank account and you are thinking about how much of this capital you should put aside to cover any losses that you might incur, should the portfolio be worth less than $1 million at the end of the year. Any capital that you don't put aside to cover losses is placed in various long term investments that will only mature in several years time. Consequently, these assets will not be available at the end of the year should you need them.

The value of the share portfolio you purchased may rise or fall. If it rises, then no problem; you sell the shares, repay the loan and take a profit. If the value of the portfolio falls however, then you may have a problem. If the drop in value is greater than the capital you put aside, then you won't have enough money to repay the loan, and you will become insolvent. For the sake of argument, assume there is a 10 percent chance that your portfolio will be worth $950,000 or less (a loss of at least $50,000), but only a 1 percent chance that it will be worth $800,000 or less (a loss of at least $200,000). The key thing you need to decide, in order to determine how much capital you need, is the level of risk (of becoming insolvent) that you are willing to accept. The more risk adverse you are, the more capital you will require. If you are willing to accept a 10 percent chance of going bust at the end of the year then all you need to do is put aside $50,000. However, if you are only willing to accept a 1 percent chance of becoming insolvent, then you need to put aside $200,000. So in VaR terminology, the value at 10 percent risk is $50,000 and the value at 1 percent risk is $200,000.

The core task when implementing a VaR methodology is to decide upon an acceptable level of risk, and then calculate the amount of capital required to cover losses at this level. For the BASEL II Accord the maximum acceptable risk of a banking institution failing has been set as a 1 in 1,000 year event; that is, a bank must hold an amount of capital such that the chance of it having insufficient funds in any 12 month period is no more than 0.1 percent. To generate a dollar value of the capital requirement the starting point is the following formula:

$$\text{Value of Risk Weighted Assets} = 12.5 * EAD * K \qquad (1)$$

where K is the 'capital requirement' and takes values in the range 0–1. EAD is the exposure at default – which was introduced in the previous section. If you rearrange equation 1 (by dividing both sides by 12.5) it can be seen that this is just another way of saying that the amount of capital put aside must be at least 8 percent of Risk Weighted Assets. To calculate the capital requirement for a 1:1,000 year event, the accord assumes that the distribution of loss follows that given by the 'Vasicek formula'[5] (Vasicek 2002; Bank for International Settlements 2005):

$$K = 1.06 * \left[LGD * N \left\{ (1 - R)^{-0.5} * G(PD) + \left(\frac{R}{(1 - R)} \right)^{0.5} * G(0.999) \right\} - PD * LGD \right]$$

where:

- PD is the estimate of default within 12 months.
- LGD is the estimated loss given default, expressed as a percentage of the exposure at default (EAD).
- N is the normal transformation.
- G is the inverse normal transformation.
- R is the asset correlation for assets within a given risk grade – as discussed earlier.

Note that the last part of the Vasicek formula subtracts the proportion of expected loss ($PD * LGD$). This is because the expected loss should, in theory, be covered by provision. Therefore, by subtracting this amount, what's left is the proportion of unexpected loss that can be expected to be incurred once every 1,000 years.

If maths is not your strong point, then the Vasicek formula can be a little daunting. A simple way to think about the Vasicek formula is as follows. If you know the average probability of loan default over the coming year (the value of PD) for a pool of loans, and you know the asset correlation (R) between the loans, the Vasicek formula generates the proportion of the loans in the pool that are likely to written-off once in every thousand years. The value of LGD in the formula provides an adjustment to take into account any money that may be clawed back after default. For example, repossession and resale of mortgaged property, or assets seized and sold following legal action to recover a credit card debt.

Figure 11.1 illustrates the output of the Vasicek formula for different PD values ranging from 0–1 (assuming an LGD value of 100%).

Figure 11.1 shows the results of applying the Vasicek formula with two different asset correlations: $R = 0.04$ (i.e. the asset correlation that applies to credit cards) and $R = 0.15$ (i.e. the asset correlation that applies to mortgages). For a given PD value, a much higher proportion of assets are at risk for $R = 0.15$ compared to $R = 0.04$. This is to be expected. The PD represents the probability of default for a pool of

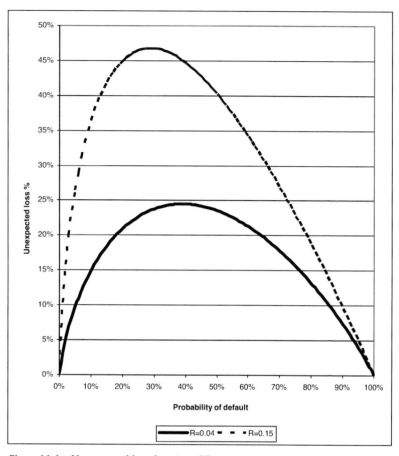

Figure 11.1   Unexpected loss for given *PD*

assets. The more highly correlated the assets are within the pool, then the greater the chance that if one of the assets defaults then so will the others. Another feature of the loss curve generated by the Vasicek formula is that as the *PD* increases from zero, at first the proportion of assets at risk increases. However, once the *PD* exceeds a certain point, then the proportion at risk begins to decrease and approaches zero as *PD* approaches 1. At first this may seem counter intuitive, but it is important to remember that the Vasicek formula gives a figure for unexpected loss, not the total loss. If you calculate that the probability that someone will default on a debt within the next 12 months is 1, then this means you expect the customer to default with absolute certainty. You should therefore, have set aside provision against it. Consequently, the unexpected loss is zero.

For a more detailed explanation of calculating credit risk using the IRB approach see the BASEL committees guidance notice (Bank for International Settlements 2005).

11.5.3 Definition of default

An important question that an organization must ask itself is, what is our definition of default? The BASEL Accord assumes a backstop position that any credit agreement that is 180 or more days past due should be considered to be in default, and a UK based lender that wishes to use the IRB approach must include 180 days past due within its default definition. In some circumstances default may be defined as less than 180 days past due, but an organization would need to argue a good case to the regulator before being allowed to do so.

Days past due is one of two drivers of default definitions. The second driver is 'ability to pay' factors. An 'ability to pay' factor is something that indicates that a customer is likely to default, even if they are currently up-to-date with repayments or only in mild arrears. In the UK, the Financial Service Authority specifies that where a customer is bankrupt, where a debt has been restructured (re-aged) or interest payments suspended; the loan should be treated as a case of default regardless of the arrears position. Individual organizations can also include additional ability to pay factors within their default definition if they believe that these factors are strongly correlated with default. For example, accounts that are found to be fraudulent can generally be expected to default even if the account is currently up-to-date. It would therefore, be reasonable to use confirmed fraud as an ability to pay factor.

11.5.4 Calculating probability of default (*PD*)

Estimates of *PD* should be based on organizations' internal rating systems and subject to use test. This means that the process an organization uses to assess the creditworthiness of individuals should also be used to drive their calculation of *PD*. Under normal circumstances it is not acceptable to develop models specifically to calculate *PD* for capital requirements calculations, which are then not used to make decisions about how customers are treated within the business. In practice, this means that most organizations use a combination of their application and behavioural credit scoring systems; as described in Chapters 4, 5, 6 and Appendix A as the basis of their *PD* calculations.

Individual estimates of default probability, such as those generated by application and behavioural credit scoring systems, can not be used directly in conjunction with the Vasicek formula. This is because the Vasicek formula provides loss estimates for pools of assets. It does not generate loss estimates for individual loans. Therefore, loans with similar credit scores must be grouped into homogenous risk groups (risk grades). The *PD* value used within the Vasicek formula is then taken to be the average default probability for all loans within the risk grade. How loans are assigned to risk grades is each organization's individual responsibility. However, some popular methods for assigning loans to risk grades are:

- Mechanical segmentation. An automated process, such as Classification and Regression Trees (CART) is applied. This places loans with similar attributes within the same risk grade (See Appendix A for more information about CART).
- Risk grade amalgamation. A large number of risk grades (perhaps 50–100 or more) are defined initially. The *PD* for each grade is calculated, and the grades sorted in *PD* order. Tests of statistical significance (t-tests) are performed to see if *PD* values of adjoining risk grades have significantly different values from one another. If there is no significant difference between the *PD*s, then the two grades are amalgamated into one. The process is repeated until the differences in *PD* between all of the remaining risk grades are statistically significant.
- Doubling of odds. A common policy is to assign risk grades such that the odds of default (The ratio of non-default to default cases) doubles in each risk grade. For example, for the highest risk grade the odds might be 1:1 (50 percent chance of loans in this grade defaulting within the next 12 months). The next risk grade has odds of 2:1 (33.33 percent chance of loan default), the next 4:1, then 8:1 and so on.
- Business sensible groupings. There may be some loans that should be grouped together (or excluded from certain risk grades) due to operational or business reasons.

Regardless of the method employed, most organizations end up with somewhere between 10 and 20 risk grades.

A further requirement of the regulator is that the value of *PD* for each risk grade must represent the long run *through the cycle* (TTC) position; that is, the *PD* estimate for each risk grade must be the average probability of default measured across the economic cycle, covering periods of growth and periods of recession. The application and behavioural scoring systems that are used to assess individuals' creditworthiness are *point in time* (PIT) rating systems. They generate estimates of the likelihood of loan default at a single point in time, and these estimates will vary as the economy changes. This means that in their raw form credit scoring systems do not provide through the cycle estimates. If the economy is booming, then the *PD* estimates made by credit scoring systems are typically lower than the through the cycle average. Likewise, if the economy is in recession then the estimated *PD*s tend to be higher than average. It is therefore necessary to transform credit scoring generated point in estimates of default into through the cycle estimates of *PD*.

The preferred way to transform credit scores into through the cycle estimates is to apply the organization's incumbent credit scorecards to historical account data, as illustrated in Table 11.2.

Table 11.2   Calculating through the cycle *PD*

Date risk grade assigned	Default rate 12 months after risk grade assigned				
	Risk grade 1	Risk grade 2	Risk grade 3	...	Risk grade 20
May 1999	55.45%	25.90%	12.22%	...	0.02%
June 1999	54.12%	25.44%	12.85%	...	0.03%
July 1999	53.92%	26.70%	13.01%	...	0.02%
...	...	...	...	...	...
...	...	...	...	...	...
February 2009	58.97%	28.98%	13.86%	...	0.04%
March 2009	57.77%	28.17%	13.59%	...	0.05%
April 2009	58.04%	28.01%	14.04%	...	0.04%
Average (TTC) default rate	55.56%	27.23%	12.89%	...	0.04%

Table 11.2 has been produced using monthly snapshots of data from the organization's account management system for a ten year period between May 1999 and April 2009. For the sake of argument, assume that the current date is April 2010 and the organization has chosen ten years because it believes that this is sufficient to cover the last economic cycle, based on national economic indicators such as unemployment, interest rates and GDP, which are published by the government. Accounts from each snapshot have then been assigned to one of 20 risk

grades, based on the behavioural credit scores they received at the time when the snapshot was taken. The number of defaults that were observed in each risk grade in the following 12 months was then divided by the total number of accounts to give the default rate. The average (through the cycle) *PD* for each risk grade is taken to be the average default rate, calculated across the entire ten year period.

The problem with this approach is the amount of data required. To generate complete through the cycle estimates it is necessary to calculate credit scores going back more than ten years. IT systems are constantly evolving, and many organizations are unable to apply the credit scoring systems they use today to account records from many years ago. Much of the information required to calculate the scores will not have been maintained historically. Arguably, organizations could use the credit scores that where available at the time when snapshots were taken as a surrogate for the scores generated by their current system, but even this data is not stored by many organizations. Consequently, many lenders have been forced to use estimated rather than actual through the cycle figures as inputs to their *PD* calculations.

The most popular estimation method when full data is not available is the variable scalar approach. The variable scalar approach assumes that while detailed account data may not be available for calculating credit scores and hence risk grades, there is information available about general trends in default rates over time. This information may come from an organization's own records or from external industry sources. For example, the Council of Mortgage Lenders in the UK maintains information on mortgage arrears, defaults and repossessions for a period going back more than 25 years. This means that average though the cycle *PD*s can be calculated for the entire UK mortgage portfolio (although not for individual risk grades). It also means that it is possible to establish how default rates today compare to the historic defaults rates that were observed throughout the economic cycle. Organizations then use the relationship between current and historic default rates to adjust their current point in time estimates. So, if industry average default rates observed today are 20 percent higher than the through the cycle average, then this would suggest that each organization should revise its *PD* estimates downwards by 20 percent to give a through the cycle figure.

The main problem that regulators have with the variable scalar approach is that it relies on a number of assumptions. If industry wide data (such as the UK Council of Mortgage Lenders data) is used to derive long run averages, then a natural assumption is that the trend in defaults seen in this data also apply to individual lender's data; that is, an individual lender's portfolio is near the industry norm. If not, then some further adjustment must be made to account for the difference. Assumptions must also be made about how the scalars are applied to individual risk grades. As a rule, loans in risk grades with low default rates display very different through the cycle behaviour than grades with high default rates, in terms of the magnitude of the differences between the top and the bottom of the economic cycle. Therefore, organizations need to apply different scalars to each risk grade. It is the responsibility of individual organizations to demonstrate to the regulator that their method for doing this is sound.

11.5.5 Calculating exposure at default (*EAD*)

The exposure at default (*EAD*) is the amount that a customer owes at the point when default occurs. *EAD* includes the current balance, plus any additional credit that may be advanced prior to default. Accrued interest, charges and fees must also be taken into account. The accord tends to be conservative in nature. Consequently, estimates of *EAD* are not allowed to include any repayments that might be made prior to default. In practice, this means that the *EAD* can not be less than the current value of the loan.

For mortgage and loan products estimating *EAD* is relatively straight forward. *EAD* can be calculated as a function of:

- Current loan amount outstanding.
- The estimated time to default. It is insufficient to simply assume the position that default will be in six months time (i.e. half way between now and 12 months). Consideration must be given to the current arrears status, the organization's definition of default and any other factors that affect the time to default. For example, if the default definition is based on accounts hitting 180 days past due (six months) and an account is currently up-to-date, then the time to default will be somewhere between six and 12 months, suggesting an average time of nine months. However, if an account is already three months in arrears, then the time to default is likely to be lower. Ideally, an organization will examine historical account data to determine how long accounts of different types (in different states of arrears) take to reach a state of default.
- The contractual rate of interest, applied from now until the estimated time of default.

- Fees and charges incurred prior to default. For example, late fees, letter charges, court costs and so on. Note that fees and charges incurred following default should be included with in the *LGD* calculation, rather than the *EAD* calculation.

A simple *EAD* calculation might be something along the lines of:

$$EAD = B * (1 + A)^{T_i} + P * T_i$$

where:

  B is the outstanding balance on a loan.
  T is the average time to default (in months) for an account in arrears status i (i months past due). Note that T_i will generally be smaller for accounts that are in a worse arrears status because they will move to default more quickly than up-to-date accounts.
  A is the contractual rate of interest, expressed as a percentage.
  P is the average monthly penalty charges and other fees applied.

For revolving credit products the calculation of *EAD* is less straight forward. A customer who is in, or is approaching, financial difficulty is likely to use a significant proportion of any headroom between their current balance and their credit limit before they default. In theory, someone may have a zero balance on their credit card today, be offered a credit limit increase next month, and then use their entire credit line before they default. Therefore, in addition to the aforementioned factors, providers of revolving credit also need to estimate how much of the available credit facility will be used prior to default. This will typically be done by taking a sample of customers who defaulted, segmenting them into different groups and observing the changes in customer balances that occurred in each group in the months prior to default. These estimates are then used to calculate conversion factors, representing the proportional increase between the original balance and the balance at default.[6] These conversion factors can then be applied to accounts today, to estimate the increase in balance that can be expected to occur in cases of default.

As for *PD*, *EAD* should be calculated for homogeneous groups. Some organizations interpret this as meaning that separate *EAD* conversion factors should be calculated for accounts within each risk grade. However, an alternative is to use historical data to produce statistically derived forecasting models (similar in principle to credit scoring models as described in Appendix A) to generate individual *EAD* estimates for each loan. Loans with similar *EAD* estimates are then grouped together.

11.5.6 Calculating loss given default (*LGD*)

Estimates of *PD* and *EAD* cover events that occur within the next 12 months. Loss given default on the other hand has no specified time limit over which it is measured. Following default, debts can continue to be recovered for many years, and it is up to each organization to decide the time following default over which it will measure *LGD*. From a regulatory perspective, the shorter the time period the better, because less recoveries will be made, meaning a higher loss and hence a larger capital requirement. For a lender, the longer the period the better because more recoveries will be made, and hence a lower capital requirement. Naturally, lenders will therefore tend towards longer periods for measuring *LGD*. However, as with *PD*, many organizations do not have detailed recovery information going back many years. In practice, some organizations measure recoveries over a 12 month period following default, but many use 3–5 years or more.

To accurately calculate *LGD* it is necessary to have an idea about how different types of defaulted debts will be dealt with and the recovery rates and costs of different types of debt recovery action. For example, what types of debt will be sold, which will be collected in-house and which will be outsourced to third party debt collectors.

The accord requires estimates of *LGD* to be based on a 'downturn scenario'; that is, recovery rates on defaulted loans are lower when the economy is in a downturn, and a downturn scenario must be considered when *LGD* calculations are made. The downturn scenario is particularly important for providers of secured credit (mortgages), as losses will be highly correlated with the sale value that the lender can achieve for repossessed properties.

11.5.7 Stress testing

Estimates of risk weighted assets (and hence capital requirements) must be subject to stress testing. Stress testing means that organizations must be able to demonstrate how their capital requirement will change, should there be significant micro or macro economic changes that effect their portfolios. In particular, regulators require organizations to estimate by how much their capital requirement is likely to change in a 1:25 year 'moderate downturn' scenario. In theory, *LGD* should already represent the loss given default for the 1:25 scenario, and *EAD* tends to be relatively invariant to the economic cycle. Therefore, stress testing tends to focus primarily (but not solely) on *PD*.

There are several approaches to stress testing. Probably the most popular is scenario testing. An organization will come up with a list of scenarios that it thinks might occur over the next 25 years. Each scenario will consider factors that may have an effect on the *PD*, *EAD* or *LGD*, such as gross domestic product, exchange rates or unemployment rates. Historical data can be used to derive likely scenarios – such as what happened to unemployment in the last recession, but the scenarios must be forward looking; that is, just because something did/did not happen in the past does not necessarily mean it will/will not happen in the future, and it is future events that are important. An estimate is then made of the effect that each scenario is likely to have on an organization's capital. Some possible scenarios might be:

- Scenario 1. In the last recession, the *PD* estimates generated by our credit scoring models were typically 5 percent lower than the observed default rate. Therefore, we will multiply all *PD* estimates by 1.05 and see what the effect is on our capital requirements.
- Scenario 2. We believe that house prices may fall by up to 15 percent in the next 12 months. Therefore, we will assume a 15 percent reduction in house prices for calculating *LGD* for our mortgage book.
- Scenario 3. With unemployment increasing from 5 to 10 percent of the workforce, and central bank interest rates increasing from 4 to 6 percent, we estimate that 40 percent of loans will migrate downwards by one risk grade.

Coming up with robust scenarios is not straightforward. The regulator will require convincing that the set of scenarios that have been considered are representative and comprehensive. The amount of statistical analysis and forecasting required, based on historical micro and macro economic trends, should not be underestimated. Scenarios should also consider 'One off' events such as a war or a flu pandemic and the effect that such events may have.

Rather than coming up with a fixed list of scenarios, a more advanced approach is to use a process called Monte Carlo Simulation to generate many different scenarios at random. The basic assumption is that the distribution of the factors that affect *PD*, *LGD* and *EAD*, such as unemployment and interest rates, follow known distributions. Values from each distribution are selected at random and these are used to adjust the values of *PD*, *LGD* and *EAD* that are input to the Vasicek formula. The process is repeated many times using different, randomly selected inputs. The outputs of the Vasicek formula from each different set of inputs is a distribution of risk weighted assets values, and hence capital requirements. Statistical measures such as the mean and standard deviation of the observed distribution can then be calculated. This allows confidence limits to be applied to determine the value of risk weighted assets and the capital requirement associated with the 1:25 year scenario.

The biggest hurdle to successful application of Monte Carlo Simulation is being able to convince the regulator that the choice of distributions used are representative of the patterns of behaviour that are present in the real world situations.

11.6 Regulatory response

Each year organizations must submit details of their capital requirements to the regulatory authorities. The regulator then decides whether or not an organization's capital reserves are adequate. In the UK all banking institutions must undertake an Internal Capital Adequacy Assessment Process (ICAAP) at least once a year, and provide the results to the Financial Services Authority. The ICAAP covers the full BASEL II capital requirements process that includes credit, market and operational risk. The ICAAP must also cover details of the organization's long term capital strategy; that is, in addition to a precise figure of their capital requirement now, organizations must also have a long term view about how their capital might change over the next three to five years or more, and have plans in place to deal with any shortfalls that are envisaged.

The Financial Services Authority uses the ICAAP as an input to its Supervisory REview Process (SREP) to assess each organization's capital position. The starting point of the SREP will be the ICAAP, but the SREP will involve further significant dialogue and investigation to ensure that any questions that the regulator has about the ICAAP are answered to their satisfaction.

A key principle of the BASEL II Accord is that an organization's senior management should take responsibility for capital requirements and be fully aware of the risks that their organization faces. Therefore, the regulator would typically expect senior managers and board members to contribute to the ICAAP/SREP process. Regulators take a dim view if oversight of the ICAAP is delegated to less senior staff within an organization.

Following the SREP, the regulator will issue an organization with Capital Guidance. If the regulator feels that there are any inadequacies

in the way in which an organization has calculated its capital requirements, or there are any risks that have not been covered or stress testing
has not been sufficiently comprehensive, then the regulator can demand
that additional capital is maintained to cover these shortcomings.

11.7　The future of capital requirements and Basel II

Given the worldwide banking crisis of 2007/8, the BASEL II Accord
clearly failed in its task of making the banking system more secure
against unexpected shocks. Arguably, more stability would have resulted
if organizations had simply continued to use the old version of the
standardized approach that was in place prior to BASEL II. Why did
BASEL II fail? There is no single reason and blame can not be placed at
any one door. However some contributory factors were:

- Complexity. One conclusion drawn by the Turner Report, produced
  by the UK government to determine the causes of the banking crisis,
  was that the complexity of the capital requirements framework
  meant that it was not well understood by many senior bankers
  (Financial Services Authority 2009 p. 22).
- Over reliance on mathematics. In the past, bankers with many years
  experience would apply their expert opinion to help inform their
  organizations about the risks they faced and the capital position
  that they should take. With the implementation of the new accord,
  far greater emphasis was placed on the raw numbers that came out
  of the capital requirements formulas. Less emphasis was placed on
  the expert opinion of senior bankers.
- Light touch regulation. In many countries regulators adopted a hands
  off approach, trusting the calculations made by banking institutions
  to be adequate.

Another criticism that has been levelled at the accord is that it exasperates
the problem of procyclicity. The mechanics of the accord means that in
times of economic downturn banks are forced to increase their capital
reserves and restrict their lending activities. This is just at the time when
individuals and businesses are most in need of new lines of credit.
Consequently, downturn conditions are made worse than they otherwise would be because individuals and businesses that can not obtain
new credit respond by reducing their expenditure. A widely accepted
view is that the accord should be amended so that a 'capital buffer' is
built up by banks in the good times, that can then be used to cover

losses and allow them to continue lending when the economy takes a downturn, thus damping the pro-cyclic effect.

At the time of writing,[7] these and other issues are being considered by national and international regulators. It is very likely that in the months following publication of this text there will be a revised Basel II or Basel III Accord, that will result in significant changes in the way in which banking institutions calculate their capital requirements.

11.8 Chapter summary

If a deposit taking institution becomes insolvent, then there is a considerable risk that depositors will lose their money and/or the banking system will become unstable. To reduce the risk of such events, deposit taking institutions are required to hold an amount of capital, in addition to provisions, in reserve to cover any unexpected losses that they might incur. This extra capital is referred to as their capital requirement.

The BASEL II Capital Accord has been adopted by regulatory authorities around the world for determining the minimum amount of capital that deposit taking institutions must hold against unforeseen events that might otherwise cause them to become insolvent. As a minimum, institutions must maintain sufficient capital such that the capital ratio is greater than or equal to 8 percent.

An institution is allowed to calculate the value of its risk weighted retail credit assets in one of two ways. These are the standardized approach and the advanced IRB approach. The standardized approach is the simplest, with the regulatory authorities providing the risk weights to apply to different types of asset. With the advanced IRB approach, an organization uses its own internal estimates of the probability of default (PD), the exposure at default (EAD) and the loss given default (LGD). This means that for organizations where the likelihood of customers defaulting is low, less capital should be required than if the standardized approach is adopted. The downside of using the advanced IRB approach is that organizations must hold very detailed financial information about the historic status of their customer's credit accounts and are subject to far more stringent regulatory oversight than those that apply the standardized approach. Many organizations have traditionally not held all of the data required for the IRB approach. They have either had to expend considerable time and cost upgrading their systems, or taken a pragmatic decision to apply the standardized approach, even if this means they need to maintain more capital than would be required under the advanced IRB approach.

Appendix A   Predictive Models of Consumer Behaviour

This appendix describes methods for constructing predictive models of consumer behaviour (also referred to as scoring models, credit scorecards or scorecards, and these terms are used interchangeably in the text that follows). The first part discusses problem formulation and the nature of the data sets employed. The second part describes the modelling approaches that are most commonly used by practitioners within the financial services industry. It is assumed the reader has some knowledge of mathematics and/or statistics.

A.1   Problem formulation

The objective is to generate a model that predicts future (or otherwise unknown) behaviour based on information currently known about individuals. This might be the likelihood that someone will respond to a mailing or the probability that a credit card application is fraudulent. Decisions about how to manage relationships with people are then made on the basis of the resulting model estimate (the score). Decisions may be based on a single score representing one type of behaviour, or several scores used in combination.

The most popular approach is to treat behaviour as a binary classification problem. Information about individuals is captured at time T (the sample point) and their behaviour recorded at time $T+t$ (the outcome point).[1] For some behaviour, such as response to a marketing text, t may be just a few hours. For other types of behaviour, such as defaulting on a credit agreement, t may be many months or years. Individuals are then classified based on their behaviour between T and $T+t$. An individual is classified as 'good' if they exhibited behaviour considered desirable and 'bad' otherwise. Often a third 'indeterminate' category is defined where the good/bad classification is for some reason ambiguous. However, indeterminates usually represent only a small proportion of the population and are usually ignored.[2] For modelling purposes goods are usually assigned a value of 1 and bads a value of 0 (or vice versa). Classification or regression methods are then applied to generate a model of good/bad behaviour. With some approaches the score generated by the model can be interpreted as an estimated probability of good or bad, but this is not true for all approaches.

A.2   Data sets and sampling

Consumer credit data sets are typically a mixture of continuous, semi-continuous and categorical variables. These are collected from a variety of sources such as the organization's prospects database, the application processing system, the account management system and credit reports obtained from credit reference agencies. Data sets are often large and highly dimensional, containing millions of records and hundreds of variables. Consequently, models have traditionally been constructed using samples rather than full populations.[3]

Robust models can be built using a few hundred cases of each class and around 1,500 to 2,000 of each class (including any validation sample) is sufficient to build good quality models (Lewis 1992; Siddiqi 2006 p. 29). However, better models usually result from taking samples several times larger than this if enough data is available (Finlay 2006). Class priors are usually uneven, and therefore, stratified sampling is recommended to ensure sufficient numbers of each class. Observations are then weighted so that the distribution of goods and bads is representative of the population from which the sample was taken.[4]

A.2.1   Development and validation samples

Given the large samples often available, a development/holdout validation methodology is standard practice. The sample taken for model construction will be split into two parts: Typically, 80 percent will be assigned as the development sample and the remaining 20 percent of cases as the holdout sample. Competing models are developed using only the development sample. The holdout sample is then used to compare the performance of each model to find out which one is best. Any decisions about how the model will be used should be based on the properties of the holdout sample.

A.2.2   Out of time sample

The performance of models of customer behaviour have a tendency to deteriorate over time due to changes in consumer population and/or changes in the relationship between individual predictor variables and the modelling objective. Consequently, a model constructed using data taken from a sample window 1–2 years in the past is not likely to perform as well as the performance metrics, calculated using the holdout sample, suggest.

A standard strategy to mitigate against population changes is to take an additional 'out-of-time' sample, towards the end of the model construction process. It may take many months from the time when the development and holdout samples are taken before a final model is ready for implementation. Therefore, a more recent sample of data can be taken just prior to model implementation. The performance of the model can then be evaluated using the more recent out-of-time sample. If necessary, the decisions rules based on the scores that people receive can be adjusted to take into account any observed change in model performance.

A.3   Data pre-processing

Data sets are rarely in a form that can be used without some work to prepare the data. The following sections describe the data pre-processing activities that usually need to be undertaken prior to model development.

A.3.1   Exclusions, data cleaning and new variable creation

In some cases it is prudent to exclude certain observations or variables from the data set. Typical exclusion reasons are:

- If it is known that operationally policy rules will be applied to override the model score. Consider a model that is being constructed to assess the creditworthiness of new loan applications. If a decision has been taken that in future loans will only be granted to people earning more than $20,000, then there is no point including observations where the income is below $20,000 in the model development sample.

- If the data set contains variables that will not be available operationally. This often occurs due to changes in data capture processes resulting in information that was available at the sample point no longer being collected[5] or new legislation that prohibits the use of certain data items.
- If an observation is classified as 'Not taken up'. Not taken up is when someone applies for credit and is deemed creditworthy, but then decides not to take up the offer.

Typical data cleaning activities include:

- Coding missing and invalid data to standard default values. Data may be missing or incorrect for a number of reasons. For example, for the variable Time in Current Employment, values could be missing because the question was asked on paper based application forms, but not for phone applications. Alternatively, it could be missing because it was asked on the application form, but not provided by the applicant. Values can also be assumed to be incorrect if they are negative or greater than the age of the applicant, or a value exists when the applicant has stated that they are not currently employed.
- Removal of duplicate data items. If the data set has been collated from a number of different sources, the same variable may feature more than once.

There may also be a requirement to derive new data items that provide a better representation of the data. For example, for a credit card the data set may contain the variables Previous Month Statement Balance and Payments Received This Month. Both variables may be predictive, but the ratio of Payments Received This Month to Previous Month Statement Balance is usually more predictive because it gives an indication of what proportion of their balance someone repays. Deciding what new variables to code is often based on experience rather than any mechanical process and can involve a great deal of trial and error.

A.3.2   Formatting of the independent variables

The most widely accepted practice is to use dummy variables for model construction (Hand and Henley 1997). A dummy variable approach can lead to better models than using either raw or transformed versions of the variables (Hand and Adams 2000). This is because dummy variables tend to provide a very good way of approximating non-linear features of a dataset using a set of linear components.

There are several different approaches to defining dummy variables. The simplest, which is generally adequate for most problems, is to create one dummy for each level within a categorical variable, and to segment continuous variables into between 5 and 20 ranges, where each range contains an equal proportion of the population (the actual number of ranges will be problem specific and deciding how many dummies to have tends to be based on expert opinion). In order to generate robust models a general rule of thumb is that each dummy should contain at least 25 cases of each class (and ideally more than 50). In cases where there are considered to be too few observations, two options are available. The first is to ignore the relevant category and exclude it from the modelling process. The second is to 'coarse classify' the variable. This means that a decision is made to combine two or more categories and represent them with a single dummy variable. For example, consider the variable marital status[6] as shown in Table A.1.

Table A.1 Distribution of cases across variable categories

| Category | Marital status | | | | |
	Number of goods	Number of bad	Total	Good:bad odds	Bad rate
Single	4,045	515	4,560	7.85	11.3%
Married	5,492	394	5,886	13.94	6.7%
Divorced	1,989	324	2,313	6.13	14.0%
Separated	189	24	213	7.88	11.3%
Widowed	783	86	869	9.10	9.9%
Cohabiting	2,896	260	3,156	11.14	8.2%
Total	**15,394**	**1,603**	**16,997**	**9.60**	**9.4%**

In Table A.1 there are only 24 bad cases in the separated category. Therefore, it is prudent to combine the separated category with another. This may be done on the basis of expert opinion, in which case to group separated and divorced together would seem sensible. An alternative is to group separated with the category with which they are most similar in terms of the bad rate (or good:bad odds). In this case those who are single. Another option is to calculate measures of how well the set of dummy variables for marital status differentiates between goods and bads for every possible coarse classification, and to choose the one that generates the best measure of discrimination. Common examples of the statistics used include Fischer's information value, the chi-squared statistic and Somer's D concordance statistic, as described by Thomas et al. (2002 pp. 132–4).

Two major criticisms have been voiced against using dummy variables. The first is the increase in the dimensionality of the problem and the corresponding increase in the computational effort required to estimate a model. This used to be a very significant problem when computer processing power was more limited, but today computational effort is rarely an issue when using standard modelling approaches such as logistic regression. The second problem is that it is common for some of the parameter coefficients of the model to have values that do not confirm with the univariate patterns that have been observed; that is, a monotonic increasing or decreasing trend will have been seen in the relationship between an independent variable and the dependent variable, but this pattern is not replicated by the parameter coefficients that enter the model. For example, when building a model of creditworthiness, it may be observed that older people are always more creditworthy than younger people – there is a monotonic increasing relationship between age and good repayment behaviour. Imagine that the model developer decides to define five dummy variables spanning the age ranges 18–25, 26–39, 40–54, 55–64 and 65+. The five dummy variables (along with any other variables) are used to generate a model with the following parameter coefficients:

–0.23, (for ages 18–25)
+0.00, (for ages 26–39)
+0.15, (for ages 40–54)
+0.07, (for ages 55–64)
+0.24, (for ages 65+)

Although the general trend is for older people to contribute more to the score than young people, there is a 'blip' for those aged 55–64. The expectation is that the parameter coefficient should be somewhere between +0.15 and +0.24 to ensure that the trend is monotonically increasing, but with a value of +0.07 this is clearly not the case. Why does this effect occur? It could be because the dummy variable contains very few observations, which means that the variance on the parameter estimate is very wide. However, the most likely reason is because of interaction and correlation effects between variables. From a purely theoretical perspective, this is not a problem for predictive modelling if the model truly reflects the nature of the data. In practice however, many users will not accept a model that does not conform to their expectations. Therefore, the model developer may have to exclude certain variables or combine (coarse classify) and/or redefine the dummy variables in order to force the parameter coefficients to follow the patterns that the user expects to see. So in this example, the model developer may feel it appropriate to combine the dummy variables for those aged 55–64 and 65+ and reproduce the model. The net result is that in order to produce a business acceptable model, the model that is developed may be sub-optimal in terms of its predictive capability because of the compromises that have been made in relation to which variables are allowed to enter the model and/or how dummy variables have been defined.

An alternative approach that overcomes some of the problems with dummy variables is to transform the independent variables so that the relationship between each independent variable and the dependent variable is log linear – a process known as a *weights of evidence* transformation (Thomas 2000). For categorical variables the value of each attribute is replaced with the natural log of: the proportion of total population goods, divided by the portion of total population bads that fall within the attribute. For continuous variables, each variable is segmented into a number of ranges (in a similar way to the dummy creation process discussed earlier) and the weight of evidence calculated for each range. Every observation within the range is then allocated the same weight of evidence. For example, for the variable income, if 10 percent of the goods and 5 percent of the bads have incomes in the range $90K–$95K the weight of evidence for any observation with incomes in this range will be LN(10/5). The major disadvantage of using weights of evidence is that the relationships between the weight of evidence and the dependent variable are forced to be log linear. If interaction effects exist (something that is not uncommon) the model may be sub-optimal. The result is that the model will overestimate the likelihood of some groups and underestimate the likelihood of others – in credit scoring terminology the model is said to be misaligned. There are a number of methods by which misalignment can be corrected, but these tend to be crude and based on univariate adjustments to model parameters. These are discussed briefly in Appendix B, but the reader is also referred to McNab and Wynn (2003 p. 81) and Thomas et al. (2002 pp. 152–4) for further discussion of misalignment issues.

In practice, dummy variable and weights of evidence approaches tend to yield models with very similar levels of performance.

A.4   Variable selection

Given the wide use of dummy variables it is not uncommon to have data sets containing hundreds of independent variables. Therefore, it is usual to perform a variable selection process to limit the number of variables included within the final modelling process. Common methods of variable selection include:

- Univariate measures of the relationship between independent variables and the dependent variable. Examples include Fischer's Information Value and the Chi-squared statistic; that is, a test of between group means is performed with a large value of the test statistic indicating a strong relationship. Only the most predictive variables are selected for inclusion. Univariate methods suffer from the drawback of not taking into account correlations or interactions between variables.
- The use of expert opinion to discard variables which, for whatever reason, the expert does not believe should be included within the model.
- The use of a stepwise procedure to select statistically significant variables. There are two main criticisms of stepwise procedures. First, they can lead to over fitting when sample sizes are small (Harrell et al. 1996). Second, they can result in an unstable selection of variables within explanatory models, in the sense that very small changes to the data set can lead to different variables being selected. However, for predictive modelling stepwise procedures are less controversial (Menard 1995 p. 63). For procedures such as logistic regression, a stepwise procedure can be included within the modelling process. For methods such as neural networks, a stepwise (regression) procedure may be applied to produce the sub-set of variables used as inputs to the network.

Given the increase in computer power in recent years the need for dimension reduction for computational reasons has become redundant for approaches such as discriminant analysis, linear regression and logistic regression for all but the very largest problems. It is possible to create models using tens of thousands of observations and hundreds of variables in a few seconds using a standard PC. However, there are a number of non-computational reasons for using variable selection methods. These include reducing multicolinearity and over fitting,[7] and for creating models that contain as few variables as possible, thus simplifying operational issues associated with implementation and testing. In some situations there may also be political, ethical or legal concerns about the use of certain variables. In these situations, where a high level of colinearity exists, a suitably applied variable selection procedure may enable suspect variables to be excluded without a significant reduction in model performance.

A.5   Methods of model construction

There is a considerable body of literature describing a wide range of different approaches to modelling consumer behaviour. However, the approach adopted by most practitioners tends to come from a set of well established techniques that can be applied using statistical packages such as SAS, SPSS and STATA. The basic principles underpinning the six most popular approaches to modelling consumer behaviour: discriminant analysis, linear regression, logistic regression, survival analysis, neural networks and classification and regression trees, are described in the sections that follow. The following conventions have been adopted:

- X is a column vector of k independent variables $(x_1, x_2,..., x_k)$.
- B is a row vector of k parameters $(b_1, b_2,..., b_{k-1})$ such that:

  $B.X = b_1 x_1 + b_2 x_2 + ..., + b_{k-1} x_k$
- Y is the dependant variable; that is, 1 or 0 representing the good and bad classes respectively.
- S is the output of the model (the score).

A.5.1   Discriminant analysis

The objective of discriminant analysis is to determine the class to which an individual belongs, based on the individual's observed characteristics. With Linear Discriminant Analysis (LDA) the probability density function of the two classes are assumed to be multivariate normal distributions with k means vectors u_1 and u_2 and common covariance matrix Σ (Lachenbruch 1982), the discriminant score function is then defined as:

$$S = [X - 0.5(u_1 + u_2)]^T \Sigma^{-1}(u_1 - u_2)$$

Where the covariance matrices of the two classes are not equal, Quadratic Discriminant Analysis (QDA) should be used instead:

$$S = 0.5 Ln \frac{|\Sigma_2|}{|\Sigma_1|} - 0.5(X - u_1) \Sigma_1^{-1}(X - u_1) + 0.5(X - u_2) \Sigma_2^{-1}(X - u_2)$$

Observations are then classified as good if:

$$S > \ln \frac{p_2}{p_1} \tag{1}$$

otherwise they are classified as bad, where p_1 and p_2 are the prior probabilities of an observation being good and bad respectively. Discriminant analysis is popular with practitioners, but has been criticized because many of the underlying model assumptions are found not to apply for consumer credit problems (Eisenbeis 1977; Eisenbeis 1978). However, as Eisenbeis explains, this is only important if the model is used along with statistical tests of significance in relation to the parameter estimates or the predicted values. In most consumer credit applications these tend not to be important issues. This is because what are of interest are the properties of the overall score distribution based on large number of observations, not individual point estimates.

A.5.2   Linear regression

(Multiple) linear regression results in a linear model of the form:

$$S = \alpha + B.X \tag{2}$$

where the score, S, is an estimate of the value of the dependent variable, Y. The model constant, α, and model parameters, B, are chosen to minimize the sum of squared errors between predicted and actual observations: that is, minimize:

$$\sum_{i=1}^{N} e_i^2$$

where N is the set of observed cases and e_i is the error term for observation i, calculated as the difference between actual and predicted values $(Y - S)$. Differentiating with respect to each of the independent variables in turn produces a set of k simultaneous equations with k unknowns. Setting these derivatives to zero and solving yields the estimated values of model parameters.

Although popular, the major criticism that has been voiced over the use of linear regression is that it is an inefficient estimator of the probability of class membership. This is because model scores can be outside the range of possible probability values (0–1).

A.5.3   Logistic regression

Logistic regression is the most widely used method for constructing models of consumer behaviour. As for linear regression, the process results in a linear model as shown in equation (2). However, whereas linear regression produces an estimate of the value of the dependent variable, logistic regression produces an estimate of the probability of class membership. The model parameters are chosen such that the likelihood across the set of n observed cases is maximized; that is:

$$\text{MAX} \prod_{i=1}^{N} (S_i^{Y_i} (1 - S_i)^{(1 - Y_i)})$$

where the score, S_i, represents the posterior probability that $Y_i = 1$, calculated as a function of independent variables.

The problem of predicted probabilities lying outside the range of possible values, found with linear regression, is surmounted by applying the logit transformation:

$$Logit(Y) = Ln \frac{P(Y = 1)}{\{1 - P(Y = 1)\}}$$

For any observed case the logit function produces values of $\pm \infty$ for $P(Y = 1)$ and $P(Y = 0)$ respectively. This means it is not possible so solve the likelihood function using traditional calculus techniques. Therefore, model parameters are found using iterative methods such as the Newton-Raphson Algorithm. To obtain a probability of class membership, the inverse logit function is applied to the resulting score, S:

$$P(Y = 1) = \frac{e^s}{1 + e^s}$$

yielding values in the range $(0,1)$.

A.5.4   Survival analysis

Survival analysis examines event times associated with a given population. For example, time to death from diagnosis of a disease or the time to failure of a machine component. The two key components of survival analysis are the survival function and the hazard function. As described by Thomas et al. (2002) the survival function, $S(t)$, represents the cumulative probability of an event not having happened by a certain time; $S(t) = P(T > t)$ where t is the current time and T is the event time. If $F(t)$ is defined as $1 - S(t)$ then the density function of F is defined as:

$$f(t)\ \delta t = P(t \leq T \leq t + \delta t).$$

The hazard function is the probability of an event happening at time t given that the event has not already occurred:

$$h(t) = \frac{f(t)}{S(t)} \Rightarrow h(t)\delta t = P(t \leq T \leq t + \delta t \mid T \geq t)$$

The major developments in survival analysis occurred in the 1960s and 1970s when regression methods were first applied to produce survival distributions for individuals within a population (Harris and Albert 1991). Of particular note was the introduction of proportional hazards methods for censored regression (Cox 1972). As described by Harris and Albert, Cox's general model is:

$$p(i) = \frac{e^{(B.X_i)}}{\sum_{m \in R_i} e^{(B.X_m)}}$$

where:

> $p(i)$ is the conditional probability of observing event i from the set of R possible events.

Model parameters are found using maximum likelihood methods. For the case where the independent variables have no effect on the hazard rate; that is, where $b_1 \ldots = b_k = 0$, all individuals in the population follow the same hazard function. This can be viewed as analogous to the logistic regression case where the only parameter in the model is the constant. Cox's model was appealing because it introduced (controversially at the time) a new likelihood function, not affected by censored data. This enabled reliable forecasts of event time to be made beyond the length of the original study on which the model was based.

Survival analysis is well suited to modelling a number of different types of consumer behaviour. From a marketing perspective, knowing the time to response from a mailing campaign can assist in logistical planning in customer contact centres to optimize resource allocation and improve customer service levels. From a risk perspective, although customer performance is usually observed at a fixed point in time, the actual time when customers default varies greatly. It is also the case that in many situations, practical issues constrain the length of the observation period, and therefore events of interest continue to occur after the outcome point.[8] A survival analysis model can predict these events where a standard classifier would not.

A.5.5   Neural networks

Artificial Neural Networks (ANNs) developed from research into Artificial Intelligence. The basic component of an ANN, the perception, was developed by Rosenblatt (1958) and consisted of a single layer of inputs and one or more outputs. These single layer networks can be shown to be equivalent to general linear models and do not deal well with non-linear problems (Minskey and Papert 1969). Therefore, modern research efforts have concentrated heavily on the use of Multi Layered Perceptrons (MLPs), as shown in Figure A.1.

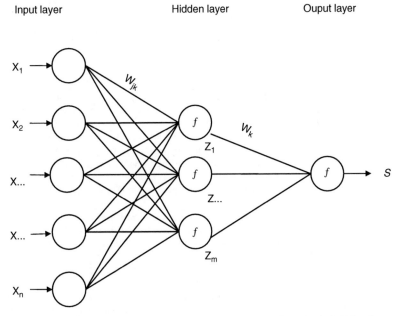

Figure A.1   Example of a multi-layered perceptron with a single hidden layer and single output

For the network in Figure A.1 the output of the perceptron is given as:

$$S = f \sum_{j=1}^{m} w_j \left(f \sum_{i=1}^{n} w_{ij} x_i \right)$$

where:

n is the number of input variables.
m is the number of elements in the hidden layer.
w_{ij} is the weight between input x_i and hidden layer neuron j
w_j is the weight between hidden neuron j and the single neuron in the output layer.
f is termed the transfer (or activation) function applied to the sum of products of inputs and weights to generate output from neurons in the network.

The transfer function is commonly chosen from the family of sigmoid functions which are easily differentiable – an important feature for training the network. The most common of these are the logistic function and the hyperbolic tangent function. The result of applying the transfer function is to normalize the output of the perceptron within the range (0,1).

The general feature of the MLP is the ability to model non-linear features of the problem space through the inclusion of one or more hidden nodes contained within one or more hidden layers. It is noted that a MLP may have more than the single hidden layer depicted in Figure A.1, and more than one output. However, a suitably structured network with a single hidden layer is able to approximate any linear or non-linear continuous function to any desired level of accuracy. In addition, most credit problems are concerned with the creation of a model that generates a single output; that is, a score representing one aspect of individual behaviour. Therefore, a network with a single hidden layer and single output is adequate for most problems found in practice.

There are two non-trivial problems involved with developing a network. The first is determining the structure of the network; that is, the number of inputs and outputs, the number of hidden layers and the number of perceptrons in each layer. This is not a precise science and there is often an element of trial and error using different network architectures to find the best network. The second problem is to determine the values of the network weights that optimize the objective function. The objective function is typically the minimization of a function of error, representing the difference between the output from the network and the observed value of the dependent variable. The error function can be represented in a number of forms, but minimized least squares is common (Haykin 1994). A number of approaches can be used to derive network weights, but the most common is back-propagation (Rumelhart et al. 1986).

There are many other parameters that are required for the construction of a MLP; for example, the activation function, the algorithm used for training and the formatting of the independent variables. In addition, the MLP is not the only network topology available (West 2000). Consequently, the literature pertaining to the design and use of neural networks is considerable. See Bishop (1995) for a detailed discussion of issues surrounding the design, training and application of neural networks.

A.5.6   Classification and regression trees (CART)

The Recursive Partitioning Algorithm was developed by Breiman and Friedman in 1973, coming to prominence in their book *Classification and Regression Trees* in 1984 (Thomas 1998). Binary splits are made recursively to produce smaller and smaller segments, with each segment containing a 'Purer' set of observations than its parent group; so that as more splits are made the resulting groups contain an increasing proportion of one of the two classes of interest. The segmentation process halts when a given set of stopping criteria are met, such as the node is >*x* percent pure, or the number of observations in the node is less than a specified minimum. A record of the segmentation process is usually captured in the form of a *classification tree* as shown in Figure A.2.

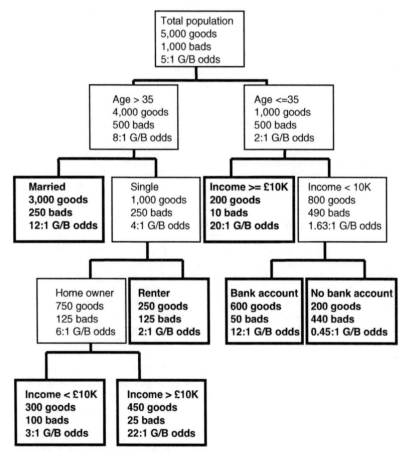

Figure A.2   Example of a classification tree

The rules for creating each branch of the tree are determined by examining the domain of all possible splits and choosing the split that maximizes the discrimination between the two classes. There are a number of possible rules available for this purpose. Details of common splitting rule are given by Thomas et al. (2002 pp. 55–9).

CART models are prone to over-fitting (Hand et al. 2002). Therefore, algorithms such as the c4.5, prune the tree to limit its size. Pruning criteria are based on the number of observations in a node or the incremental change in classification performance when a node is removed; that is, if removing a node leads to a significant loss of performance then pruning does not occur.

Classification trees are attractive because they are easy to understand and use and can utilize both continuous and categorical data. The drawback is that they do not generate a score, although the end nodes can be ranked in purity order to provide a score of sorts. For practical applications each end node of the tree will be classified according to the good:bad odds (or bad rate) associated with that node.

A.5.7   Alternative methods

Many alternative methods have been applied by researchers to classification problems in credit management. These include graphical and longitudinal models (Sewart 1997), bump hunting (Becker and Fahrmeir 2001), Markov chains (Cyert et al. 1962; Bierman and Hausman 1970), nearest-neighbour clustering algorithms (Chatterjee and Barcun 1970; Henley and Hand 1996), probit and tobit models (Grablowsky and Talley 1981), genetic algorithms (Fogarty et al. 1992; Yobas et al. 2000), linear programming (Orgler 1975), genetic programming (Ong et al. 2005) and support vector machines (Baesens et al. 2003). However, there is little evidence to suggest that any of these significantly outperform traditional methods when applied in practice, or that there is much, if any, use within the credit industry.

A.6   Assessing model performance

The primary use of consumer behaviour models is to make decisions on the basis of the model score. Therefore, credit practitioners are not very interested in standard statistical measures of model fit, such as the R^2 coefficient for linear regression or the likelihood ratio for logistic regression.[9] Instead, they are interested in the misclassification properties of the model for the cut-off score that maximizes their business objectives. Observations with scores above the cut-off will be classified as good, while observations below the cut-off will be classified as bad. In particular, two measures tend to be of greatest interest:

1. The misclassification rate/cost for the cut-off defined by the probability at score. For example, for a mailing campaign it may only be cost effective to mail individuals where the probability of them responding is at least 1 in 50. Therefore, the cut-off will be the score where the probability of response is 0.02 (1/50).
2. The misclassification rate/cost for the cut-off score that defines a pre-determined proportion of the population. For example, a provider of retail credit may wish to define a cut-off that results in 90 percent of all credit applicants

being accepted. Therefore, the cut-off score will be defined as the score above which 90 percent of the population score.

Once a cut-off score has been chosen, model performance is determined by producing a two-way classification table showing actual and predicted outcomes as shown in Table A.2.

Table A.2   Example of a 2*2 classification table

		Actual class	
		Good	Bad
Predicted class	Good (above cut-off)	A	B
	Bad (below cut-off)	C	D

Total population = $A + B + C + D$
Total correctly classified = $A + D$

The figures in Table A.2 are then used to calculate the Percentage Correctly Classified (PCC):

$$PCC = \frac{A + D}{A + B + C + D}$$

The PCC can be calculated for any given cut-off score, allowing the properties of the accept/reject population to be compared for a range of cut-off strategies. Where two competing models are being compared, the one with the highest PCC is generally taken to be the better of the two.

A.6.1   K-S statistic and GINI statistic

Sometimes the precise cut-off to be applied to a scoring model will not be known. In other situations multiple cut-off scores may be applied at different points in the score distribution. For example, where a credit reference agency develops a model that is then used by many difference lenders. In these cases, measures of group separation may be used to assess the global performance of a model in addition to, or instead of the PCC for a single cut-off.

The K-S statistic is a measure of group separation, defined as the maximum difference between the cumulative proportion of each class across the range of model scores:

$$MAX(B(S) - (G(S))$$

where $G(S)$ and $B(S)$ are the cumulative proportion of good and bad cases scoring $\leq S$ for all S. For example, for the score at which 50 percent of the bads score at or below that score and 10 percent of the goods score at or below the score, then the difference is 40. If this is the maximum difference found across all possible scores, then the K-S statistic is 40.

The Lorentz diagram or ROC (Receiver Operator Curve) is defined as the cumulative proportion of goods at score versus the cumulative proportion of bads at score over the range of model scores.[10] An example of a ROC curve is shown in Figure A.3.

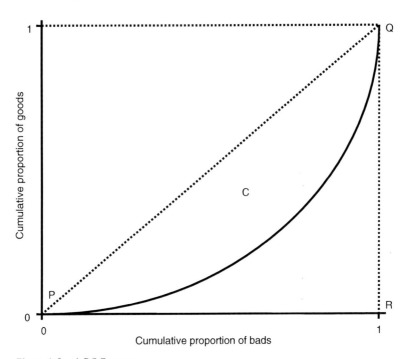

Figure A.3   A ROC curve

where G and B represent the cumulative proportion of goods and bads in each class respectively. The GINI statistic is a measure of how well the model score discriminates between good and bad cases, compared to the ideal model. Graphically, the GINI statistic can be expressed as the ratio of the two following areas of Figure A.3:

1. Region C; that is, the area between the ROC curve (represented by the curve in Figure A.3.) and line PQ. The line PQ represents the ROC curve produced from a model that provides no discrimination at all between goods and bads; that is, where the cumulative proportion of goods and bads is the same for all scores;
2. The region defined by triangle PQR. This is the ROC curve for a perfect model; that is, a model for which there exists a score where all of the bads score below the score, and all of the goods score at or above the score.

The greater the GINI the better the model. For a model that provides perfect discrimination (where the area C is equal to the area PQR) the GINI statistic will be 1. For a model that provides no discrimination the GINI statistic will be 0.

For a discrete two class population of n observations ranked by model score, the GINI statistic can be calculated using the Brown formula (also known as the trapezium rule):

$$GINI = 1 - \sum_{i=2}^{n} [G(i) + G(i-1)][B(i) - B(i-1)]$$

What can be classified as a 'Good' GINI is problem specific and one can not say that a model constructed on one population is more predictive than a model built on a different population just because the GINI statistic is higher. However, GINI statistics between 0.40 and 0.80 are common.

Note that for binary classification problems the GINI is equivalent to Somer's D concordance statistic.

A.7   Comparison of alternative modelling techniques

A feature of consumer behaviour modelling is the flat maximum effect (Lovie and Lovie 1986). The flat maximum effect exists where there are many optimal or near optimal solutions to a given objective function. Support for the existence of the flat maximum effect is strong. Several studies have concluded that the performance of many classifiers is almost identical and there is no consensus as to which is the best classifier in practice (Boyle et al. 1992; Henley 1995; King et al. 1995; Desai et al. 1996; Arminger et al. 1997; West 2000; Baesens et al. 2003). As noted by Thomas et al. (2002) results such as these should be taken as indicative only, as they are based on low dimensional data sets containing relatively few observations compared to those used in real world applications. One must also be careful not to confuse the difference between general and specific findings (Hand 2005). While there is support for a wide range of classification and regression approaches yielding very similar levels of performance on average, it may be the case that for an individual dataset one method may be substantially better than another. Therefore, for practitioners it makes sense to develop a number of competing models using different methodologies in order to see which one generates the best model for their particular problem.

There is also evidence that combining models can yield better performance than any single model on its own (Kittler 1997, 1998). So, for example, logistic regression, linear regression and neural network models could be constructed. An observation would be classed as good or bad when the majority (two or more) of the models agree. Ensemble strategies such as Bagging and Boosting have also demonstrated potential, where many different models are constructed using different sub-sets of the data and then combined (West et al. 2005).

Another important consideration is the effect of pre-processing on model performance (Crone et al. 2006). As Crone et al. observed, data pre-processing is almost never considered an important factor in comparisons of competing methods. Yet, their empirical research based on a large database from a direct mailing campaign, suggested that the type of pre-processing applied was an important (arguably the most important) feature in determining the relative performance of competing models. An example of the effect that pre-processing has on model performance, is when neural networks and logistic regression are compared. If untransformed versions of continuous independent variables are used, then a neural network will often be seen to outperform a logistic regression model. This is because the hidden neurons in the network allow non-linear features in the data to be modelled. However, if a dummy variable or weights of evidence approach is adopted, then the performance of neural networks and logistic regression is often about the same.

Given the pragmatic nature of customer modelling in an applied environment quantitative measures of performance are not the only (or even the most important) consideration when deciding which type of model to use. Thomas et al. (2001) surveyed a number of credit practitioners who had attended an industry conference. They were asked about the model features that were desirable to them and their organization. From 58 respondents, 39 said that the parameters of the model for a continuous variable (represented by a number of dummies) should normally or always follow monotonic trends. In another question, 50 respondents from a sample of 64; said that there was never a requirement for the predicted score to be in the range (0, 1) which somewhat weakens the argument favouring methods that generate probabilistic estimates over ones that do not. It also supports the case that the most important factor when measuring scorecard performance is the relative ranking of scores, not the accuracy of individual estimates of the probability of default.

One perceived advantages of simple linear classification models, such as those produced using linear and logistic regression, is the ease of understanding for non-professionals and the operational ease of explaining decisions to customers who have been declined. Detailed explanation of the working of more complex model forms such as neural networks is possible, but requires a good deal more effort to express in a format that is readily understandable by laypeople.

A.8   Reject inference

Models of consumer behaviour developed on credit applicant populations (such as those used to decide whether or not to grant credit) suffer from sample bias. This is because the outcome point data used to construct these models is only available for applicants who were granted credit. Nothing is known about how rejected applicants would have behaved if they had been accepted.[11] The effect of this bias is that a model constructed using only previously accepted cases may generate over-optimistic estimates. Therefore, when the model is applied to the entire population of credit applicants, some individuals who should be rejected because they represent a poor credit risk will be accepted.

To try and counter sample bias a process known as 'reject inference' is often applied. A sample of rejected applications where good/bad performance is unknown is included in the data set, and an estimate of how these rejects would have behaved, if they had been granted credit, is made. A final model is then constructed using all observations; that is, those with known performance who were accepted and rejected applicants whose performance has been inferred.

There are several different approaches to reject inference. Four of the most popular approaches; reject acceptance, augmentation, iterative reclassification and data substitution, are discussed here.

A.8.1   Reject acceptance

The easiest way to address sample bias is to accept some applicants who should be rejected. Repayment performance of 'accepted rejects' can then be observed and included within the model development process (Rosenberg and Gleit 1994). However, this approach is not popular due to the costs associated with accepting non-profitable customers (Thomas et al. 2002) – although the costs can be vastly reduced if only marginal cases are taken from just below the existing accept/reject cut-off rule.

A.8.2   Augmentation

Augmentation, as described by Hsia (1978), is probably the most widely used reject inference method (Banasik and Crook 2003). The key assumption underpinning augmentation is that marginal accepts that just passed the previous cut-off rule are more like the rejected population than higher scoring accepts. Therefore, by giving greater weight to marginal accepts in the modelling process, better estimates of rejects performance will result.

The first stage of the augmentation process is to construct a model to predict the likelihood of cases being accepts or rejects, based on the incumbent decision making system. In the second stage, observations in the accepted population are weighted according to the inverse probability of them having been accepted, using the probability estimates generated by the first stage model. A final model to predict good/bad behaviour is then produced using the weights assigned in the second stage. The net result is that observations that were only just accepted have the greatest influence in determining the structure of the final model.

A related approach is bi-variate probit analysis described by Heckman (1976) and demonstrated by Boyes et al. (1989) and Jacobson and Roszbach (2003). In some ways augmentation can be considered a form of boosting, in which models are repeatedly constructed with greater and greater emphasis being placed on harder to classify (more borderline) cases.

A.8.3   Iterative reclassification

Iterative reclassification is described by Joanes (1993) as follows:

Step 1. Construct a model for the accepted population, for which account performance is known. Apply this model to the rejected population and classify rejected applications as either good or bad based on the posterior probabilities from the model.
Step 2. Re-estimate the model parameters using both the accepted and rejected cases.
Step 3. Reclassify rejects using the updated model posterior probability.
Step 4. Repeat steps 2 and 3 until the difference between subsequent iterations is sufficiently small.

A common (although rarely mentioned) problem with most reject inference procedures is that they attempt to assign each reject as either good or bad. No cases are assigned to be indeterminate, which will arguably lead to an overestimate of the number of goods and bads within the total application population. An attractive feature of iterative reclassification is that it can be easily adapted to include an indeterminate class for rejects. The algorithm in step 1 is modified to assign rejects to one of three, instead of two classes.

A.8.4   Data substitution

Rejected applicants may have credit accounts with other lenders. Therefore, information about how these accounts performed can be used as a surrogate for the application that was declined (McNab and Wynn 2003 p. 58). Although attractive, this approach has a number of drawbacks. First, data about repayment behaviour with other lenders needs to be obtained, usually from a credit reference agency, which will incur cost. Second, it must be assumed that the way in which rejected customers behaved with other lenders is representative of the way they would have behaved, should their application have been accepted. Third, some individuals will have no other credit accounts. Therefore, a different reject inference method must be applied to these cases.

A.8.5   Assessment of reject inference

There are three questions about the appropriateness of reject inference. The first question is; what is the scope for reject inference? To put it another way, if information about the repayment behaviour of rejects is known, does this enable better predictive models of behaviour to be developed? In a number of papers Banasik et al. (2003), Banasik and Crook (2005) and Crook and Banasik (2004) report on their research into reject inference using a sample of accounts that should have been rejected, but were for some reason accepted. Therefore, the actual repayment performance was known. Their analysis concluded that there was indeed scope for improving the quality of decision making by having information about rejects, and this tended to be greater when the reject rate was high. Independent research by Verstraeten and Van den Poel (2005) came to the same conclusion.

Assuming there is scope to apply reject inference, the second question is; is it possible to apply reject inference to develop models that are better than models developed exclusively on the accept population? An often cited review of reject inference methods came to the conclusion that, regardless of the scope for reject inference, reliable reject inference is impossible based on information solely extracted from the development sample in question (Hand and Henley 1993); that is, using methods such as augmentation and extrapolation. Later work by Crook and Banasik (2004) agreed with these findings, concluding that augmentation is more or less useless (although in a previous paper, they did report modest improvements when using the bi-variate probit method (Banasik et al. 2003) as did Kim and Sohn (2007)). Importantly, they also concluded that in some cases reject inference could lead to worse results than if no reject inference had been applied. This is because there is potential to increase bias within the population rather than reduce it. This leads to the third question. If reject inference is applied, how is it validated? In practical application, reject performance is not available (otherwise reject inference would not be needed). Therefore, it is impossible to know whether the performance of rejects has been estimated correctly when a model is developed.

In conclusion, there is agreement that bias exists in credit application data and there is scope for reject inference to be applied. If additional data is available in the form of 'accepted rejects' or via data substitution then this is worthwhile and may allow superior models to be constructed. However, the case for applying methods such as augmentation and iterative reclassification, which are applied by many practitioners, has yet to be proved.

A.9   Calibration and presentation

In practical usage there is often a requirement to calibrate scores to a specific scale. Calibration does not affect the predictive power of a model, but is undertaken for historic and/or operational reasons. In particular, if a new model has been developed to replace an existing one, then there may be a requirement that the scores generated by the new model have the same meaning as those generated by the old model it replaces. Most credit granting institutions use logistic regression to construct their credit scoring models, but most do not apply the inverse logistic function to generate probability estimates. Instead, lending decisions are based on the untransformed score, S, which is calibrated to yield a specific relationship between the score and the good:bad odds, where the good: bad odds are defined as:

Good:Bad odds $= 1/(P(Y = 0)) - 1$

where $Y = 1$ for goods and $Y = 0$ for bads and $P(Y = 0) = 1 - P(Y = 1)$

Alternatively, a simple way to think about the good:bad odds (or just odds going forward) is that for a given population, the odds is the number of goods divided by the number of bads. If a population contains 400 goods and 100 bads then the good:bad odds are 4:1. (This is the same as saying that the proportion of bads in the population – the bad rate – is 20 percent. In fact, odds and bad rate are really different ways of expressing the same thing. The good:bad odds is equal to: $1/(\text{bad rate}) - 1)$.

Standard practice is to calibrate model scores such that the good:bad odds are A:1 at a score of B, and the odds double every C points. A very commonly used calibration scale is to have odds of 1:1 at score of 500 and for the odds to double every 20 points ($A = 1$, $B = 500$, $C = 20$). So at a score of 500 the odds will be 1:1, at 520 they will be 2:1, at 540 4:1 and so on.

The nature of the logistic regression process means that the score, S, is equal to the natural log of the odds of the development sample. A score of 1 indicates odds of e^1 (2.718), a score of 2 odds of e^2 (7.388) and so on. Therefore, for models produced using logistic regression, a calibrated score can be calculated as:

$$S_{calibrated} = \{B - (C/ln(2) *Ln(A) \} + S * C/Ln(2)$$

As the model is linear, this has the same effect as multiplying the model intercept and each of the parameter coefficients by $C/Ln(2)$ and then adding $B - (C/Ln(2) *Ln(A))$ to the value of the intercept.

For methods that don't automatically generate scores that are equal to $Ln(odds)$ – such as linear regression, then as long as the relationship between the score and $Ln(Odds)$ is approximately linear,[12] then an initial step can be undertaken to transform the score so that the score is equal to the $Ln(Odds)$. This is achieved by applying logistic regression to predict the good/bad classification, using the original score as the independent variable, to produce a model in the form:

$$S' = \alpha + bS$$

where α and b are the intercept and parameter coefficient of the logistic regression model. S' can then be used instead of S in the calibration formula to produce $S_{calibrated}$.

Following calibration, common practice is to round parameter coefficients (and hence scores) to the nearest integer. This is for two reasons. The first is historic, dating back to the time when computers had only a fraction of the processing power of modern computers and arithmetic using real numbers required 2–3 orders of magnitude more processing power than integers. The second reason is that many people find integer representations of models easy to understand. Therefore, having simple models comprising integer coefficients helps non-technical managers understand the model that their analysts have developed. Using integers does result in a slight loss of model accuracy. However, as long as the calibration scale is sufficiently large, then the effect of rounding is trivial.[13] For a typical application or behavioural credit scorecard, calibrated to odds of 1:1 at a score of 500 and a doubling of odds every 20 points, scores will typically range from around 400 to around 800; yielding about 400 possible scores that someone may receive.

The final calibrated scorecard (if developed using linear or logistic regression together with dummy variable or weight of evidence transformed predictor variables) will then be presented in a form similar to that shown in Figure A.4.

Figure A.4 is an application scorecard used to credit score applications for personal loans. A high score indicates that someone is likely to repay the loan (good), a low score that they are likely to default (bad). To generate someone's score, one starts with the constant, and then adds/subtracts points depending

Constant	+663

Applicant's age		Number of children	
<23	−49	0	0
23–27	−29	1–3	+7
28–30	−8	4+	0
31–35	0		
36–40	+6		
41–60	+17		
60+	+25	Occupation status	
		Full-time employed	0
		Part-time employed	−23
Accomodation status		Self employed	−11
Home owner	+48	Homemaker	−21
Renting	−9	Student	−48
Living at home	0	Unemployed	−85

Time at current address		Time in current employment	
< 1 year	−70	< 1 year	−71
1–3 years	−31	1–2 years	−21
4–5 years	−9	3–4 years	−8
6–8 years	0	5–7 years	0
9+ years	+30	6–12 years	0
		13–19 years	+5
		20+ years	+13
Gross annual income $		Not in employment	0
125,000+	+40		
90,000–124,999	+8	Number of credit card	
50,000–89,999	0	0	−14
30,000–39,999	−28	1	0
0–29,999	−51	2+	+8

Figure A.4   Example of a personal loan application scorecard

upon the person's attributes. So for someone aged 25, who owns their own home and has lived there for the last two years, then their initial score will be 663. 29 points are subtracted because of their age, 48 points added because they are a home owner, 31 points subtracted because of the time they had lived at their address and so on.

If the predictor variables have been transformed into dummy variables, then the points in the scorecard are just the parameter coefficients of the model after calibration has been applied. If weights of evidence transformations have been applied to the predictor variables, then the points in the scorecard are equal to the calibrated parameter coefficients of the model, multiplied by the weight of evidence for the given parameter interval. So if the weight of evidence for the attribute age <23 was –1.7 and the parameter coefficient (following calibration) was 28.231, then the points given to those aged <23 would be 28.231 * –1.733 = –48.924 (49 rounded to nearest integer).

A.10   Continuous models of consumer behaviour

Binary classification models are popular. However, in many cases the two classes of interest only approximate measures of financial interest that are relevant to lenders' strategic objectives and bottom line measures. Therefore, there is increasing emphasis on producing models that predict continuous financial measures rather than binary outcomes.

The traditional way to incorporate continuous financial information into the decision making process is to weight the results produced from a binary model of behaviour with prior information about costs and revenues. For example, when using discriminant analysis to decide which credit applicants to accept on the basis of their likelihood to default, the decision rule described in equation (1) may be augmented with average profit and loss information:

Classify as good if:

$$S > \ln \frac{Lp_2}{Rp_1}$$

where L is the average cost of misclassifying a bad as good, $L > 0$, R is the average cost of misclassifying a good as bad, $R > 0$. In general, for any method that generates likelihood estimates of class membership (such as logistic regression), the general form of the decision rule to optimize the use of the model will be:

$$S = R^* p(G/X) - L (1 - p(G/X)) \qquad (3)$$

Classify as good if $S > 0$:

where $p(G/X)$ is the posterior probability of an observation being good given X, the set of independent variables. S will therefore be positive where:

$$p(G/X)/(1 - /P(G/x)) > R/L.$$

This strategy is widely used by practitioners, but it is simplistic because it assumes a uniform distribution of R and L over the range of model scores, a situation that is rarely found to exist in practice. Therefore, a more appropriate formulation of the score function is:

$$S = E(R/X,G)\, p(G/X) - E(L/X, B)\, (1 - p(G/X)) \tag{4}$$

where $E(R/X,G)$ and $E(L/X,B)$ are the expected misclassification costs given X and the good/bad status respectively. Therefore, a practical implementation of (4) would involve building models to estimate $p(G/X)$, $E(R/X, G)$ and $E(L/X, B)$. Variations on this theme are used to estimate expected loss for the advanced IRB approach to calculating capital requirements to comply with the BASEL II Accord.

Other approaches to dealing with continuous financial measures have also been proposed. Cyert et al. (1962) adopted a Markov chain approach, looking at the probability of accounts moving between different delinquency states over a number of time intervals to forecast the amount of bad debt an account was likely to generate, and such models are now commonly used to generate provision estimates of future bad debt. The idea of using Markov processes was developed further by Thomas et al. (2001) who proposed a profit maximization model based on a Markov processes/dynamic programming approach to determine optimal credit limits to assign to accounts. Oliver and Wells (2001) and Beling et al. (2005) suggested the definition of efficient frontier cut-off strategies. This approach was based on the development of a binary classification model, but with decisions about how to manage accounts based on multiple objectives that included, expected losses, profitability and the number of new accounts opened. However, the approach that is most widely applied in practice is the one discussed in Chapter 4 and described by Thomas et al. (2002). This is to develop several binary models of different aspects of customer behaviour, such as mailing response, risk of default, product usage and attrition, which are used in combination to segment a population. Decisions are then based on the profitability profile of the resulting segments.

A.11   Implementation

Sometimes implementing a model is a relatively simple task. All that is required is to apply the model to an existing database to produce a sub-set of cases. For example, in planning a mail shot, a response model might be applied to a prospects database just once, to create a list of people where the likelihood of response is say, greater than 2 percent. The list will then be passed to whoever is responsible for producing the mail shot. In many cases however, models are used within operational systems on an ongoing basis. For example, to automatically credit score all new applicants when they apply for credit. These models form part of a business critical system that may be responsible for making billions of dollars of lending decisions each year. In situations like this, considerable planning is required across a number of business functions and the implementation may need to be scheduled months ahead to ensure correct implementation and avoid business disruption.

The first question is; how is the model to be implemented? Today, many organizations use parameterized decision engines, such as Experian's Strategy Manager and FICO's Blaze. These allow credit professionals to directly input credit scoring models and decision rules into their organization's IT systems. Most decision engines are designed to implement linear models; that is, models in the form $\alpha + b_1x_1 + b_2x_2 + ,..., + b_kx_k$. Some packages can implement other model forms such as neural networks and decision trees, but many do not. Therefore, it is imperative that consideration is given to the types of models that the decision engine can deal with at an early stage. There is no point in developing a fantastic model using a cutting edge statistical technique if it can't be implemented within the operational environment.

Another issue is data. Systems change and evolve over time, and certain data items that were available for model construction may no longer be available within the operational system. An example of this that I came across was where the model development database contained information about the number of cars in the applicant's household, and this proved to be a highly significant variable within the model. However, a few months prior to implementation a decision was taken to simplify the loan application form and the question was no longer asked. Therefore, the model could not be implemented and had to be rebuilt.

Once an implementation route has been established there is a need to test a model before it goes live. This ensures that the score is correctly calculated and that the right cut-off decisions are being applied on the basis of the score. It is surprising how often errors are introduced during model implementation, particularly from simple typing errors. For example, coding a parameter coefficient as positive rather than negative or adding an extra zero. To avoid such pitfalls a comprehensive testing facility should exist that enables a significant volume of test cases to be processed within the live system.

Testing should continue for some time after the model goes live, to confirm that scores continue to be calculated correctly, and to monitor model performance.

Appendix B   Scorecard and Portfolio Monitoring

The predictive ability of models of consumer behaviour (scorecards) deteriorate over time. This is due to economic and social effects that results in changes to the underlying relationships between the independent variables and the predicted behaviour. As a general rule, scorecards have a lifespan of between one and five years before their performance has degraded to such an extent that it's worthwhile replacing them. To determine how well a model is performing and when to replace it, financial institutions undertake monitoring of their scorecards on a regular basis. Monitoring is usually carried out on a monthly (or sometimes quarterly) basis. Each reporting period, a set of reports will be produced to identify if the following has occurred:

- Score misalignment: This is when the relationship between peoples' scores and the good:bad odds changes. If the economy enters a downturn then write-off rates will rise across the board. All other things being equal, applicants will receive the same credit score that they once did, but the probability of bad associated with this score will have increased. As a result, some credit applications with a credit score that would once have indicated that they would have been creditworthy are now uncreditworthy.
- Scorecard degradation: This is when changes in social and economic conditions leads to changes in the relationships between the independent variables and predicted behaviour. As more change occurs, so the ability of a model to discriminate between good and bad customers deteriorates.

If the monitoring reports indicate that significant changes have occurred, then corrective action will be taken. If score misalignment is observed, then it is a relatively easy process to recalibrate the model so that the desired score:odds relationship is restored.

If minor degradation in performance is observed, then small adjustments may be made to one or more of the parameters of the model to improve its predictive ability – a process sometimes referred to as 'fine tuning'. If more major changes are observed, then the usual course of action is to construct a completely new scorecard to replace the incumbent one.

In addition to scorecard monitoring, organizations also undertake portfolio monitoring. Portfolio monitoring is used to determine if any population shifts (changes to the geo-demographic make up of the population) have occurred.

Sometimes population shifts are indicative of scorecard misalignment or scorecard degradation, but this is not necessarily the case. A credit card provider may observe a doubling of credit applications from people with below average incomes, but the relationship between income and good/bad repayment behaviour, as captured in the scorecard, continues to hold true. If low income is indicative of poor credit risk, then the net result is that a higher proportion of credit applications will be rejected, even if the scorecard that the organization uses to assess credit-worthiness continues to be optimal.

Changes to the profile of a population often occur when a new marketing strategy is employed, resulting in different types of customers being targeted for the product. Likewise, changes to the competition's marketing strategies will have a similar effect.

In the remaining two sections of this appendix we take a brief look at the reporting that organizations undertake to evaluate the first two of these effects that is, score misalignment and scorecard degradation.

B.1   Score misalignment

As discussed in section A.9, models developed using linear or logistic regression usually display a linear relationship between the score and the natural log of the

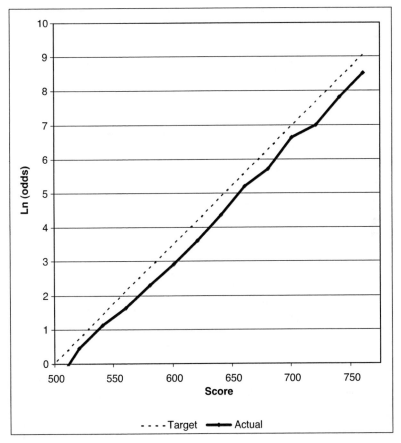

Figure B.1   Actual vs expected score odds relationship

good:bad odds. Common practice is to calibrate the model so that it yields a specific relationship between the score and the odds. The standard method for assessing score misalignment is to examine the observed score odds relationship against the target (expected) score odds relationship, as illustrated in Figure B.1.

In Figure B.1, the target score odds relationship is for good:bad odds of 1:1 at a score of 500 and a doubling of odds every 20 points, which is shown by the dotted line. The solid line shows the actual (observed) relationship between the score and the good:bad odds. The actual score odds relationship has been produced by taking a sample of accounts whose performance has been observed over a period of time.[1] Observations have been ranked by score, and segmented into about 20 intervals. The *Ln*(odds) within each score interval has then been calculated and plotted against the mean score of each interval. If the model is well aligned then the actual and target good:bad odds lines should be the same. In Figure B.1 the actual odds for any given score are consistently lower than the

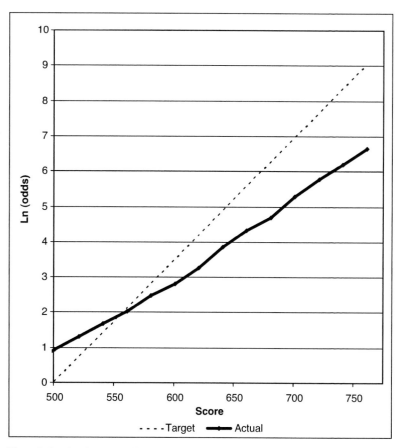

Figure B.2   Gradient misalignment

target odds. This means that the model is generating over optimistic estimates, and is described as being negatively misaligned. For example, at a score of 600, the target odds are 32:1, but the actual odds are 18.2:1. When the target and actual score:odds lines are different, but parallel, this means that all scores are too high/low by the same amount. Therefore, the misalignment can be corrected by simply applying an intercept adjustment; that is, adding/subtracting a fixed amount to the scorecard constant (the model intercept). For the model used to produce Figure B.1 a negative adjustment to the constant is required, resulting in the actual score odds line in moving to the left so that it becomes aligned with the target score odds line.

Figure B.2 illustrates a slightly different situation. In Figure B.1 the actual score:odds line was parallel to the target score odds line, meaning that a simple intercept adjustment was all that was required to re-align the scorecard. In Figure B.2 the target and actual score odds relationships have different gradients. The actual score odds line has shallower gradient than the target score odds line. This type of misalignment is corrected by applying a multiplier to all of the parameter coefficients. A multiplier >1 will increase the gradient, a multiplier <1 will decrease the gradient.

As long as the actual good:bad odds are approximately linear, then the easiest way to deal with both types of misalignment, as illustrated in Figures B.1 and B.2, is to use logistic regression to derive an intercept and gradient adjustment. This is the same process as described in section A.9 for calibrating scorecards where the score can not be interpreted directly as the *Ln*(Odds).[2]

If the actual score odds relationship is non-linear, then the calibration process is more complex. It may be possible to apply a non-linear transformation to the scorecard or alternatively, different calibrations may be applied to different sub-populations, effectively creating different scorecards for each sub-population. It should be noted that replacing a single scorecard with two or more new ones increases complexity and can result in considerable cost operationally. This is in terms of the cost of implementation/testing and ongoing monitoring. Therefore, careful consideration should be given to the costs/benefit case of taking this option – against the two alternative solutions which are:

1. To redevelop the model.
2. To adjust the decision rules around the use of the model, taking into account the change in the score odds relationship.

B.2   Scorecard degradation

Misalignment, as discussed in the previous section, is relatively easy to remedy via calibration. Deterioration in model performance on the other hand, tends to be more difficult to deal with. To determine how well the model is performing, performance measures will be calculated each reporting period. Typically, this will be measures such as the K–S statistic, GINI coefficient and/or the percentage misclassified for a given cut-off strategy, which are the same measures that were used to evaluate the model when it was originally constructed.

If one is using models with censored data – such as application scorecards to assess whether or not someone is creditworthy and should therefore be granted credit, then it is important to take the degree of censoring into account when measuring performance. This is because performance can only be measured for the part of the population that has not been subject to censoring; that is, the accepted population whose good/bad repayment performance can be observed. The better the model is at distinguishing between good and bad cases, the worse the model will appear to be using measures such as the GINI/K–S statistic, because most of the bads will have been declined, leaving a relatively homogenous pool of accepted (mostly good) cases. What this also means is that if an organization tightens it's lending criteria by raising its cut-off scores, perhaps in response to deteriorating economic conditions, then the model will appear to show less discrimination than before the change was made, even if the model is still performing optimally. The easiest way to get around this problem is to measure performance using only the highest scoring x percent of cases, where x percent or more of the population are accepted at all times. For example, an organization may see reject rates vary from between 20 and 50 percent over a number of years. Therefore, they will compare performance measures each month using only the highest scoring 50 percent, because each month there will always be at least 50 percent of the population that are accepted, and which therefore have repayment behaviour associated with them.

As a rule of thumb, if model performance has decreased by more than about 5–10 percent since the model was originally deployed, then there will be a financial case for fully redeveloping the model. If the drop in performance is of a lower order than this, then it may be possible to 'fine-tune' the model by making minor changes to one or more of the parameter estimates within the scorecard.

If model performance has decreased, then this will be as a result of changes in the underlying relationships between the independent variables and the predicted behaviour. To establish what changes have occurred, standard practice is to produce univariate (characteristic) misalignment reports for every variable that features within the model. A typical univariate misalignment report is shown in Table B.1.

Table B.1 is a univariate misalignment report for the variable: Loan amount requested/Applicant's net annual income. This variable is often a strong predictor of creditworthiness for unsecured loans and features in many application scorecards. The left most column shows the intervals in the scorecard. So the first interval (>=1.00) displays information for credit applicants that are making loan applications for amounts that are equal to or greater than their net annual income. The left hand side of the table (columns one to seven) shows the actual behaviour that was observed. Columns one through four show the total number and of accepted applications in each interval, the proportion of loans in the interval and the number of loans that subsequently displayed good or bad repayment behaviour. The next three columns show the bad rate, odds and natural log odds, calculated from the numbers of goods and bads in each interval. The right hand side of the report (columns eight to 12) shows the expected numbers of goods and bads, given the scores that individuals received, together with the expected bad rate, expected odds and expected Ln(odds). Each row in the expected columns have been calculated using the following steps:

1. Calculate the average interval score; $S_{average}$; that is, the scores for each observation in each interval are summed together and divided by the total number of cases in the interval, as given in column one.[3]

Table B.1 Univariate misalignment report

Column		1	2	3	4	5	6	7	8	9	10	11	12	13	14
				Actual					**Expected**						
Interval	Range	Total cases	% total	# Goods	# Bads	Bad rate	Odds	Ln (odds)	# Goods	# Bads	Bad rate	Odds	Ln (odds)	Delta score	Scorecard points
1	≥1.00	5,768	2.16%	3,998	1,770	30.69%	2.26	0.81	3,693	2,075	35.97%	1.78	0.58	7	−55
2	0.93–0.99	9,334	3.50%	7,072	2,262	24.23%	3.13	1.14	6,712	2,622	28.09%	2.56	0.94	6	−41
3	0.81–0.92	31,923	11.96%	28,033	3,890	12.19%	7.21	1.97	27,700	4,223	13.23%	6.56	1.88	3	−22
4	0.69–0.80	41,866	15.69%	40,666	1,200	2.87%	33.89	3.52	40,674	1,192	2.85%	34.11	3.53	0	−9
5	0.55–0.68	55,765	20.90%	54,565	1,200	2.15%	45.47	3.82	54,579	1,186	2.13%	46.00	3.83	0	−5
6	0.42–0.54	29,887	11.20%	29,215	672	2.25%	43.47	3.77	29,215	672	2.25%	43.47	3.77	0	0
7	0.35–0.42	27,133	10.17%	26,809	324	1.19%	82.74	4.42	26,826	307	1.13%	87.36	4.47	−2	15
8	0.27–0.35	26,773	10.03%	26,497	276	1.03%	96.00	4.56	26,520	253	0.95%	104.70	4.65	−3	25
9	0.10–0.26	28,805	10.80%	28,678	127	0.44%	225.81	5.42	28,701	104	0.36%	277.20	5.62	−6	37
10	<0.10	9,554	3.58%	9,514	40	0.42%	237.85	5.47	9,525	29	0.31%	325.98	5.79	−9	45
		266,808	100.00%	255,047	11,761	4.41%	21.69	3.08	3,693	4,223	4.75%	254,145	12,663		

Ratio of loan amount requested to applicant's net annual income

2. Calculate the expected Ln(odds) for the average score, using the calibration scale that the scorecard is meant to be aligned to. This is achieved by applying the calibration procedure, described in section A.9 in reverse:

$$Expected\ Ln(Odds) = [S_{average} - \{B - (C/ln(2)\ *Ln(A)\}]/\{C/Ln(2)\}$$

where, if you remember, the calibrated score has target odds of A:1 at a score of B, and the odds double every C points. Also remember that the uncalibrated score, S, was equal to $Ln(Odds)$.

3. Once the expected Ln(odds) for the interval are known, the expected (good: bad) odds can be calculated as: $e^{expected\ Ln(odds)}$, and the expected bad rate as $1/(odds+1)$. The expected numbers of bads is then just the bad rate multiplied by the total number of observations in the interval (as given in column one).

Column 14 shows the parameter coefficients in the scorecard, and column 13 is the delta score. The delta score is a measure of the misalignment (the difference) between the actual odds and the expected odds for each interval. It is calculated as:

$$\delta = C\ *\ Ln[(Actual\ odds)/(expected\ odds)]/Ln(2)$$

The delta score, δ, represents the difference between the points observations receive in practice and the points they should receive in theory, for a scorecard that is perfectly aligned with the target score odds relationship. In theory, if there is no correlation between variables within the scorecard, then the misalignment can be corrected by simply adding the delta score to the current score. So for the first interval ($>=1.00$), the misalignment would be corrected by adding seven to the scorecard points, so that in going forward observations receive -48 points, instead of the -55 points that they currently receive.

All scorecards display some level of misalignment due to random fluctuations in the sample used to monitor it. Therefore, one only tends to be concerned if the delta score for an interval exceeds acceptable tolerances. Statistical tests can be performed. For example, a chi-squared test to see if the actual and expected number of goods and/or bads are significantly different. Alternatively, one may perform a test of population proportions to see if actual and expected bad rates are significantly different. However, in practice, simple rules of thumb are often applied, such as:

$\|\delta\| < (0.125\ *\ C)$	No significant misalignment.
$(0.125\ *\ C) \le \|\delta\| < (0.25*\ C)$	Minor level of misalignment.
$(0.25\ *\ C) \le \|\delta\| < (0.5*\ C)$	Moderate level of misalignment.
$(0.5\ *\ C) \le \|\delta\|$	Serious level of misalignment.

where C is the point that doubles the odds. So in Table B.1, if the scorecard has been calibrated to a scale where 20 points doubles the odds, then intervals 1, 2, 9 and 10 show moderate misalignment and intervals 3 and 8 minor misalignment.

Usually, corrective action is only taken if moderate or serious misalignment is observed, and even in these cases action may not be taken unless the misalignment is seen consistently across several reporting periods. This is to ensure that the misalignment that is observed is not a feature of the reporting period, and is representative of a permanent shift in the relationships in the scorecard.

In practice, most variables in most credit scorecards are not correlated, or only correlated to a small degree. Therefore, simple univariate adjustments (adding or subtracting delta scores) to individual parameter coefficients can often be used to realign a scorecard, improve its predictive performance and extend its operational life by several months or years. However, if predictor variables are highly correlated with each other, and/or many intervals are misaligned across several variables, then simple univariate fine-tuning may not be sufficient, and it may be necessary to rebuild the model from scratch.

Appendix C   US and UK Legislation

This appendix lists the major national (federal) legislation relevant to the management of consumer credit agreements in the US and UK. Table C.1 details US legislation and Table C.2 UK legislation.

Table C.1   US consumer credit legislation

Act	Main points
Fair Credit Reporting Act 1970 (FCRA)[1]	Empowers individuals to obtain copies of their credit reports from a credit reference agency, and to challenge any information in their credit report that is not accurate. Prohibits the sending of unsolicited credit cards or other credit tokens to individuals without their consent.
Fair and Accurate Credit Transaction Act 2003 (FACT)	An amendment to the FCRA granting further rights to individuals to access their credit reports and to challenge the accuracy of the information they contain. It also places greater responsibilities on lenders and credit reference agencies to deal with cases of identify theft.
Truth In Lending Act 1968 (TILA)	Places an obligation on lenders to clearly state the terms of credit agreements within credit agreements and promotional materials. For example, the total charge for credit (the finance charge) and the APR must be clearly displayed.
Consumer Leasing Act 1976	An amendment to the TILA covering personal leasing agreements.
Fair Credit and Charge Card Disclosure Act 1988	An amendment to the TILA covering credit and charge cards.
Fair Credit Billing Act 1986	An amendment to the TILA, placing an obligation on credit card providers to investigate and correct errors on customers' statements. For example, if a customer reports that their statement contains details of transactions they didn't make, or if interest charges have been calculated incorrectly.

Table C.1 US consumer credit legislation – *continued*

Act	Main points
Equal Credit Opportunity Act 1974 (ECOA)	Prohibits the use of certain information in deciding who to grant credit to. This includes gender, marital status, race, colour, nationality and religion.
Fair Debt Collection Practices Act (FDCPA) 1977	Restricts the actions third party debt collectors can take to recover debt. For example, contacting people in the middle of the night and threatening behaviour.
Bankruptcy Abuse Prevention and Consumer Protection Act 2005	Updates the Federal Bankruptcy Code 1978, making it harder for individuals to file for Chapter 7 Bankruptcy.[2]
Patriot Act 2001	The Patriot Act deals with a range of legislative issues with the aim of preventing terrorism. In relation to consumer credit it requires financial institutions to verify the identity of individuals when opening new bank accounts.
Credit Card Accountability Responsibility and Disclosure Act 2009	The Act is meant to protect consumers from unfair treatment by card providers, and make the terms of credit agreements more transparent. Amongst other things, the Act requires card providers to issue statements at least 21 days before payment is due and to give customers at least 45 days written notice before changing interest rates or other charges.

Notes:
1. The FCRA, ECOA, FDCPA and the TILA are sub-chapters of the Consumer Credit Protection Act 1968.
2. Five categories of bankruptcy are defined by the Federal Bankruptcy Code 1978. Chapters 11 & 9 deal with public and commercial institutions and Chapter 12 provides special provisions for farmers. Chapters 7 & 13 bankruptcy covers personal insolvency. If someone files for Chapter 7 bankruptcy they surrender their assets (less essential items exempted under Federal or State law). The surrendered assets are then used to repay the bankrupt's creditors. Usually, the bankrupt is then discharged and any remaining debts are written-off and cannot be collected later. The entire process from filing to discharge usually takes between four and six months (The American Bar Association 2006). Under Chapter 13 bankruptcy, the debtor agrees a repayment plan with creditors that may last anything up to five years. For a wage earner with considerable assets, Chapter 13 bankruptcy is often preferred to Chapter 7 because the debtor can retain ownership and use of their assets, which they would be required to surrender under Chapter 7. However, for those with few assets Chapter 7 is preferable because debts are written-off more quickly.

Table C.2   UK consumer credit legislation

Act	Main points
Consumer Credit Act 1974	The main legislation covering UK consumer credit agreements.[1] In particular, the act states the terms and conditions that must be included within a credit agreement for it to be legally enforceable, the action that can be taken to recover unpaid debts, and when a customer has the right to cancel an agreement. The act requires anyone engaged in consumer lending activities to obtain a credit license from the Office of Fair Trading (OFT).
Consumer Credit Act 2006	Updated a number of areas of the 1974 Act. In particular, the £25,000 limit for regulated agreements was removed, greater powers were granted to the courts to amend credit agreements that are deemed to be unfair, and more information was required to be provided to customers about their accounts. The process for granting credit licences was also revised, giving the OFT greater powers over the granting and withdrawal of credit licences.
Data protection Act 1998	Requires organizations to obtain consent to hold or process personal data. Empowers individuals to obtain copies of any information held about them by any organization.[2] For example, their credit reports from a credit reference agency or a copy of their account records from their bank.
Financial Services (Distance Marketing Regulations) 2004	Provides additional protections to consumers who buy products or services via post or the internet. In particular, it provides a 14 day cooling off period, during which an individual may cancel an agreement for any reason.
Consumer Credit (Early Settlement) Regulations 2004	Specifies the charges that can be levied and the rebate that a customer must receive in cases where they repay a loan early.
Consumer Credit (Advertisements) Regulations 2004	Details the terms and conditions that must be stated within promotional materials. For example, the total cost of credit and the APR.
Enterprise Act 2002	The Enterprise Act covers a number of areas, but the parts that are most relevant to consumer credit deal with the way in which bankruptcy (personal insolvency) is dealt with. In particular, it allows an individual to be discharged from bankruptcy after 12 months (prior to the Act the period was three years).

Table C.2   UK consumer credit legislation – *continued*

Act	Main points
Tribunals Courts and Enforcement Act 2007	Introduced a number of changes to the administration of unpaid debts that are dealt with by the courts. In particular, the Act introduced debt relief orders, which allow people with assets of <£300 and unsecured debts of less than £15,000 to apply for cheap 'fast-track' bankruptcy proceedings. The Act also replaced the age old system of court appointed Bailiffs with certified enforcement officers to collect debts on behalf of creditors.

Notes:
1. Some types of credit agreements are classified as 'unregulated agreements' and are exempt from many sections of the Act (although confusingly, some sections of the Act do apply to unregulated agreements). Unregulated agreements include credit agreements for a period of a year or less where there are four or fewer instalments, loans secured on land (a mortgage) and loans where the interest rate is no more than 1 percent above the Bank of England base rate.
2. A few government organizations, such as the security services MI5 and MI6 are exempt from the Act on the grounds of national security.

Appendix D   Recommended Reading

Bailey, M. (ed) (2002). *Consumer Collections and Recoveries: Operations and Strategies*. White Box Publishing. This book is targeted primarily at practitioners working in industry. Each chapter has been written by an industry expert, focusing on a specific aspect of debt management. Bailey has also edited a number of similar books about credit scoring and other aspects of credit management – all of which provide useful insights into the day-to-day operation of a consumer credit business.

Bank for International Settlements (2005). *An Explanatory Note on the BASELL II IRB Risk Weight Functions*. Basel. This provides a guide to calculating credit risk for BASEL II using the two IRB approaches. The BIS website http://www.bis.org/ also provides a wealth of information on BASEL II.

De Chernatony, A. and McDonald, M. (2003). *Creating Powerful Brands*. Elsevier Butterworth-Heinemann. This is ideal for anyone who wants to gain a comprehensive understanding of brand management.

Chryssides, G. D. and Kaler, J. H. (1993). *An Introduction to Business Ethics*. Chapman and Hall. This remains the definitive introduction to business ethics, providing a comprehensive overview of ethics and its application to business in a very readable format, making it accessible to a wide audience.

Edwards, H. (2004). *Credit Management Handbook*. Gower. This is a down to earth guide to credit management, providing a great deal of information about all aspects of credit management from a UK practitioner perspective.

Evans, D. and Schmalensee R. (2005). *Paying With Plastic. The Digital Revolution in Buying and Borrowing*. The MIT Press. This book gives a detailed account of the US credit card market and a wealth of information about the history and economics of credit card provision in the US.

Financial Services Authority, *FSA Handbook (BIPRU)*. This contains the full set of rules for UK banks and building societies for calculating their capital requirements. The FSA also maintains an archive of discussion and guidance documents. Available on line at http://www.fsa.gov.uk/Pages/handbook/

Finlay, S. (2009). *Consumer Credit Fundamentals*. Palgrave Macmillan. Chapter 3 provides a history of consumer credit from ancient times until the present day. Chapter 4 provides a discussion of some of the ethical arguments surrounding the use and misuse of credit, and Chapter 5 provides further information on US and UK legislation.

Hand, D. J., Mannila, H. and Smyth, P. (2002). *Principles of Data Mining*, MIT Press. This is a general text about data mining and describes, with many practical examples, many of the techniques that can be used to interrogate, analyse and model large data sets. Many of the techniques described are applicable to credit management problems.

Harrison, T. (2008). *Financial Services Marketing*. FT Prentice Hall. There are very few good books about the marketing of financial services. This is one of them.

Johnson, G., Scholes, K. and Wittington, R. (2007). *Exploring Corporate Strategy*. Pearson Education. Chapter 12 discusses the merits and drawbacks of the management structures that can be adopted by organizations.

Lewis, M. (1990). *The Credit Card Industry: A History*. Twayne Publishers. Lewis provides a superb history of the credit card industry from its origins in the 1950s until the late 1980s.

McNab, H. and Taylor, P. (2008). *Consumer Credit Risk Management*. Global Professional Publishing. This book has been written to complement The Chartered Institute of Bankers' Diploma in Financial Services Management in the UK. It has a practical focus and is suitable for anyone wishing to gain a broad understanding of how credit departments operate.

Siddiqi, N. (2006). *Credit Risk Scorecards*. John Wiley and Sons. This is a well written and practically focused book about the construction of predictive models of customer behaviour for credit risk assessment, as discussed in Appendix A. The book is a good accompaniment to the text by Thomas et al. (2002).

Slawsky, J. and Zafar, S. (2005). *Developing and Managing a Successful Payment Card Business*. Gower Publishing Limited. This is a great book for explaining the detail underpinning how a credit card operation works. It is very worthwhile reading this book in conjunction with *Paying with Plastic. The Digital Revolution in Buying and Borrowing*, by Evans and Schmalensee (see above).

Tapp, A. (2008). *Principles of Direct and Database Marketing*. FT Prentice Hall. Tapp gives a detailed and comprehensive, yet very readable, introduction to direct marketing and database marketing.

Thomas, L. C., Edelman, D. B. and Crook, J. N. (2002). *Credit Scoring and Its Applications*. Philadelphia, Siam. This book provides comprehensive coverage of the mathematical methods that can be employed to construct models of consumer behaviour. The book's main emphasis is on the construction of such models for credit assessment.

Thomas, L. C. (2009). *Consumer Credit Models: Pricing, Profit and Portfolios*. Oxford University Press. Many organizations have recently begun to look beyond simple credit scoring models to predict default/non-default and other binary behaviours. This book presents some of the methods that are being proposed to construct models that predict customer profitability and other financial measures.

Notes

Chapter 1

1 Although this is an interesting theory, there is as yet no substantive evidence to support it.
2 A definitive definition of 'consumer credit' is somewhat elusive. 'Consumer credit' is not defined in the Oxford Dictionary of English (Soanes and Stevenson 2005). The Dictionary of Banking and Finance (Collin 2003) defines consumer credit as 'The credit given by shops, banks and other financial institutions to consumers so that they may buy goods.' The Oxford Dictionary of Finance and Banking (Smullen and Hand 2005 p. 88) defines consumer credit as 'short term lending to the public' but this is somewhat unsatisfactory as it does not give any indication as to what short term might mean. It is also worth pointing out that for most types of credit the term can vary enormously. A debt on a credit card (usually classified as consumer credit) may be only for a few days or months, but could be for many years if only the minimum repayments are made. Likewise mortgages (often excluded from definitions of consumer credit) are often for 15–30 years, but there are no barriers to terms far shorter than this. It is therefore possible for a credit card debt to take longer to repay than a mortgage.
3 If a credit agreement is unsecured, no specific assets are named in the agreement. However, a court may authorize seizure of a borrower's assets if default occurs.
4 The most common of these are personal contract purchase agreements (a form of hire-purchase) used for motor finance. During the agreement the customer repays capital and interest, but at the end of the agreement a portion of the original debt remains outstanding. The customer then has the option of returning the vehicle or paying the outstanding balance in full.
5 Normally this will be that all the required payments have been made, but other conditions could apply.
6 The hirer always has the choice not to exercise their option to buy and hence withdraw from the agreement – although there may be penalty charges specified in the agreement if this occurs. With most hire-purchase agreements the option to buy is exercised automatically when the final rental instalment is paid resulting in the title (ownership) of the goods transferring to the hirer.
7 In some countries this principle does not apply. The credit relationship is considered to be completely separate from any linked transaction. For example, credit card companies in Japan have no liability for goods or services bought using their cards.
8 There are many other types of credit products such as pawn loans, mail order catalogue accounts, payday lending and so on, but these form only a very small part of the consumer credit market and are not provided by most large credit granting institutions.
9 Retail banks are also known as commercial banks.

10 Restrictions on credit union lending vary by country. In some, credit unions can only lend funds that have been provided by members. In others, they can borrow from and lend to other credit unions, and in some, they can obtain funds from other financial institutions to support of their lending activities.

11 In the UK for example, banks, building societies and finance houses account for about 98 percent of total consumer credit by value. However, in terms of numbers, minority lenders are used by anything up to 20 percent of the UK population (Finlay 2005).

12 Historically this was called a cycle because when the agreement terminated the process began anew, with promotional activity to encourage the customer to enter into another credit agreement. Today this is a somewhat outdated model. This is because many lenders now adopt a customer centric view rather a product centric one; that is, they look to satisfy the entire spectrum of the customer's credit needs on an ongoing basis, rather than selling them single products one at a time.

13 It is sometimes possible for funds to be recovered after a debt has been written-off. This is discussed in more detail in Chapter 8.

Chapter 2

1 In many organizations mailing is contracted out to a third party rather than undertaken in-house.

2 Of course there should be more strategic planning of resources than this. For example, if customer services forecasts that they will have spare capacity at some point in the future, then they should inform the other areas of the business (such as credit and marketing) so that suitable use can be made of the resources when they become available.

3 Other types of structure do exist, such as matrix, team and project based structures, but these are not very common within large financial services organizations. See Johnson and Scholes (2007) for more information about organizational structures.

4 By worldwide I mainly refer to first world countries with established financial infrastructures. This including the US, most EU member states, Canada, Australia and Japan. Consumer credit legislation in less developed regions can be patchy or virtually non-existent.

5 The APR is a standardized measure of the cost of credit presented in the form of an interest rate. As well as interest, the APR also includes other mandatory fees or charges, such as arrangement fees for a mortgage or an annual fee for a credit card. Optional charges, that a borrower chooses whether or not to pay, such as payment protection insurance, are not included within the APR calculation.

6 In many countries, including the UK, creditors may not recover assets themselves. Instead the court will appoint enforcement officers (bailiffs) to recover assets which are then passed on to the creditors.

7 Normally essential items such as clothing, food, basic furniture and so on are exempt from bankruptcy orders.

8 There are some types of debts, such as court fees, that may not be written-off.

9 In many regions cancellation rights are not universal and there are certain exceptions where cancellation rights do not apply. In the US and UK for example, there is no right to cancel if a credit agreement is signed on the lender's premises.

10 Of course the goods could be faulty, which creates a different set of issues and places certain liabilities on the vendor, but for the purposes of debate this scenario is not considered further.

11 The debt was in pounds sterling. Dollar values calculated using an exchange rate of 1.70 dollars to the pound.

12 If the debt had increased in line with inflation, then between 1989 and 2004 it would have increased by about 60 percent.

13 In the original court ruling the credit agreement was considered unenforceable for a number of reasons, one of which was that it was an extortionate credit agreement. Therefore, it was unlawful under the terms of the UK Consumer Credit Act 1974. In the court of appeal the ruling was upheld, but only on the basis that the original agreement was incorrectly drawn up. It therefore remains somewhat unclear as to whether the credit agreement was extortionate under UK law.

14 This report identifies three separate measures for literacy. The 34 percent figure relates to document literacy. This measures the ability of the reader to identify and understand information from different parts of a text, where the information may be presented in a number of different formats.

Chapter 3

1 The calculation of APR is not simple and is determined by regional legislation. Therefore, a detailed explanation of APR calculation is not entered into here.

2 'Large and complex' can usually be taken to mean beyond the scope of an individual to understand the data without resorting to some type of mechanical process to aid interpretation. So, any data set containing more than a few hundred cases and more than about ten different data items would be a suitable candidate for data mining.

3 This is not to say that using existing customer data would be completely useless, but only limited inferences can be drawn from the data. There is also a risk that the conclusions drawn do not accurately reflect the true behaviour of the target market.

4 In decision analysis the value of a decision is usually referred to as its utility. So the objective in this example is to find the set of features that maximize an individual's utility when using the credit card. Utility can be used to represent monetary value, but it can also be used to measure non-monetary aspects of decisions that are important to the decision maker.

5 The complexity of the mathematical models used in this process can vary enormously. A simple model might assume a fixed amount for each type of card expenditure. Hence, the model would predict that the same revenues would be generated regardless of the product features chosen. A more comprehensive model might include estimates of how revenues and costs would vary depending on the features that the individual chooses.

6   Tapp quotes figures in pounds sterling. Dollar values calculated using an exchange rate of 1.70 dollars to the pound.

Chapter 4

1   If the proportion of responders that convert is known, then it is a relatively easy task to apply a scaling factor to the response cost to estimate the average conversion cost. So if 80 percent of responders convert, the conversion cost will be 1.25 (1/80%) times greater than the response cost.
2   For a test mailing it is usual to wait somewhere between four and six weeks for responses to be received; for e-mails up to 14 days, and for texts 1–2 days. Obviously responses could be received after this period, but the number of late responders is usually very small.
3   This is obviously a simplified scenario. If the goods turn out to be faulty or result in some other problem then a sale may actually result in a loss.
4   It is generally a good idea to exclude people who are highly indebted, but if a consolidation loan or balance transfer feature is being promoted, then it may be prudent to retain these individuals on the list if the new offer is more affordable than their current credit commitments.
5   Models that predict the likelihood of future default tend to be called different things within different phases of credit management, even though the models are predicting the same type of behaviour. Models used to screen contact lists are usually referred to as risk pre-screening models, while similar models that are used when someone applies for credit are commonly referred to as credit scoring models.
6   'Good' and 'Bad' are standard terms used within the credit industry to describe customers on the basis of their repayment behaviour.
7   This approach to marginal bad rate assumes every customer will generate the same profit/loss depending on whether credit is repaid or default occurs. Obviously this is a simplification of the true state of affairs and more complex methods consider the marginal bad rate for different customer segments.
8   Beyond two dimensions it becomes difficult to produce cost trade-off graphs such as Figure 4.4. Instead, the relevant calculations will be performed using a computer that will then rank prospects in value order.

Chapter 5

1   There are generally two reasons for this. First, credit reference data is usually charged on a volume basis. Therefore, to acquire it for the entire contact list may not be cost effective given that the majority of prospects do not go on to apply for a product. Second, in some countries (the UK for example) industry agreements exist that prohibit the use of some credit reference data for marketing purposes. Full credit reference data can only be used at the point of application to assess the risk of future default.
2   Although it may only take a few days or weeks for individuals to respond to direct marketing activity, the data used to produce the contact list is likely to have been gathered some time before the contact list was used.

3   In some countries people have a unique identifier allocated by the government that is permitted to be used for commercial purposes. Therefore, this can be used to identify someone quickly if they have their details to hand. For example, social security numbers in the US.

4   In Figure 5.1 separate databases have been used to illustrate the difference between active and completed applications. In practice, active and completed applications will reside on the same database and a marker will be placed on the applicant's record to indicate whether their application is active or complete.

5   Common practice is to request previous address information if someone has lived at their current address for less than three years.

6   In the UK, if someone believes that the information on their credit report is incorrect or requires some explanation, then they are allowed to add an explanatory statement to it.

7   In the US use of marital status for credit assessment is illegal.

8   If detailed information about other credit agreements can be obtained from a credit report, then there is little reason to ask this type of question.

9   A lender could of course create their own summarized data if they wished, and some organizations do take this approach. However, many organizations rely on the summarized data that the credit reference agencies provide because credit reference agencies often have far more experience of using and processing this type of data than their clients.

10   In the UK it is illegal under data protection legislation to use associated individual data unless there is a proven financial link between individuals. For example, they have applied for, or taken out a loan in joint names.

11   This is usually the case for low value unsecured credit such as store and credit cards. However, for higher value lending such as mortgages and motor finance, additional proofs of identity and residence will usually be required. For example, passport or driving licence, together with a recent utility bill or other document that contains both name and address.

12   The other reason is that the average value of retail credit agreements is low. Therefore, higher interest rates need to be charged to cover costs.

13   In many regions a credit agreement must contain full details of the credit offered, including the amount, term and APR. If any of these details are unknown when a credit application is made, the credit agreement can only be signed after the application has been processed and the full terms of the offer have been agreed in principle. However, if the full terms of the credit agreement are known prior to the applicant applying, then a credit agreement can be signed by the applicant as part of the application form that they complete – if the form contains all of the relevant terms and conditions.

14   Most card providers allow an additional card holder, but the credit agreement only exists between the applicant and the credit provider. Therefore, the applicant is ultimately responsible for any spending that the additional card holder incurs.

15   There are several ways this can be done, but usually financial information such as income will be summed across all applicants, or an average taken. For account status information, such as number of months in arrears with existing credit agreements, the worst status across all applicants is usually taken.

16   It could be argued that taking a best case approach could be a good strategy to adopt. This is because if two people are signatories to a credit agreement,

then in many countries, both are equally liable for the whole debt; they are not individually liable for half the debt each. Therefore, as long one of the individuals is willing and able to make repayments, the attitude of the other towards the debt is not an issue.

Chapter 6

1 In this context, an account management system is taken to include all customer data held by an organization. In practice a distinction is made between the 'live' system used to process transactions and manage customer accounts and 'off-line' reporting systems used to provide management information.
2 The account creation date may be some days or weeks after the application date. This is often due to the customer needing to sign and return a credit agreement by post, or if the customer is asked to provide further documentary evidence; for example, recent payslips as proof of earnings.
3 For credit cards it is common for a customer to be sent a statement of account each statement period. However, for some products, particularly mortgages and personal loans, statement details will only be sent to the customer once a year, even if statement processing occurs on a monthly basis.
4 In the US, the Credit Card Accountability, Responsibility and Disclosure Act of 2009 requires card issuers to mail statements to customers at least 21 days before the due date.
5 The cycle date is usually constrained to be between 1 and 28 so that problems do not arise in months that do not contain 29, 30 or 31 days.
6 Some merchants have pre-determined floor limits. If the value of a card transaction is below the merchant's floor limit, authorization is not required from the card issuer before the transaction occurs.
7 Some organizations act as both card issuers and merchant acquirers. For example HSBC, Wells Fargo and Barclays bank.
8 In September 2007 the average interchange fee was limited to 0.55 percent of a transaction's value. This figure is subject to regular review by the Reserve Bank of Australia.
9 In some organizations account management processes occur at month end, and then applied to accounts the next time they cycle.
10 This situation can also arise if someone's name or address is incorrectly captured during data entry.
11 Organizations that maintain separate account management systems will often create links between systems to facilitate a partial customer management strategy. For example, if an organization maintains separate card and loan account management systems, then data about delinquent accounts may be transferred between each system to prevent further credit being extended on one product if the customer is delinquent on another.

Chapter 7

1 With credit cards customers are normally permitted to continue using their cards when they first become delinquent. A block will only be put on the account in high risk cases, or when the account becomes more seriously delinquent.

2 It is assumed that the lender operates a product or customer level management strategy, and can therefore, match accounts across customers.
3 Note that in the UK, the Office of Fair Trading issued a ruling in 2006 that late payment fees of more than £12 were not justifiable under normal trading conditions.
4 Ethical concerns can be raised about the appropriateness of encouraging a delinquent borrower to clear one debt by increasing another, particularly if the new debt places a greater financial burden on the individual due to balance transfer fees or a higher rate of interest being charged.
5 Most collections letters are pre-scripted and produced automatically by the collections system with no human involvement. Therefore, they are very cheap to produce.

Chapter 8

1 The process of repossessing residential property is also referred to as foreclosure.
2 Power dialler technology is also widely used within the marketing arena. A power dialler based system will be linked to the prospects database and used to manage telemarketing activity.
3 In some countries debts must be of a certain size before bankruptcy proceedings can be brought. For example, in the UK an individual's debt must be greater than £750.

Chapter 9

1 £428 million at a conversion rate of $1.70 to the pound.
2 Age is usually a good indicator of creditworthiness, and often features in credit scoring models employed to make lending decisions.
3 Standard practice in this situation is to close the account. A new account will then be created and a copy of all the information from the old account copied over to the new account.

Chapter 10

1 A balance sheet is one of several standard reports that all companies are required to produce as part of their annual accounts. The report contains two parts. Assets and liabilities. Assets are things of value that the organization owns, liabilities debts or other obligations that the organization has. Overall, the total assets and total liabilities are always equal; that is, they balance – hence balance sheet.
2 In practice, some securitization agreements leave some or all of the risk with the originator.
3 IAS standards are not universally applied. In the US for example, US GAAP (Generally Accepted Accounting Principles) are widely used in the production of company accounts.

4 The general calculation of net present value is: $A/(1+P)^N$, where A is the amount, P is the interest rate and N is the number of time periods ahead for which the net present value is calculated.

Chapter 11

1 In the UK for example, provision can only account for a maximum of 1.25 percent of risk weighted assets; i.e. about one-sixth of the minimum 8 percent capital requirement.
2 For the purpose of calculating capital requirements, lending to small businesses (turnover less than 1 million Euros) is included within the retail category.
3 The 8 percent minimum capital requirement is a carry over from the previous Basel I Accord that was implemented in 1988. 8 percent is a somewhat arbitrary figure. At the time of the original BASEL I Accord some regulators argued for a lower figure than 8 percent, some for a higher one. Consequently, 8 percent represents something of a compromise position.
4 There is a third method called the foundation IRB approach, but this is applicable to other types of credit risk. The foundation IRB approach can not be applied to retail credit.
5 Note that for credit exposures other than retail credit there is an additional maturity component to the Vasicek formula.
6 It would be simpler just to estimate the absolute increase in customer balances prior to default. However, regulators seem to prefer the use of conversion factors as an intermediary step for the calculation of *EAD* for revolving credit.
7 Readers should be aware that it takes about eight months to get a book into print. So while this book was published in 2010, the text was completed in the summer of 2009.

Appendix A

1 For some problems insufficient numbers of observations may be available at any one *T*. Therefore, a sample period, $T+\Delta T$, will be defined over which observations are collected. Correspondingly, there will be an outcome period $t+\Delta T$. For example, credit applications may be collected from January to December 2008 and their behaviour recorded 12 months later, between January and December 2009.
2 An example of indeterminates is commonly found with models of repayment behaviour. Those who keep to the terms of the credit agreement are classified as good while those whose accounts become seriously delinquent are classified as bad. However, there will be accounts that are mildly delinquent (typically 0–30 days past due), but are not seriously in default. Therefore, while not being wholly good, they can not be considered to be completely bad either. One possibility is to treat the problem as comprising three classes instead of two (Reichert 1983); that is, good, indeterminate and bad; but this approach is not popular.

3 With the continuing improvement in performance of modern PCs, taking all available data is increasingly an option.

4 Some people argue that a better approach is to use equal unweighted numbers of goods and bads to create a balanced sampled. This is achieved either by undersampling (throwing away goods so that the number of goods and bads are equal) or over-sampling (bads are replicated a number of times so that the proportion of goods and bads used for model development are approximately equal). Weighting is only applied to the holdout sample after the model has been developed, so that any reporting based on the holdout sample is reflective of the full population. This approach is particularly popular where class priors are grossly unequal. For example, when modelling fraud the incidence of frauds (bads) in the population is usually well below 1 percent. See Weiss (2004) for a more detailed discussion of the different balancing strategies that can be employed.

5 A common example where this occurs is when a credit application form is redesigned, resulting in a different set of questions being asked.

6 For US readers it is pointed out that the use of marital status in credit granting decisions is illegal under the ECOA 1974.

7 Note that a stepwise procedure will reduce, but not eliminate colinearaity between variables that feature within a model. Therefore, a model developer should undertake additional analysis to establish if colinearity is a problem between variables that feature in the final model. As a rule of thumb if two variables have a correlation coefficient above about 0.75 then one of them should be removed from the model. Alternatively, variance inflation factors in excess of ten are also indicative of colinearity problems.

8 When estimating future default it is often infeasible to observe a sample of accounts over the full term of the credit agreement. For example, a typical mortgage runs for 20+ years. Therefore, common practice is to define accounts as good or bad on the basis of a limited outcome period, which is often between 12 and 24 months in length.

9 In terms of the explained variance consumer behaviour models are actually quite poor. For example R^2 values of only 0.1–0.3 are common.

10 Which is the same as the graph of sensitivity vs (1 – specificity).

11 It should be noted that most rejected applicants would actually turn out to be good payers. However, the proportion of bad payers with the same score means that on average it is unprofitable to accept applicants with such a profile.

12 One way to do this is to rank observations by score, divide the population into about 20 intervals and calculate the ln(good:bad odds) for each interval and the mean score in each interval. The odds of each interval are then plotted against the average score. If the observed relationship appears to be roughly a straight line, then this is usually adequate.

13 For any scorecard where the points that double the odds is more than about ten, the loss of accuracy will be trivial from a usage perspective.

Appendix B

1 Usually this will be the outcome period used when the scorecard was constructed. However, alternative forecast horizons are sometimes used in addition to or instead of the original outcome period.

2 It should be noted that some organizations do not calibrate their scorecards when they become misaligned. Instead, they will alter the decision rules (the cut-off scores) used to make decisions about how individuals are treated, to take into account the change in the score odds relationship that is observed.

3 Note that using the average score gives an approximation (although quite a good one) for the expected numbers. Slightly more accurate results will be obtained if the individual scores are used to calculate the proportion of each individual observation that is expected to be good or bad, and then summing these proportions across all of the observations in the interval to arrive at expected good and expected bad figures.

Bibliography

APACS (2008). *Credit Fraud: The Facts 2008.* APACS

Arminger, G., Enache, D. and Bonne, T. (1997). Analyzing credit risk data: A comparison of logistic discrimination, classification tree analysis, and feed-forward networks. *Computational Statistics* **12**(2).

Baesens, B., Gestel, T. V., Viaene, S., Stepanova, M., Suykens, J. and Vanthienen, J. (2003). Benchmarking state-of-the-art classification algorithms for credit scoring. *Journal of the Operational Research Society* **54**(5).

Bailey, M. (ed.) (2004). *Consumer Credit Quality: Underwriting, Scoring, Fraud Prevention and Collections*, 1st edition. White Box Publishing.

Balmer, N., Pleasence, P., Buck, A. and Walker, H. C. (2005). Worried sick: The experience of debt problems and their relationship with health, illness and disability. *Social Policy & Society* **5**(1).

Banasik, J. and Crook, J. (2003). Lean models and reject inference. Credit Scoring & Credit Control VIII, Edinburgh.

Banasik, J. and Crook, J. (2005). Credit scoring, augmentation and lean models. *Journal of the Operational Research Society* **56**(9).

Banasik, J., Crook, J. N. and Thomas, L. C. (2003). Sample selection bias in credit scoring models. *Journal of the Operational Research Society* **54**(8).

Bank for International Settlements (2005). *An Explanatory Note on the BASEL II IRB Risk Weight Functions.* Bank of International Settlements.

Bank of England (2009). Statistical Interactive Database. Retrieved 10/06/2009. http://www.bankofengland.co.uk/mfsd/iadb/NewIntermed.asp

Barron, J. M. and Staten, M. (2000). *The Value of Comprehensive Credit Reports: Lessons from the U.S. Experience.* Credit Research Centre McDonough School of Business Georgetown University.

Becker, U. and Fahrmeir, L. (2001). Bump hunting for risk: A new data mining tool and its applications. *Computational Statistics* **16**(3).

Beling, P. A., Covaliu, Z. and Oliver, R. M. (2005). Optimal scoring cutoff policies and efficient frontiers. *Journal of the Operational Research Society* **56**(9).

Bierman, H. and Hausman, W. H. (1970). The credit granting decision. *Management Science* **16**(8).

Bishop, C. (1995). *Neural Networks for Pattern Recognition*, 1st edition. Oxford: Oxford University Press.

Boyes, W. J., Hoffman, D. L. and Low, S. A. (1989). An econometric-analysis of the bank credit scoring problem. *Journal of Econometrics* **40**(1).

Boyle, M., Crook, J. N., Hamilton, R. and Thomas, L. C. (1992). Methods applied to slow payers. *Credit Scoring and Credit Control.* L. C. Thomas, J. N. Crook and D. B. Edelman. Oxford: Clarendon Press.

Chatterjee, S. and Barcun, S. (1970). A non-parametric approach to credit screening. *Journal of the American Statistical Association* **65**(329).

CIFAS (2009). *2008 Fraud Trends.* Retrieved 23/06/2009, http://www.cifas.org.uk/default.asp?edit_id=896-57

Colin, P. H. (2003). *Dictionary of Banking and Finance*, 3rd edition. Bloomsbury.

Consumer Affairs Directorate (2001). *Report by the Task Force on Tackling Overindebtedness*, Department of Trade and Industry.

Consumer Affairs Directorate (2003). *Second Report by the Task Force on Tackling Overindebtedness*, Department of Trade and Industry.

Cox, D. R. (1972). Regression models and life tables. *Journal of the Royal Statistical Society Series B* **34**(3).

Crone, S. F., Lessmann, S. and Stahlbock, R. (2006). The impact of preprocessing on data mining: An evaluation of classifier sensitivity in direct marketing. *European Journal of Operational Research* **173**(3).

Crook, J. and Banasik, J. (2004). Does reject inference really improve the performance of application scoring models? *Journal of Banking & Finance* **28**(4).

Cyert, R. M., Davidson, H. J. and Thompson, G. L. (1962). Estimation of the allowance for doubtful accounts by Markov chains. *Management Science* **8**(3).

Cyrus, W. (2006). *It's a sellers' market, for now.* Credit Today: Debt Sale & Purchase. **October 2006**.

De Chernatony, L. and McDonald, M. (2003). *Creating Powerful Brands*, 3rd edition. Elsevier Butterworth-Heinemann.

Department for Constitutional Affairs (2004). *A Choice of Paths. Better Options to Manage Over-indebtedness and Multiple Debt*. Department for Constitutional Affairs.

Desai, V. S., Crook, J. N. and Overstreet, G. A. (1996). A comparison of neural networks and linear scoring models in the credit union environment. *European Journal of Operational Research* **95**(1).

Dobson, P. (1996). *Sale of Goods and Consumer Credit*, 5th edition. Sweet and Maxwell.

Drentea, P. and Lavrakas, P. J. (2000). Over the limit: The association among health, race and debt. *Social Science & Medicine* **50**(4).

Durand, D. (1941). *Risk Elements in Consumer Instatement Financing*, 1st edition. New York: National Bureau of Economic Research.

Ehrlich, E. and Fanelli, D. (2004). *The Financial Services Marketing Handbook: Tactics and Techniques That Produce Results*, 1st edition. Bloomberg Press.

Eisenbeis, R. A. (1977). Pitfalls in the application of discriminant analysis in business, finance and economics. *The Journal of Finance* **Vol. 32**(3).

Eisenbeis, R. A. (1978). Problems in applying discriminant analysis in credit scoring models. *Journal of Banking & Finance* **2**(3).

Evans, D. and Schmalensee, R. (2005). *Paying With Plastic: The Digital Revolution in Buying and Borrowing*, 2nd edition. Cambridge, Massachusetts: The MIT Press.

Everson, S. (ed.) (1988). *Aristotle: The Politics*, 1st edition. Cambridge: Cambridge University Press.

Experian (2007). *Explaining Experian May 2007*. Retrieved 04/09/2007 http://www.investis.com/corporate/financial/reports/2007/expexperian/explaining_070807.pdf

Financial Services Authority (2009). 'The Turner Review. A regulatory response to the global banking crisis', The Financial Services Authority.

Finlay, S. (2005). *Consumer Credit Fundamentals*, 1st edition. Palgrave Macmillan.

Finlay, S. (2006). *Modelling Issues in Credit Scoring*. Department of Management Science. Lancaster: Lancaster University.

Finlay, S. (2009). *Consumer Credit Fundamentals*, 2nd edition. Palgrave Macmillan.

Finlay, S. M. (2006). Predictive models of expenditure and indebtedness for assessing the affordability of new consumer credit applications. *Journal of the Operational Research Society* **57**(6).

Fogarty, T. C., Ireson, N. S. and Battle, S. A. (1992). Developing rule-based systems for credit card applications from data with the genetic algorithm. *IMA Journal of Mathematics Applied in Business and Industry* **4**(1).

Gelpi, R. and Julien-Labruyere, F. (2000). *The History of Consumer Credit: Doctrines and Practice*, 1st edition. New York: St. Martin's Press.

Goth, P., McKillop, D. and Ferguson, C. (2006). *Building Better Credit Unions*, 1st edition. The Policy Press.

Gow, D. (2009). *MasterCard Cuts International Fees*. Retrieved 10/06/2009. http://www.guardian.co.uk/business/2009/apr/01/mastercard-cuts-fees.

Grablowsky, B. J. and Talley, W. K. (1981). Probit and discriminant functions for classifying credit applications: A comparison. *Journal of Economics and Business* **33**(3).

Gup, B. E. (2004). *The New Basel Capital Accord*, 1st edition. Thomson.

Hand, D. J. (2005). Good practice in retail credit scorecard assessment. *Journal of the Operational Research Society* **56**(9).

Hand, D. J. and Adams, N. M. (2000). Defining attributes for scorecard construction in credit scoring. *Journal of Applied Statistics* **27**(5).

Hand, D. J. and Henley, W. E. (1993). Can reject inference ever work? *IMA Journal of Mathematics Applied in Business and Industry* **5**(1).

Hand, D. J. and Henley, W. E. (1997). Statistical classification methods in consumer credit scoring: A review. *Journal of the Royal Statistical Society, Series A-Statistics in Society* **160**(3).

Hand, D. J., Mannila, H. and Smith, P. (2002). *Principles of Data Mining*, 1st edition. MIT Press.

Harrell, F. E. Jr, Lee, K., L. and Mark, D. B. (1996). Multivariable prognostic models: Issues in developing models, evaluating assumptions and adequacy, and measuring and reducing errors. *Statistics in Medicine* **15**(4).

Harris, E. H. and Albert, A. (1991). *Survivorship Analysis for Clinical Studies*, 1st edition. Marcel Dekker.

Harrison, T. (1999). *Financial Services Marketing*, 1st edition. FT Prentice Hall.

Harrison, T. (2008). *Financial Services Marketing*, 2nd edition. FT Prentice Hall.

Haykin, S. (1994). *Neural Networks: A Comprehensive Foundation*, 1st edition. New York: Macmillan College Publishing Company Inc.

Heckman, J. (1976). The common structure of statistical models of truncation, sample selection and limited dependent variables and a simple estimator for such models. *Annals of Economic and Social Measures* **5**(4).

Henley, W. E. (1995). *Statistical Aspects of Credit Scoring*. Milton Keynes: Open University.

Henley, W. E. and Hand, D. J. (1996). A k-nearest-neighbour classifier for assessing consumer credit risk. *Statistician* **45**(1).

Horan, R. D., Bulte, E. and Shogren, J. F. (2005). How trade saved humanity from biological exclusion: An economic theory of Neanderthal extinction. *Journal of Economic Behavior & Organization* **58**(1).

Howells, P. and Bain, K. (2004). *Financial Markets and Institutions*, 4th edition. Pearson Education.

Hsia, D. C. (1978). Credit scoring and the equal opportunity act. *The Hastings Law Journal* **30**(2).

Jacobson, T. and Roszbach, K. (2003). Bank lending policy, credit scoring and value-at-risk. *Journal of Banking & Finance* **27**(4).

Jacoby, M. B. (2002). Does indebtedness influence health? A preliminary inquiry. *Journal of Law Medicine & Ethics* **30**(4).

Joanes, D. N. (1993). Reject inference applied to logistic regression for credit scoring. *IMA Journal of Mathematics Applied in Business and Industry* **5**(1).

Johnson, G. and Scholes, K. (2002). *Exploring Corporate Strategy*, 6th edition. Pearson Education.

Johnson, G. and Scholes, K. (2007). *Exploring Corporate Strategy*, 8th edition. Pearson Education.

Jones, R. (2006). Banks write off £100,000 after irresponsible lending claims. *The Saturday Guardian*. London.

Kempson, E. (2002). *Over-indebtedness in Britain*, Department of Trade and Industry.

Keeney, R. L. and Oliver, R. M. (2005). Designing win-win financial loan products for consumers and businesses. *Journal of the Operational Research Society* **56**(9).

Kim, Y. and Sohn, S. Y. (2007). Technology scoring model considering rejected applicants and effect of reject inference. *Journal of the Operational Research Society* **58**(10).

King, R. D., Henery, R., Feng, C. and Sutherland, A. (1995). A comparative study of classification algorithms: statistical, machine learning and neural networks. *Machine Intelligence*. K. Furukwa, D. Michie and S. Muggleton. Oxford: Oxford University Press. Volume **13**.

Kittler, J. (1997). Statistical classification. *Vistas in Astronomy* **41**(3).

Kittler, J. (1998). Combining classifiers: A theoretical framework. *Pattern Analysis and Applications* **1**(1).

Kutner, M., Greenberg, E. and Baer, J. (2005). 'A first look at the literacy of America's adults in the 21st century', US Department of Education: Institute of Education Sciences.

Lachenbruch (1982). Discriminant analysis. *Encyclopaedia of Statistical Sciences*. S. Ketz and N. L. Johnson, Wiley & Sons Inc. Volume 2.

Lee, J. and Hogarth, J. M. (1999). The price of money: Consumers' understanding of APRs and contract interest rates. *Journal of Public Policy & Marketing* **18**(1).

Legrady, P. (2006). *The Debt Buying Marketplace: The UK and Worldwide*. Credit Today: Debt Sale & Purchase. **October 2006**.

Levitt, T. (1960). Marketing Myopia. *Harvard Business Review* **38**(6).

Lewis, E. M. (1992). *An Introduction to Credit Scoring*, 2nd edition. San Rafael: Athena Press.

Lovie, A. and Lovie, P. (1986). The flat maximum effect and linear scoring models for prediction. *Journal of Forecasting* **5**(3).

McNab, H. and Wynn, A. (2003). *Principles and Practice of Consumer Risk Management*, 2nd edition. Institute of Financial Services.

McNab, H. and Taylor, P. (2008). *Consumer Credit Risk Management*, 1st edition. Global Professional Publishing.

Menard, S. (1995). *Applied Logistic Regression*, 2nd edition. Sage.

Miller, M. J. (ed.) (2003). *Credit Reporting Systems and the International Economy*, 1st edition. The MIT Press.

Minskey, M. L. and Papert, S. A. (1969). *Perceptrons*, 1st edition. Cambridge MA: MIT Press.

Nettleton, S. and Burrows, R. (1998). Mortgage debt, insecure home ownership and health: An exploratory analysis. *Sociology of Health & Illness* **20**(5).

Office of Fair Trading (2003). *MasterCard Interchange Fees: Preliminary Conclusions*, Office of Fair Trading.

Office of Fair Trading (2005). *Investigation of the Multilateral Interchange Fees Provided for in the UK Domestic Rules of Mastercard UK Members Forum Limited (formerly known as MasterCard/Europay UK Limited)*. Office of Fair Trading.

Oliver, R. M. and Wells, E. (2001). Efficient frontier cutoff policies in credit portfolios. *Journal of the Operational Research Society* **52**(9).

Ong, C.-S., Huang, J.-J. and Gwo-Hshiung, T. (2005). Building credit scoring models using genetic programming. *Expert Systems with Applications* **29**(1).

Orgler, Y. E. (1975). *Analytical Methods in Loan Evaluation*, 1st edition. London: Lexington Books.

Perreault, W. D. and McCarthy, E. J. (2004). *Basic Marketing: A Global Managerial Approach*, 15th edition. McGraw Hill.

Reading, R. and Reynolds, S. (2001). Debt, social disadvantage and maternal depression. *Social Science & Medicine* **53**(4).

Reichert, A. K., Cho, C. C. and Wagner, G. M. (1983). An examination of the conceptual issues involved in developing credit scoring models. *Journal of Business Economics and Statistics* **1**(2).

Reichheld, F. F. (2001). *The Loyalty Effect*, 1st edition. Boston, Mass: Harvard Business School Publishing.

Reserve Bank of Australia (2001). *Reform of Credit Card Schemes in Australia*. Reserve Bank of Australia.

Reserve Bank of Australia (2006). *Payment Systems (Regulation) Regulations 2006*. Reserve Bank of Australia.

Rosenberg, E. and Gleit, A. (1994). Quantitative methods in credit management: A survey. *Operations Research* **42**(4).

Rosenblatt, F. (1958). The Perceptron: A probabilistic model for information storage and organisation in the brain. *Psychological Review* **65**.

Rumelhart, D. E., Hinton, G. E. and Williams, R. J. (1986). Learning representations by back-propagating errors. *Nature* **323**(6088).

Savery, J. (1977). Numerical points systems in Credit Screening. *Management Decisions* **15**.

Sewart, P. J. (1997). *Graphical and Longitudinal Models in Credit Analysis*. Lancaster, UK: Lancaster University.

Shaw, A. (2007). *The Complete Package*. Credit Today: Debt Sale & Purchase. **September 2007**.

Siddiqi, N. (2006). *Credit Risk Scorecards: Developing and Implementing Intelligent Credit Scoring*, 1st edition. John Wiley & Sons.

Skipworth, G. and Dyson, D. (1997). *Consumer Credit Law*, 1st edition. LAG Education and Service Trust Limited.

Smith, A. and Sutherland, K. (1998). *The Wealth of Nations*. Oxford: Oxford Paperbacks.

Smullen, J. and Hand, N. (eds) (2005). *Oxford Dictionary of Finance and Banking*, 3rd edition. Oxford: Oxford University Press.

Soanes, C. and Stevenson, A. (2005). *The Oxford Dictionary of English*. Oxford University Press.

Tapp, A. (2008). *Principles of Direct and Database Marketing*, 4th edition. FT Prentice Hall.

The American Bar Association (2006). *Guide to Credit and Bankruptcy*, 1st edition. Random House.

The Federal Reserve Board (2006). *Statistics: Releases and Historical Data*. Retrieved 02/01/2007, 2007, http://www.federalreserve.gov/releases/.

The Federal Reserve Board (2009). *Charge-off and Delinquency Rates*. Retrieved 30/08/2009, http://www.federalreserve.gov/releases/chargeoff/chgallnsa.htm

Thomas, L. C. (1998). Methodologies for classifying applicants for credit. *Statistics in Finance*. D. J. Hand and S. D. Jacka. New York: John Wiley and Sons Inc.

Thomas, L. C. (2000). A survey of credit and behavioural scoring: Forecasting financial risk of lending to consumers. *International Journal of Forecasting* 16(2).

Thomas, L. C. (2009). *Consumer Credit Models: Pricing, Profit and Portfolios*. Oxford University Press.

Thomas, L. C., Banasik, J. and Crook, J. N. (2001). Recalibrating scorecards. *Journal of the Operational Research Society* 52(9).

Thomas, L. C., Edelman, D. B. and Crook, J. N. (2002). *Credit Scoring and Its Applications*, 1st edition. Philadelphia, Siam.

Thomas, L. C., Ho, J. and Scherer, W. T. (2001). Time will tell: Behavioural scoring and the dynamics of consumer credit assessment. *IMA Journal of Management Mathematics* 12(1).

Vasicek, O. (2002). Loan portfolio value. *RISK*, December 2002.

Verstraeten, G. and Van den Poel, D. (2005). The impact of sample bias on consumer credit scoring performance and profitability. *Journal of the Operational Research Society* 56(8).

Webley, S. and More, E. (2003). *Does Business Ethics Pay?* Institute of Business Ethics.

Weiss, G. M. (2004). Mining with rarity: A unifying framework. *ACM SIGKDD Explorations Newsletter* 6(1): 7–19.

West, D. (2000). Neural network credit scoring models. *Computers & Operations Research* 27(11–12).

West, D., Dellana, S. and Qian, J. X. (2005). Neural network ensemble strategies for financial decision applications. *Computers & Operations Research* 32(10).

Williams, J., Clemens, S., Oleinikova, K. and Tarvin, K. (2003). *The Skills for Life Survey*. Department of Education and Skills.

Wonderlic, E. F. (1952). An analysis of factors in granting credit. *Indiana University Bulletin* 50.

Wood, F. and Sangster, A. (1999). *Business Accounting 1*, 8th edition. Financial Times Professional Limited.

Yobas, M. B., Crook, J. and Ross, P. (2000). Credit scoring using neural and evolutionary techniques. *IMA Journal of Mathematics Applied in Business and Industry* 11(2).

Index